The Edwardian Modiste

The Edwardian

Modiste

85 Authentic Patterns With Instructions, Fashion Plates, And Period Sewing Techniques

Edited and with Additional Material by
Frances Grimble

Lavolta Press
20 Meadowbrook Drive
San Francisco, CA 94132

First edition

ISBN: 0-9636517-1-4

Published by
Lavolta Press
20 Meadowbrook Drive
San Francisco, CA 94132

Book design, cover design, scan editing and coloring, page layout, and production management by Frances Grimble and Allan Terry

Printed and bound in the United States of America by Thomson-Shore

Library of Congress Catalog Card Number: 96-75989

Publisher's Cataloging in Publication
(Prepared by Quality Books Inc.)

Grimble, Frances.
    The Edwardian modiste: 85 authentic patterns with instructions, fashion plates, and period sewing techniques / Frances Grimble.
        p. cm.
        Includes bibliographical references and index.
        ISBN: 0-9636517-1-4

    1. Dressmaking–Patterns. 2. Vintage clothing–United States.
3. Costume–United States–History–20th century.   I. Title.

TT520.G75 1996   646.4'78'04'09'041
                                            QBI96-40069

Acknowledgments

I'd like to thank my husband Allan Terry, who reconstructed the American System of Cutting rulers from the patent application, drew them for this book, edited the halftone scans, and colored the cover scans. He also provided invaluable assistance in the myriad tasks of running a publishing company.

The printer, Thomson-Shore, scanned the period artwork and provided electronic prepress advice, as well as printing the book. I'd like to thank Dave Raymond, Laurie Briegel, Larry Meilleur, and the many other employees involved.

I'd also like to thank Bob Grimble and Benedict O'Mahoney for their legal assistance, and Sam and Aileen Terry for business advice and support.

For my parents, Ralph and Helen Grimble

Contents

Introduction 1
    The American System of Cutting 1
    Drafting with the American System 2
    Projecting a Pattern 2
    Finishing a Drafted or Projected Pattern 2
    Using the Edwardian Modiste Patterns 3

1905 American Garment Cutter Instruction and Diagram Book

Using the American Garment Cutter System 7
    Practice Waist 10
    Draft for Medium and Slender Forms 13
    A Good Draft for Medium Stout Forms 14
    Draft for Medium and Slender Forms 15
    Draft for Medium and Slender Forms 16
    Ladies' Empire Coat 17
    Ladies' Shirtwaist Suit 21
    A Reception Toilette 26
    Ladies' Dressy Paletot 31
    Ladies' Princess Gown 35
    A Dressy Reception Gown 40
    Visiting Costume 45
    Ladies' Street Costume 49
    Ladies' Empire Gown 55
    A Dressy Separate Waist 58
    Ladies' Evening Waist 61
    A Dressy Shirtwaist 63
    Ladies' Dressing Sack 65
    Seamless Corset Cover 67
    Ladies' Corset Cover 68

January 1907 American Modiste 69
    Ladies' Evening Gown 70
    Ladies' Separate Waist 74
    Ladies' Reception Gown 76
    Ladies' Auto Fur Coat 81
    Ladies' Dinner Gown 86
    Advanced Styles in Tailored Waists 91

Contents

April 1907 American Modiste 96
   A Dressy Street Costume 98
   Spring Costume 102
   Ladies' Reception Gown 107

July 1907 American Modiste 112
   Ladies' Jumper Suit 113
   Ladies' Visiting Gown 118
   Ladies' Afternoon Gown 123
   Ladies' Jumper Blouse 128
   Ladies' Street Suit 131
   Ladies' Chemise 136

October 1907 American Modiste 138
   Ladies' Traveling Suit 139
   Ladies' Reception Gown 144
   Dressy Tailor-Made Suit 151
   Ladies' Auto Coat 156
   Japanese Robe 161
   Ladies' Separate Waist 164
   One-Piece Corset Cover 167

January 1908 American Modiste 168
   Dressy Redingote 169
   A Stylish Street Suit 175
   Ladies' Evening Dress 181
   Dainty Waist 186

April 1908 American Modiste 189
   White Linen Suit 190
   Easter Model 195
   The Season's Newest Mode 201
   Afternoon Toilette 206
   Shirtwaist and Skirt 210
   Kimono Wrapper 214
   Storm and Motor Coat 217

July 1908 American Modiste 221
   Ladies' Visiting Gown 222
   Attractive Model for Summer 227
   A Chic Toilette 232
   A Pretty Creation for Summer 236
   Golf and Outing Suit 240
   Ladies' Combination Suit 245

October 1908 American Modiste 247
   Effective Street Design 248
   Ladies' Reception Gown 253

Contents

Artistic Directoire Coat	260
For Autumn and Winter	264

January 1909 American Modiste — 269

A Practical Street Suit	270
A Gown for Dressy Occasions	275
For Day or Evening Wear	280
A Smart Creation for Street Wear	285
Evening or Opera Coat	290
A Pretty Net Waist	294
Fitted Corset Cover	297

April 1909 American Modiste — 298

A Dressy Street Suit	299
Stylish Street Gown	304
Stylish Evening Gown	309
Smart Design for Easter	313
Dressy Afternoon Waist	318

July 1909 American Modiste — 320

Unique Style for Summer	321
Silk and Net Waist	325
Outing Suit	327
Ladies' Bathing Suit	332
Ladies' Reception Gown	337
Ladies' Empire Raincoat	341
Princess Slip	344

October 1909 American Modiste — 347

Ladies' Reception Gown	348
A Stylish Street Suit	352
French Corset Cover	358
Ladies' Petticoat	360

The Complete Dressmaker

From Chapter II, Underwear — 365

How to Make Drawers	365
Petticoats	366
Nightgowns	366
To Make an Under Waist	367

From Chapter VII, Skirts — 368

The Lining Skirt	368
The Pleated Skirt	369
Another Style of Pleated Skirt	369
A Slot-Seam Skirt	370
A Circular Skirt	370

Contents

Cutting a Bias 370
Tailor's Tacking 370

From Chapter VIII, Making a Waist 371
Cutting the Lining 371
Fitting the Lining 371
Finishing the Lining 372
Featherbone 372
The Sleeves 373
How to Sew Hooks and Eyes on a Waist 373
The Collar 374
Draping the Waist 374
A Plain Draped Waist 374
Draping the Sleeves 376
The Belt or Girdle 377
Trimming Waists 377

From Chapter IX, Lingerie Waists and Shirtwaists ... 379
Lingerie Waists 379
Shirtwaists 379

From Chapter X, Coats and Wraps for Women and
Children 381
Sponging the Cloth 381
Making the Foundation 381
Trimming Off the Foundation 382
Padding 382
Making the Back 383
Making the Collar 383
Fitting the Revers to the Collar 384
Finishing Off the Edges 384
The Lining 384
A Coat Sleeve 384
Pressing 385
An Eton Coat 385
A Box Coat 385
A Tight-Fitting Coat 386
Capes 386

From Chapter XI, Girdles, Collars, Sleeves, Etc. 388
Separate Girdle, Closed at Back 388
Girdle, Closed in Front 389
Flowered Ribbon Girdle, Opening in Back 389
Trimmed Girdle 390
Tucked Net Collar 391
Fancy Sleeves 391

Contents

From Chapter XII, Gowns: Their Choosing and Making — 393
Materials — 393
Good Taste and Economy in Dressing — 393
Choosing the Design — 393
Measurements — 394
Dressmakers' Terms — 394

From Chapter XV, Useful Hints — 399
Miscellaneous Hints for Sewing — 399
Pleating and Shirring — 399
Braid Trimming — 399

From Chapter XVII, Gowns for Various Occasions — 400
Outing Suits — 400
The Rainy-Day Costume — 400
Maternity Gowns — 400
Correct Mourning — 401
A Bridal Trousseau or Outfit — 402

Appendices and Index
Appendix A: American System of Cutting Rulers — 407
Appendix B: Patent Application for the American System — 422
Appendix C: Metric Conversion Table — 424
Appendix D: Further Reading — 426
Index — 427

Introduction

Today we take sewing patterns for granted. We can walk into any fabric store, thumb through half-a-dozen books illustrating hundreds of styles, and buy whichever we like in a standard size. But sized patterns are the result of about 200 years of technological development.

The American System of Cutting

One-size and roughly sized patterns were used well before the 19th century. They were made widely available by 19th-century fashion publications. Except for loose undergarments and wraps, garments cut from such patterns required tricky, time-consuming fitting. From the early 19th century into the early 20th, there was a continual search for improvements on traditional cutting methods. One of the most important was the development of patent drafting systems. These were widely used by professional garment makers, by amateurs, and by companies that mass-produced patterns and garments.

Some of the earliest drafting systems projected all garment dimensions in proportion to one crucial body measurement (which varied with the system). Such systems didn't produce a good fit for most individuals, leading to the development of systems requiring additional measurements. There were also hybrid systems that combined proportional and inch measurements. Late in the 19th century direct measure systems based entirely on inch measurements became popular. Some were just procedures for using ordinary drafting tools, but some were patent systems designed to simplify drafting. Most patent systems, of whatever type, required special tools sold by the patent owner. Patent owners also published books and/or magazines with patterns to be drafted using their system.

The patterns in *The American Garment Cutter Instruction and Diagram Book* and *The American Modiste* were designed for the American System of Cutting. This was patented by Jonathan Nelson in 1902 (see appendix B). It was sold by the Page H. Gregg company of Chicago. In addition to selling the system and pattern publications, Page H. Gregg ran a school that taught design, dressmaking, and ladies' tailoring. Ads were aimed at amateurs who wished to attain professional skill, whether to go into business or just sew well at home.

The American System of Cutting is a sophisticated proportional system. It requires apportioning scales, rulers that eliminate the need for arithmetic. (See appendix A.) Instead of inches, the patterns are labeled with numbered (whole) units and lettered (fractional) ones. Unit size varies with the ruler, so the same number of units is used for any size. The rulers have size labels that correspond to inch measurements. To draft a bodice with a 34-inch bust, you would use the size 34 ruler to draw all horizontal lines. To draft a bodice with a 36-inch bust you'd use the size 36 ruler, and so on. Two rulers are required for each pattern piece, one to draw horizontal lines and the other to draw the vertical baseline. The rulers are uniformly scaled, enabling you to draft patterns for any size even if no specific ruler is supplied.

The American System rulers have been reconstructed using the information in the patent application. However, the "form piece or curve" referred to in *The American Garment Cutter* is not mentioned in the application. The instructions claim the system applies measurements to curves. But I suspect the tool was an all-in-one french curve with marks to help find the right place, but no measured units. Pattern measurements refer only to straight lines. And it's unlikely that units for all sizes would fit on one tool.

Drafting with the American System

Using the American System to draft the patterns in *The Edwardian Modiste* is quite easy. First take your measurements over the foundation garments and

undergarments you will wear. Choose the right rulers for your measurements and the garment section. Because ruler lengths are limited by the book size, the rulers in Appendix A are partial. Directions are given for copying, cutting, and pasting to full length. The rulers may then be glued to cardboard or inexpensive yardsticks and used for drafting. Or they may be used for measurement only, and lines drawn with a yardstick.

From my experience the fitted bodice patterns, such as tight linings, were designed with practically no ease. For these I'd recommend using a width ruler one to two sizes larger than your bust and leaving large seam allowances. I successfully experimented with choosing a sleeve length ruler by the modern method of measuring from the shoulder point to the wrist. If you measure skirt length from your waist to the skirt bottom, the pattern will lack the hem allowance and waistband seam allowance. Either add these after drafting or use a larger ruler. The proportionally determined hip size is large for most modern women. But numerous seams and pleats allow ample scope for fitting.

After choosing your rulers, lay out a big piece of pattern paper printed with marks at 1-inch intervals. Pencil a vertical baseline and use your length ruler to mark off the measurements shown on the pattern piece. From these, use your width ruler to draw horizontal crosslines to the measurements shown. Step-by-step instructions are given in *The American Garment Cutter Instruction and Diagram Book*.

You then draw the curves, for which you need a modern hip/armhole curve and a set of french curves. Choose a curve that fits to the ends of the lines you drew and looks like the pattern shape. You may need parts of two curves. A flexible curve (available from art and quilting suppliers) comes in handy.

Projecting a Pattern

These patterns can also be enlarged by projection. (The originals were reversed from white lines on black blocks to aid projection.) Most pattern pieces are drawn to some scale, but the original publisher reduced them to whatever fit on the page. The re-

sulting scales are unusual. More than one may be used in a single pattern, requiring different projector adjustments.

Use the American System rulers to determine what size each piece should be projected to. Use the bust ruler to size bodices, the waist to size skirts, and the sleeve length to size sleeves. Back waist length and skirt length can be corrected after projection using standard pattern alteration techniques.

Photocopy the pattern piece onto transparency film. Tape a large piece of dotted pattern paper to a wall. Place the transparency on the projector so the pattern's baseline is aligned with a vertical row of dots and the top crossline is aligned with a horizontal row. Adjust the projector till the key measurement is correct on the pattern paper. Draw the pattern using a clear plastic yardstick, ruler, and french curves (clear tools don't block projection). Or draw freehand and clean up the lines later. Projected lines look thick; you'll have to decide whether to trace the outsides or the insides. Trace stars, pleat lines, and other internal pattern marks; but note that seam allowances were not drawn to scale.

A few wide skirt pieces were drawn to scale at the waist, but narrowed at the bottom to fit on the page. Check the proportions of all wide skirt pieces till you become familiar with these patterns. Measure the waist-to-hem ratio in units, then inches. If the ratios differ, use the rulers to determine the correct waist width, hem width, and skirt length along the baseline. Draw the baseline. Mark where the waist and hem will meet it. Put the pattern piece on the projector and draw the waist curve. Mark the places diagonal seam and pleat lines should start. Then readjust the projector and draw the hem curve, marking where diagonal lines should end. Take the pattern paper off the wall and draw the diagonal lines from waist to hem.

Finishing a Drafted Or Projected Pattern

Measure edges that will be seamed together. If they're different lengths, check the original measurements and redraw as necessary. Add pattern markings such as pleat lines and stars (which cor-

respond to pattern notches). Sometimes you must true seam lines where fabric will be folded into darts, pleats, or facings. Fold the pattern like the fabric and redraw nonmatching lines.

According to the instructions, marked seam allowances are built into the pattern. From my experience some unmarked allowances may also be built in–and some not. Add any seam allowances you're not sure about and extend any that are too small to alter. Use 1-inch to 2-inch allowances on side seams, and 1-inch allowances on all seams of tight sections. To add a seam allowance, measure out from the pattern edge with a clear plastic ruler. For straight edges measure each end and connect the lines. For curved edges draw short lines at such frequent intervals that they connect. Or use a double tracing wheel to indent the paper, then pencil over the indents.

To finish the pattern piece, draw a grain line following a vertical row of pattern paper dots. Label the piece with the pattern source, garment type, and style date. Indicate how many times each piece will be cut from fashion fabric, lining, underlining, and/or interfacing. Add any marks or notes you find helpful.

Although the American System produces a good fit, Edwardian patterns assume the sewer adjusts a muslin or lining before cutting garment fabric. I strongly recommend this. You can measure pattern pieces first to correct proportionally determined measurements. But I find it easier to pinpoint problems in the muslin.

Although trim guidelines are given in the fashion plates and descriptions, pattern pieces and placement markings are often omitted. This is because Edwardian sewers adapted trims to their tastes, substituted trims from other patterns, or copied them from friends' clothes. Of course, you're free to adapt trims too. Draft and mark them with an ordinary ruler after completing the rest of the pattern. You can test size and placement on the muslin.

Using the Edwardian Modiste Patterns

The original sewing instructions are terse, though they are supplemented by the construction, fabric, and trim suggestions in the *American Modiste* fashion columns. This is typical of Edwardian patterns–even ready-made ones provided only a few sentences of instructions. Sewers were expected to refer to a dressmaking manual. To aid you I have included sections from *The Complete Dressmaker,* edited by Clara E. Laughlin and published by D. Appleton and Company in 1907. It gives detailed directions for most garment types in this book, plus special recommendations for wedding gowns, maternity wear, and mourning. It includes hard-to-find tailoring instructions and a glossary of dressmakers' terms. Due to space limitations I omitted sections on still-familiar seams and stitches.

When I began organizing *The Edwardian Modiste,* I wanted to include all the patterns in my 1905 *American Garment Cutter Instruction and Diagram Book* and my complete 1907–1909 run of the quarterly *American Modiste.* However, this would have made the book too large. I compromised by selecting the widest range of women's fashions available in the magazines. These include home wear, day dresses, formal dresses, suits, coats, blouses, lingerie, and sports clothes. If an issue included similar patterns, I chose one. I omitted the (many) children's patterns and the (few) men's.

I have edited the pattern and sewing manual instructions for clarity. I substituted a few modern spellings and terms (such as "darts" for "bust plaits"). I also edited the fashion columns to include only information that's useful in recreating the styles. I arranged the pattern pieces the way they are sewn together, as well as the page size allowed. However, I've made every effort to preserve the style and substance of the originals.

I hope you find *The Edwardian Modiste* enjoyable and useful.

——Frances Grimble

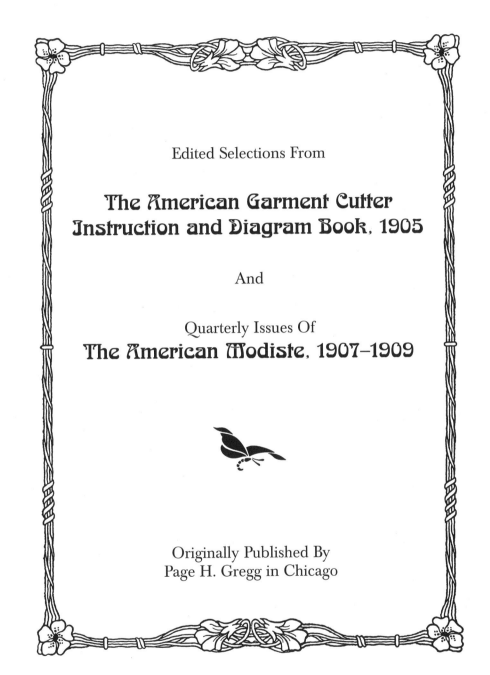

Edited Selections From

The American Garment Cutter
Instruction and Diagram Book, 1905

And

Quarterly Issues Of
The American Modiste, 1907–1909

Originally Published By
Page H. Gregg in Chicago

1905 American Garment Cutter Instruction and Diagram Book

Using the American Garment Cutter System

Taking Measurements. Five measures are required: Bust, length of waist, around the waist, sleeve, and length of skirt. In some cases a front or full-length measure is required.

Bust measure: Stand behind the person being measured. Place measuring tape over largest part of bust, close to armhole, and over shoulder blade. Be very careful not to get this measure too tight.

Front measure: This measure is used only for persons with extreme dip or very short waisted in front.

Length of waist: Great care should be used in taking this measure. Place a belt around waist and press down to hips. Then measure from bone in neck to bottom of belt.

Around the waist: Take to suit the person being measured.

Sleeve measure: Raise arm so that elbow is level with shoulder, with wristbone 6 inches in front of face. Then measure from center of back to 1 inch below wristbone.

Skirt measure: This measure is taken from waistline in front to the desired length. In some cases you need two extra measures, side and back.

Full-length measure: This measure is taken from bone in neck, down back, to the desired length of garment.

Selecting Scales. This system applies actual measurements, not only to straight lines, but also to curves. The tools consist of a square, measuring tape, set of graduated scales, and a form piece or curve.

The set of scales contains 28 distinct pieces, numbered from 19 to 46, inclusive. The odd numbers are on one side and the even on the other. The scales give the correct length and breadth of all patterns in a perfect, simple, and practical manner. The form piece is divided into spaces; each space is lettered with corresponding letters in the draft. The index hand pointing out each special letter in the draft makes it very plain how to apply the curve.

Waists, jackets, coats, collars, trimmings, etc.: Select bust and length of waist scales. To obtain scale for length of waist, always double the length of waist. For example: Bust 35, length of waist 16; use bust scale 35 for all crosslines and 32 for baseline.

Sleeves: Measure back of pattern with measuring tape from seam in back to armhole. Subtract that amount from full sleeve measure. This will give you the desired scale for baseline. For example: Bust 35, length of sleeve 31, width of back 6; this gives you scale 25 for baseline. Always use bust scale for crosslines.

Skirts: Take waist measure and desired length of skirt. For example: Waist 24, length of skirt 41. Use scale 24 for crosslines and 41 for baselines.

Full-length garments: If the garment has a waistline, draft to that point with length of waist scale. Then subtract length of waist from full-length measure. This will give the scale from waistline down. For example: Bust 33, length of waist 15, full length 56, less 15 (length of waist). This will give you scale 41 for skirt part of garment. Use bust scale on all crosslines.

Stout forms (over 46 bust): Take half of bust measure and double all points on crosslines. For example: Bust 50, length of waist 16. Use scale 32 for baseline and scale 25 for crossline. Double all points with scale 25.

Drafting Waist Patterns. Assume the measures are bust 34 inches, length of waist 15 inches, and around the waist 24 inches. Place bust measure scale number 34 on short arm of square. Double length of waist measure 15, which will make 30, and place scale 30 on long arm of square. Place your square on the paper parallel with the edges. Draw a line on the outside of the square. The first line made at the short arm of the square is called the *first crossline,* and the line made at the long arm of the square is called the *baseline.* Any part of the waist may be drafted first, but for convenience take the back. Place square with length of waist scale even with first top crossline and baseline. Then make a point opposite D, then 2A, 5D, and 10. Make an X at 10, which denotes ten spaces. Move the square down even with the X and make a point at 5D. Make points at 8A and 9F, which makes 18A and 19F. This completes all points on baseline.

Starting at 0 on first crossline with bust measure scale, locate a point at 2 1/2. Move square down to the second point on baseline 2A, omitting the first point, as there is no crossline there. Square out from point 2A and make a point at 6. Draw a line to baseline. Move square down to 5D and make a point at 6. Move down to 10X and make points at B and 3E. Move down to 15D waistline, and make points at 1/2 and 2C. Move down to 18A and make a point at 2 1/2. This completes all points on crosslines. Be careful to get all of your crosslines perfectly square.

Applying the form piece or curve: If you are careful to distinguish between inward and outward curves, and follow the rule in applying the form piece, you will soon be able to measure all curves correctly.

The index hand is used for two purposes. First, to show the direction the large part of the form piece should point. Second, to show the inward and the outward curve.

In this first draft the index hand points to a certain letter in the draft, denoting that this letter on the form piece is to be placed at the first point in front of the letter in the draft. To get the correct curve for the neck, notice the letter M. Place the

letter M on the form piece at 2 1/2. Draw a line from this point to D on baseline, making an inward curve.

For the shoulder, notice the letter G. Place the letter G on the form piece at 2 1/2. Draw an inward curve from this point to 6. To get the curve from 6 to 6 at armhole, use inside of small end of form piece. This is the only place the inside of the form piece is used. From 6 to 3E you have the letter K. Place the letter K at 6 and draw an inward curve from this point to 3E. Reverse form piece and place the letter K at 2C, at waistline. Draw an inward curve from this point to 3E. Reverse form piece again and place the letter K at 2C. Draw an inward curve from this point to 2 1/2. Draw a straight line from 2 1/2 to 19F.

Place the letter I at 1/2 (waistline) and draw an inward curve from this point to 19F. Reverse form piece and place the letter G at 1/2 (waistline). Draw an inward curve from this point to B. Reverse form piece and draw an outward curve from B to 2A. This completes the draft, as all seams are laid off in the same manner. Front, side back, and underarm pieces are drafted the same as the back.

Waist and sleeve lengths that are not whole numbers: The double scale which is used for length of waist on baseline will bring the desired length of waist on all odd or even numbers. For example, if the length of waist is 14 1/2 inches use scale 29. For 15 inches use scale 30. For 15 1/2 inches use scale 31. But should the length of waist be 14 3/4, 15 1/4, or 15 3/4 inches, then the waist must be raised or lowered 1/4 inch. This amount is the extreme change in all cases. If waistline of back has been raised or lowered 1/4 inch, you must change waistline of front, side back, and underarm piece the same amount.

If the sleeve measure is 24 1/2 inches instead of 24, use scale 24. Lengthen the upper and under part of sleeve 1/2 inch at wrist by lowering the points 28C and 31 on baseline of upper part of sleeve 1/2 inch. Also lower points on baseline of under part of sleeve, at 24 1/2 and 27B, 1/2 inch.

In sleeves, skirts, and all full-length garments, the change, if any, will not be over 1/2 inch.

To test size around waist: If pattern drafted does not correspond with waist measure, change at front and underarm seams. In extreme cases the darts may be changed.

Always read the directions given with each garment.

Cutting and Basting. You cannot be too careful in this branch of work. You cannot expect good results from a poorly basted garment.

Waists: Fold waist lining crosswise. Place pattern on lining so that all waistlines run perfectly straight with grain of goods. Pin in position. Then trace all seams, darts, and waistlines carefully.

In basting, always begin at waistline. Baste from the waistline up and from the waistline down, except for darts. Baste from top of dart down, paying no attention to waistline.

Sleeves are cut on lengthwise fold of lining. Lay pattern on lining so that crosslines on pattern are straight with grain of goods. Follow the same rule in cutting outside goods.

To baste the sleeve, pin seams at top, bottom, and center. Then baste from the bottom up. Should there be gathers at elbow, arrange them 1 1/2 inches to each side of elbow.

A good rule for basting sleeve in armhole: Measure 1 inch back of shoulder seam. Then fold armhole, placing inseam of sleeve at center of armhole. Baste sleeve in plain from side form of waist, to 1 1/2 inches in front of inseam of sleeve. Gather the remainder to fit armhole. In basting, always hold the sleeve toward you.

Skirts: Lay pattern on lining or goods so that crosslines on patterns run straight with grain of goods.

To baste, pin seams at top, bottom, and center. Always baste with the bias seam toward you. Thus you will baste half of the skirt from the top down, and the other half from the bottom up.

If you are careful in drafting, cutting, and basting, you will never have any trouble with these patterns.

Practice Waist

The measurements used for this and the following four basic drafts are: Bust, length of waist, around the waist, and (for drafts with sleeves) length of sleeve. The main part of the bodice is drafted using the bust and length of waist scales. Sleeves are drafted using the bust and length of sleeve scales.

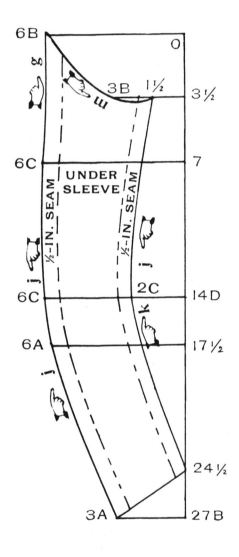

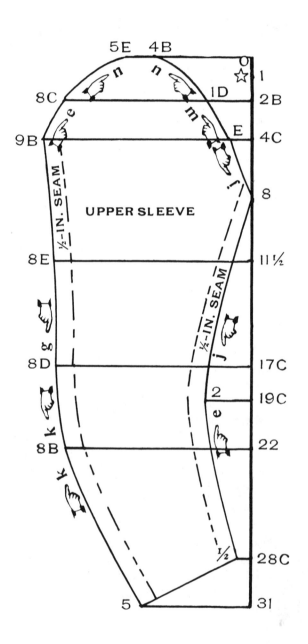

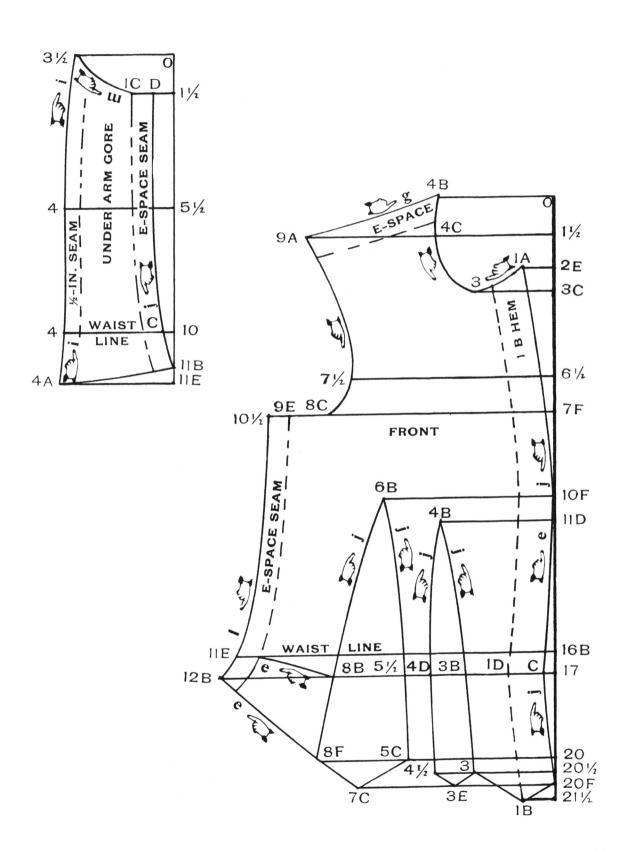

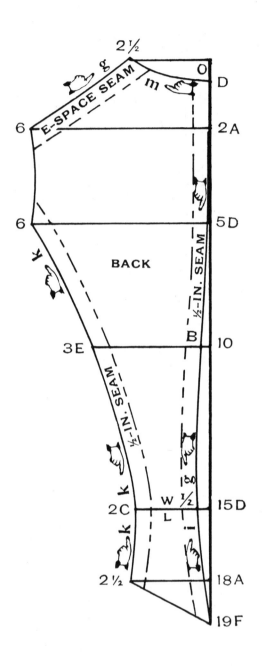

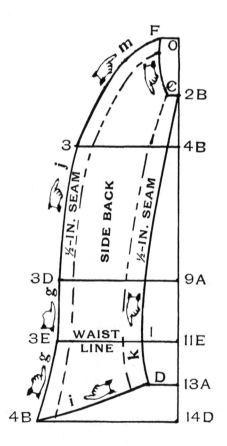

For Medium and Slender Forms

Draft for Medium and Slender Forms

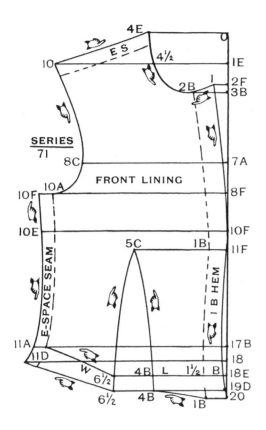

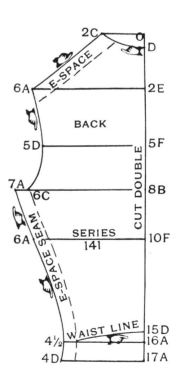

A Good Draft for Medium Stout Forms

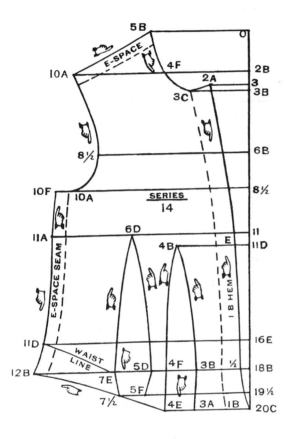

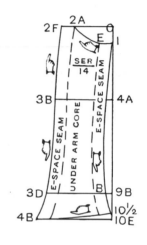

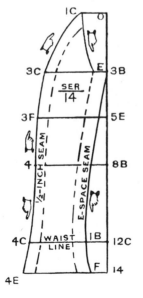

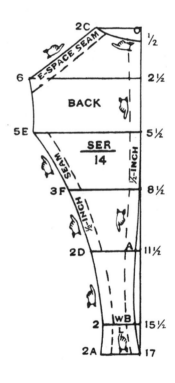

Draft for Medium and Slender Forms

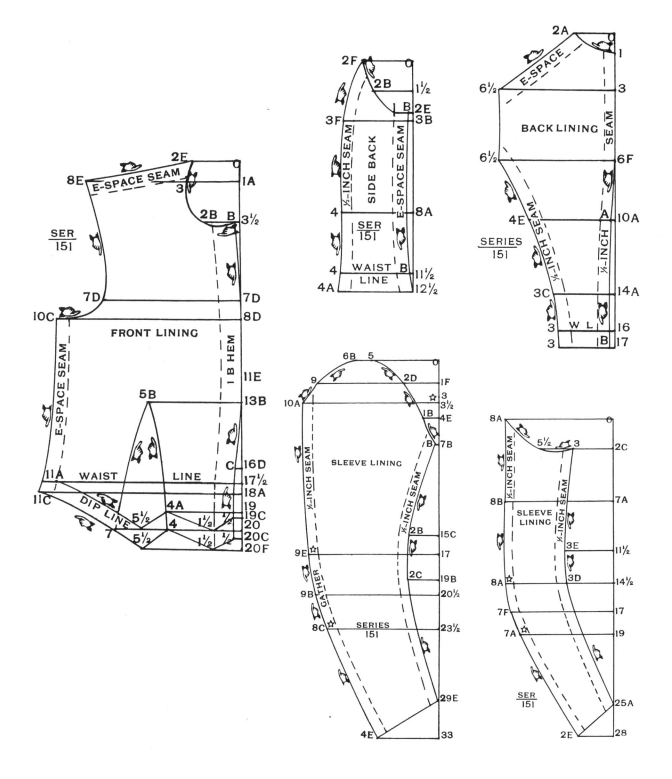

Draft for Medium and Slender Forms

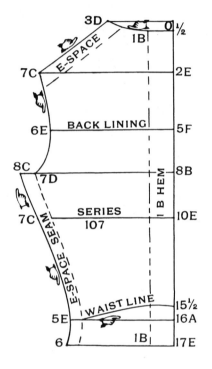

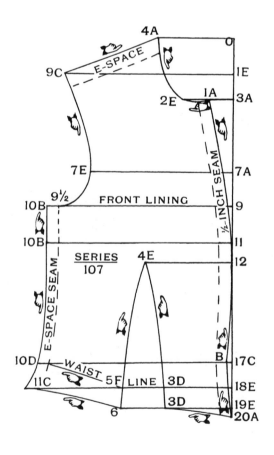

Ladies' Empire Coat

Four measures are taken for this coat: Bust, length of waist, full length, and length of sleeve. It is drafted in eight pieces: Back and front of coat, back and front yoke, collar, sleeve (two pieces), and cuff.

To Draft. Select bust and length of waist scales for yokes, collar, and skirt part of coat to star point 5 1/2 and 5B. Then subtract length of waist from full-length measure. This will give desired scale for baseline from waistline down. Use bust scale for all crosslines. For sleeve and cuff, use bust and length of sleeve scales.

To Make. Fold dotted lines to heavy lines, bringing first one to center of back, making eight inward-turning tucks for back. Follow same direc-

tions for front of coat, making six outward-turning tucks as shown in illustration. Stitch to any desired length. Join to yokes. No allowance is made for tucks in yoke.

The skirt is a nine-gore flare, drafted in five pieces. Join according to stars, and finish in the usual way.

White chiffon broadcloth is the material used for this coat, with a fancy black silk braid to trim front of coat and lower part of yokes. Collar, cuffs, and lining are of ermine.

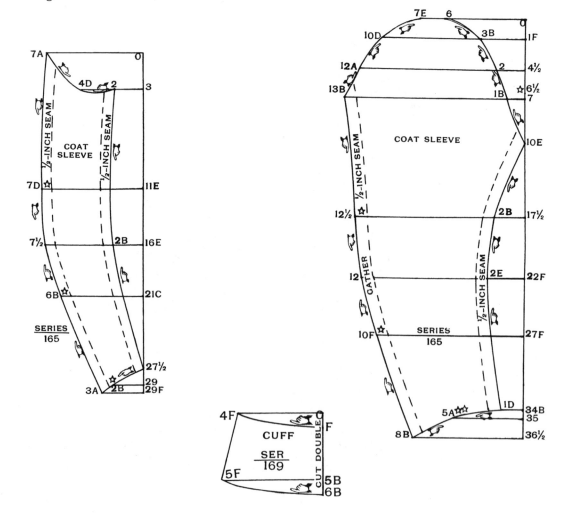

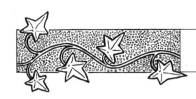

Ladies' Empire Coat

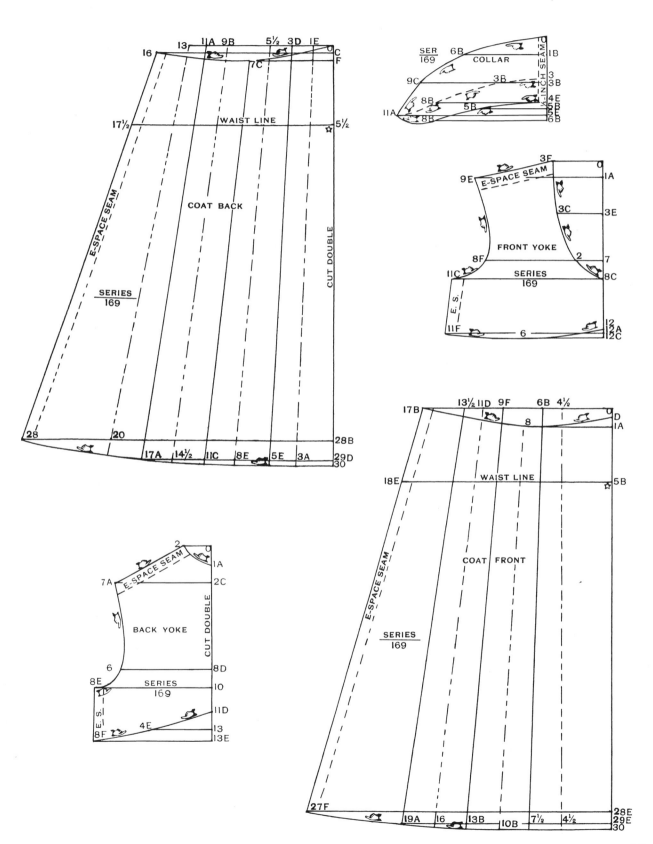

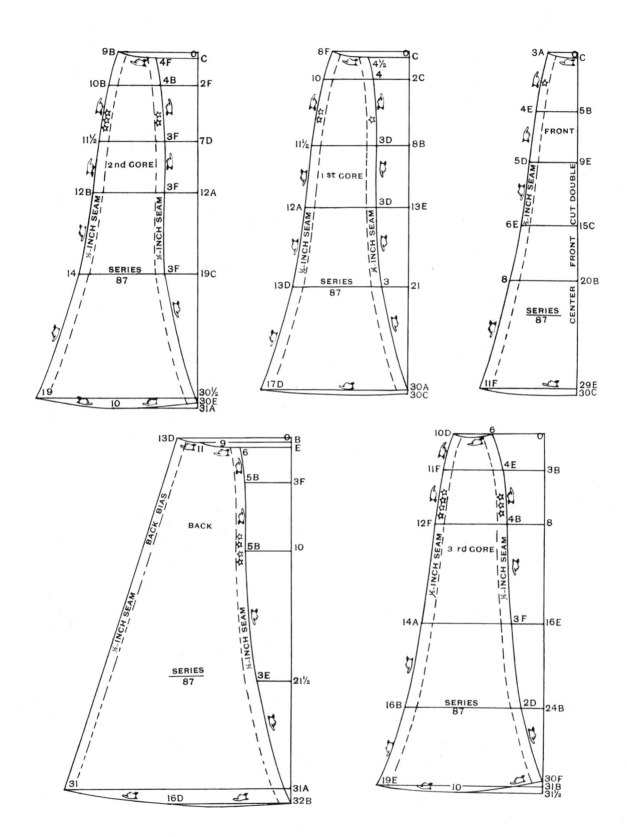

1905

Ladies' Shirtwaist Suit

Five measures are taken for this garment: Bust, length of waist, length of sleeve, around the waist, and length of skirt. It is drafted in 16 pieces: Back and front of waist, sleeve, cuff and turnover cuff, neckband, collar and turnover collar, and 15-gore kilt skirt (8 pieces).

To Draft. Select bust and length of waist scales for back and front of waist, neckband, collar, and turnover collar. For sleeve and cuffs, use bust and length of sleeve scales. For skirt, use waist and length of skirt scales.

Before drawing shoulder seam on front of waist pattern, fold tucks on dotted lines, making tucks 1 inch wide, then scroll from 4D to 15F.

To Make. Join shoulder and underarm seams. Gather to fit waist measure. Join seam of sleeve, and gather to fit armhole and cuff.

Join skirt according to stars. Stitch and press. Then arrange tucks by folding all heavy lines to dotted lines, making nine tucks on each side of skirt. Press and stitch to any desired depth.

Silk finished mohair was used for this garment, with mohair braid for trimming.

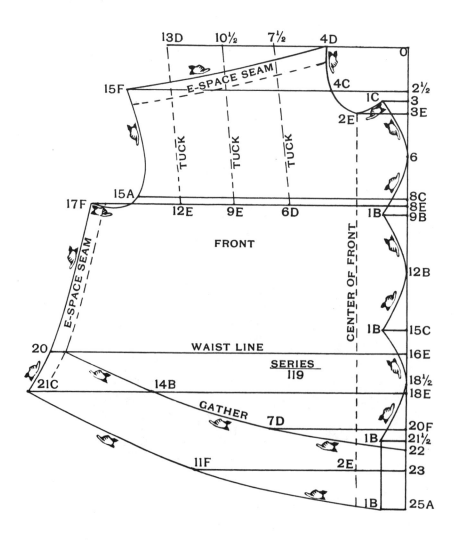

22

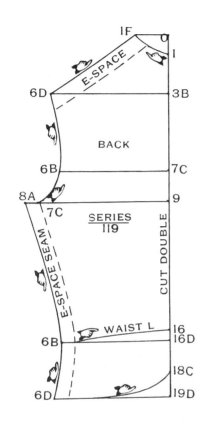

BACK

SERIES
119

E-SPACE

E-SPACE SEAM

CUT DOUBLE

WAIST L

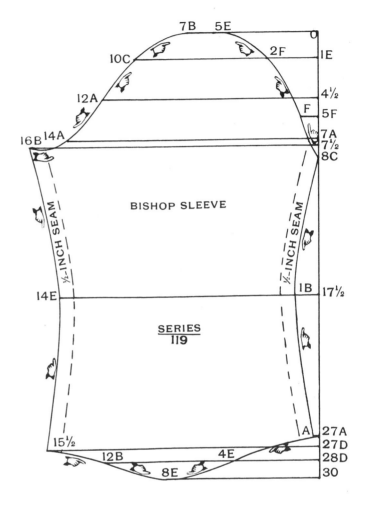

BISHOP SLEEVE

½-INCH SEAM

½-INCH SEAM

SERIES
119

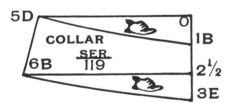

COLLAR
SER
119

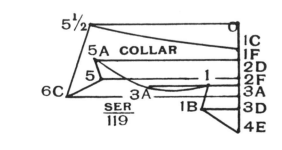

COLLAR

5A

SER
119

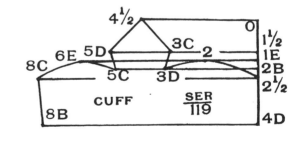

CUFF

SER
119

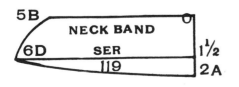

NECK BAND

SER

119

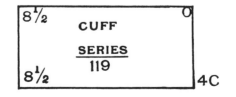

CUFF

SERIES
119

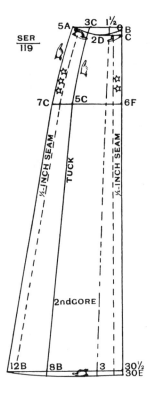

5A 3C 1½
SER
119
2D 4
B
C
7C 5C 6F
½-INCH SEAM
TUCK
½-INCH SEAM
2nd GORE
12B 8B 3 30½
30E

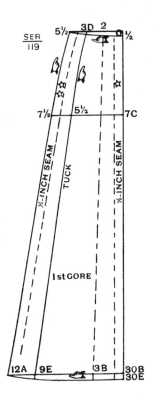

5½ 3D 2
SER
119
½
7½ 5½ 7C
½-INCH SEAM
TUCK
½-INCH SEAM
1st GORE
12A 9E 13B 30B
30E

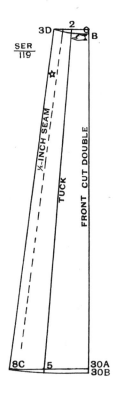

3D 2 B
SER
119
½-INCH SEAM
TUCK
FRONT CUT DOUBLE
8C 5 30A
30B

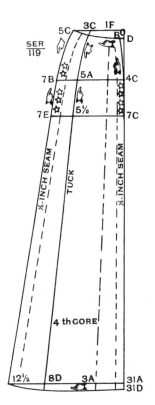

5C 3C 1F
SER
119
B D
7B 5A 4C
7E 5½ 7C
½-INCH SEAM
TUCK
½-INCH SEAM
4th GORE
12½ 8D 3A 31A
31D

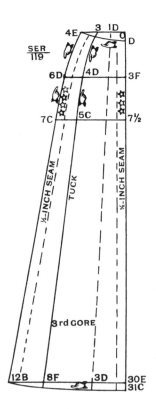

4E 3 1D
SER
119
D
6D 4D 3F
7C 5C 7½
½-INCH SEAM
TUCK
½-INCH SEAM
3rd GORE
12B 8F 3D 30E
31C

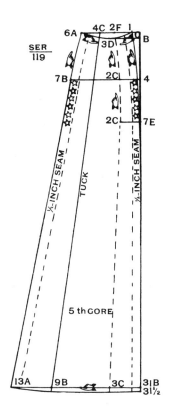

SER
119

6A 4C 2F I
3D B
7B 2CI 4
2C 7E
½-INCH SEAM
TUCK
½-INCH SEAM
5 th GORE
13A 9B 3C 31B
31½

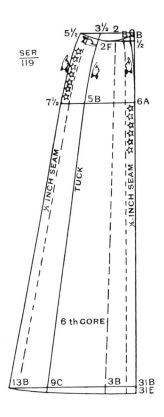

SER
119

5½ 3½ 2 B
2F B ½
7½ 5B 6A
½-INCH SEAM
TUCK
½-INCH SEAM
6 th GORE
13B 9C 3B 31B
31E

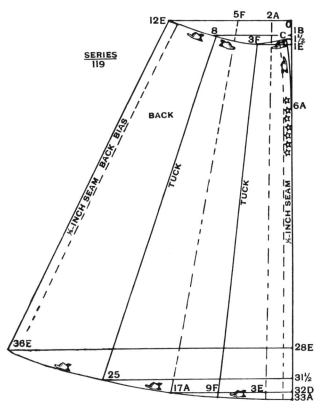

SERIES
119

12E 5F 2A
8 3F C IB
I½
IE
6A
½-INCH SEAM BACK BIAS
BACK
TUCK
TUCK
½-INCH SEAM
36E 28E
25 31½
17A 9F 3E 32D
33A

25

A Reception Toilette

Five measures are taken for this gown: Bust, length of waist, length of sleeve, around the waist, and length of skirt. It is drafted in 14 pieces: Back and front of lining, upper back and front, back and front yoke, bertha, front shirring, sleeve lining (2 pieces), sleeve puff, and 5-gore skirt (3 pieces).

To Draft. Select bust and length of waist scales for tight lining, upper back and front, two yoke portions, bertha, and front shirring. For sleeve lining and puff, use bust and length of sleeve scales. For skirt, use waist and length of skirt scales.

To Make. Take up darts in front of lining. Gather upper back and front to fit lining. Arrange yokes to same so as to cover gathers. Join shoulder and underarm seams. Gather lower part of waist to fit lining. Arrange bertha and front shirring like illustration.

Join skirt according to stars and finish in the usual way. No draft is given for skirt ruffles, as they are plain, with the exception of a point at front, side, and back.

A pretty shade of brown voile was the material used for this garment, adorned with satin ribbon of the same shade; with lace for yokes, collar, and sleeves.

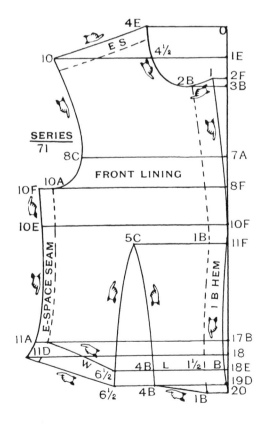

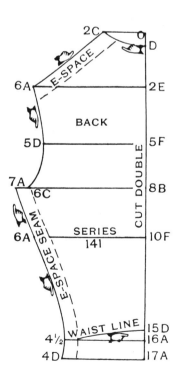

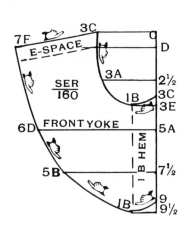

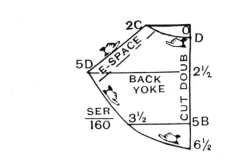

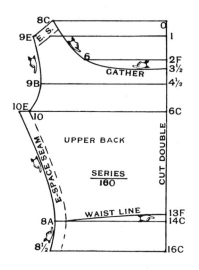

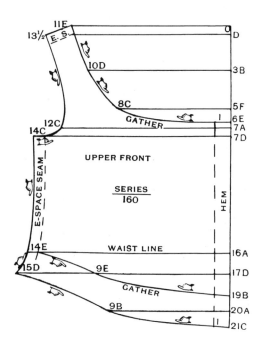

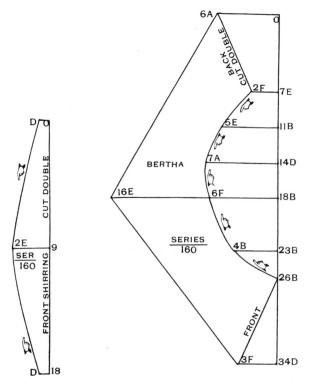

28

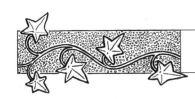

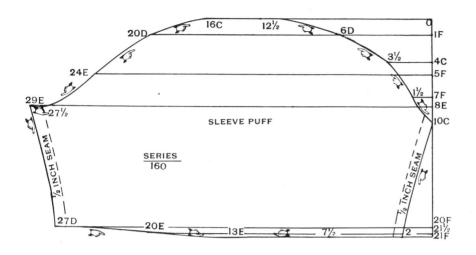

SLEEVE PUFF

SERIES
160

½ INCH SEAM

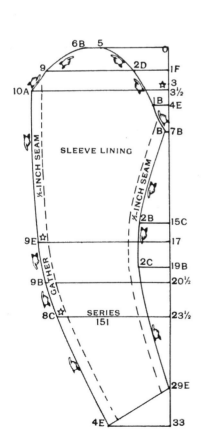

SLEEVE LINING

½-INCH SEAM

SERIES
151

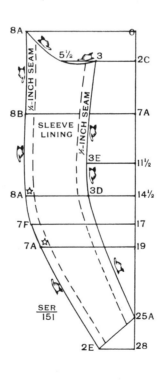

SLEEVE LINING

½-INCH SEAM

SER
151

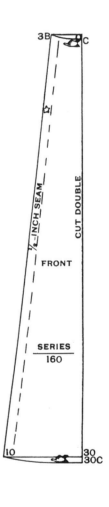

½-INCH SEAM

FRONT

CUT DOUBLE

SERIES
160

29

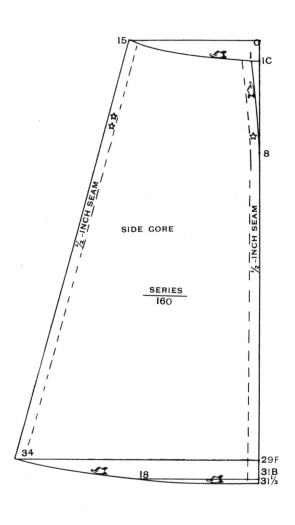

SIDE GORE

SERIES
160

½-INCH SEAM

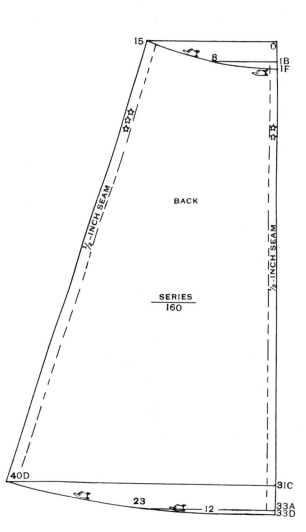

BACK

SERIES
160

½-INCH SEAM

Ladies' Dressy Paletot

Four measures are taken for this coat: Bust, length of waist, full length, and length of sleeve. It is drafted in nine pieces: Back and front of coat, coat ruffle, cape, coat revere, two collar pieces, sleeve, and cuff.

To Draft. Select bust and length of waist scales and draft back and front of coat to star. Then subtract length of waist from full length. This will give correct scale for baseline, from star to bottom of coat. Use same scale on baseline for coat ruffle and coat revere. Use bust scale for all crosslines. For cape and two collar portions, use bust and length of waist scales. For sleeve and cuff, use bust and length of sleeve scales.

To Make. Join shoulder and side seams of coat. Gather ruffle to bottom of coat. Join coat revere to cape (notice stars) before cutting goods. Line cape and revere with silk. Join to front of coat (notice diagram), then roll to outside of coat like illustration. The collar is in two sections, stock and rolling. Make sleeve in the usual way.

Black velvet was used for this French model. The shawl-shaped pelerine, cuffs, collar, and top of coat ruffle are trimmed with gimp passementerie. The coat is lined with fur. This will be a very good style for summer wear, made from heavy silk, with trimmings of lace.

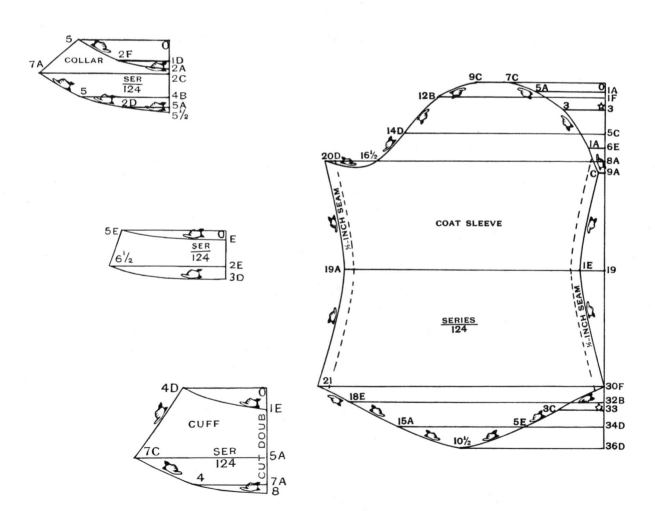

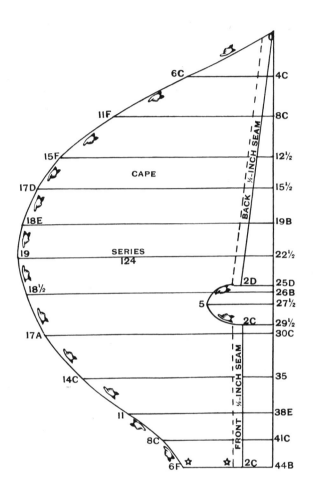

6C   4C

11F   8C

15F   12½

CAPE   15½

17D   19B

18E

19   SERIES 124   22½

18½   2D   25D
26B
5   27½
2C   29½
17A   30C

14C   35

11   38E
8C   41C
6F   2C   44B

BACK ½-INCH SEAM

FRONT ½-INCH SEAM

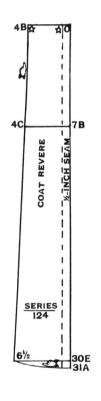

4B   0

4C   7B

COAT REVERE

½-INCH SEAM

SERIES 124

6½   30E
31A

63

COAT RUFFLE

SERIES 124

BACK CUT DOUBLE

63   9E

33

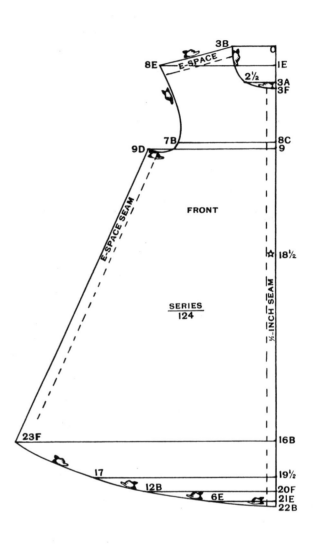

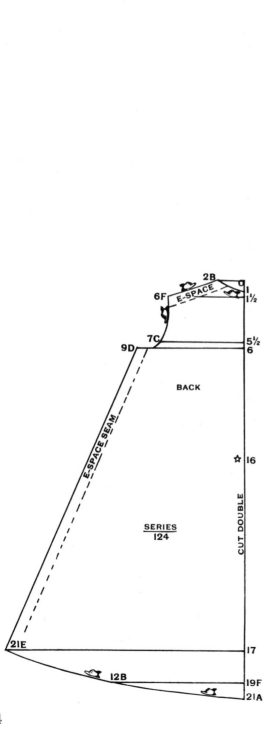

Ladies' Princess Gown

Five measures are taken for this gown: Bust, length of waist, length of sleeve, around the waist, and length of skirt. It is drafted in 13 pieces: Back, first and second side back, front, first and second side front, underarm gore, yoke (2 pieces), collar, sleeve lining (2 pieces), and sleeve puff.

To Draft. Select bust and length of waist scales for yokes, collar, back, first and second side back, underarm gore, front, and first and second side front to waistline (notice star). Then select length of skirt scale and copy all points on baseline from waistline down. Use bust scale for all crosslines. For sleeve lining and sleeve puff, use bust and length of sleeve scales.

Sleeves may be made elbow or full length.

To Make. Join the different parts of the princess together, basting from waistline up and from waistline down. At each gore below the hips there is a side pleat which gives the fullness to the lower part of the princess. The seams may be stitched like the illustration or not, as desired.

Light fawn-colored cloth was used for this gown, with lace yoke and buttons for decorations.

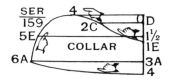

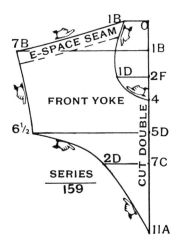

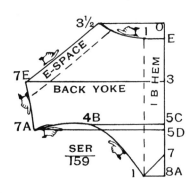

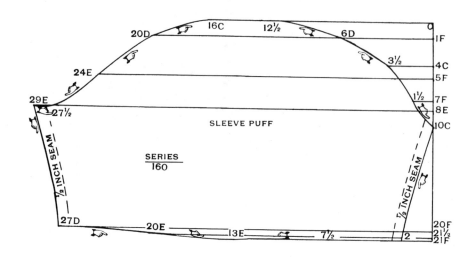

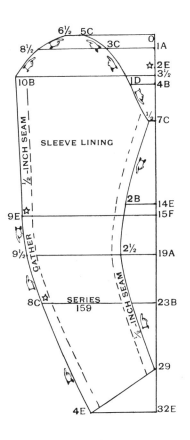

SLEEVE LINING

½-INCH SEAM

GATHER

SERIES
159

½-INCH SEAM

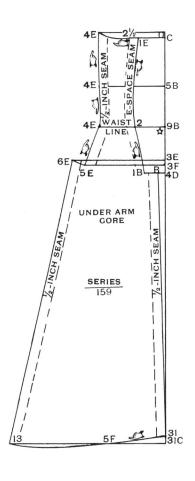

E-SPACE SEAM

½-INCH SEAM

WAIST LINE

UNDER ARM GORE

SERIES
159

½-INCH SEAM

½-INCH SEAM

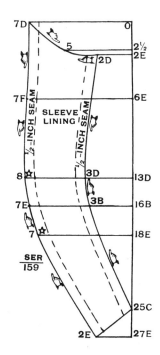

SLEEVE LINING

½-INCH SEAM

½-INCH SEAM

SER
159

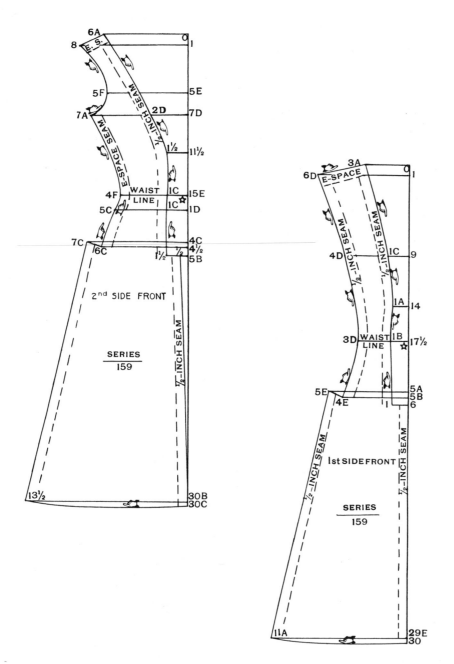

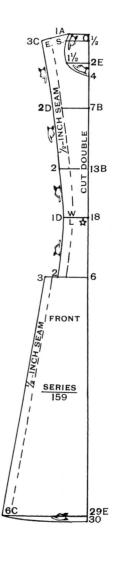

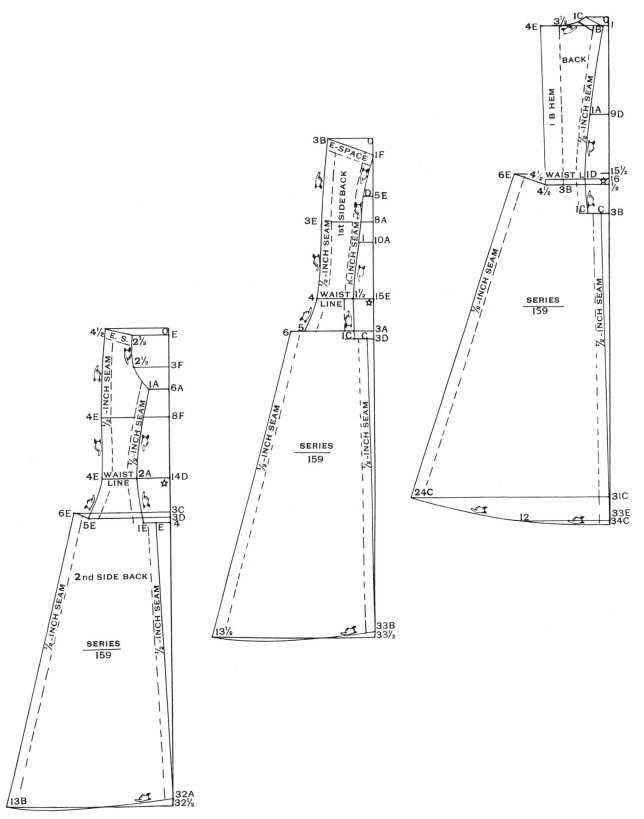

A Dressy Reception Gown

Five measures are taken for this garment: Bust, length of waist, length of sleeve, around the waist, and length of skirt. It is drafted in 16 pieces: Back, front, and side back of lining; upper back and side back; front and side front; back and front yoke; cape; girdle; sleeve puff; and a 7-gore skirt (4 pieces).

To Draft. Select bust and length of waist scales for tight lining, upper back, side back, front, side front, two yoke portions, cape, and girdle. For skirt, use waist and length of skirt scales. For sleeve puff, use bust and length of sleeve scales.

Two capes are given in one diagram.

To Make. Sew back and side back of lining together. Take darts in front. Baste side back to lining and fold back on dotted line, one space form-

ing the first tuck or fold. The other two folds are cut on the bias fold of the material and are stitched to side back. Sew back and back yoke to lining. Follow same directions with front. Close the waist where front and side front join. Arrange capes to seam of side back and side front. Finish elbow sleeve in the usual way.

Skirt is very full, with panel front. Join according to stars and gather to fit waist measure. The folds on skirt are the same width as those on waist.

Pongee in natural color was used for this gown. The trimming consists of embroidered silk braid and princess lace.

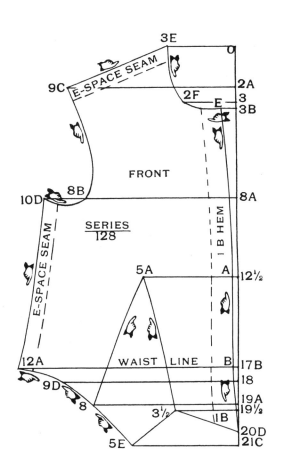

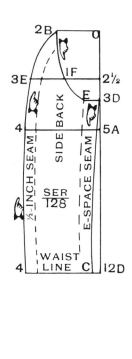

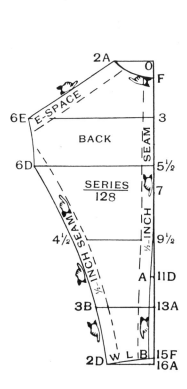

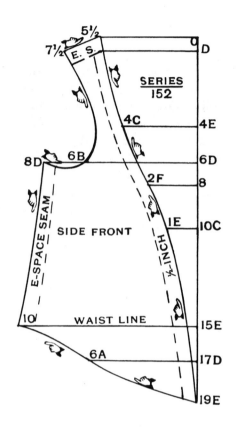

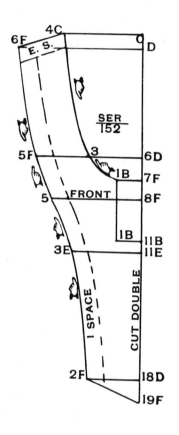

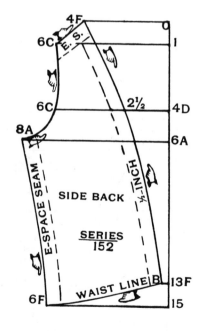

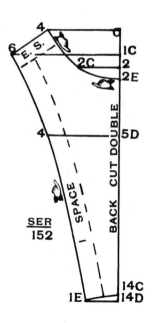

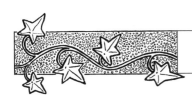

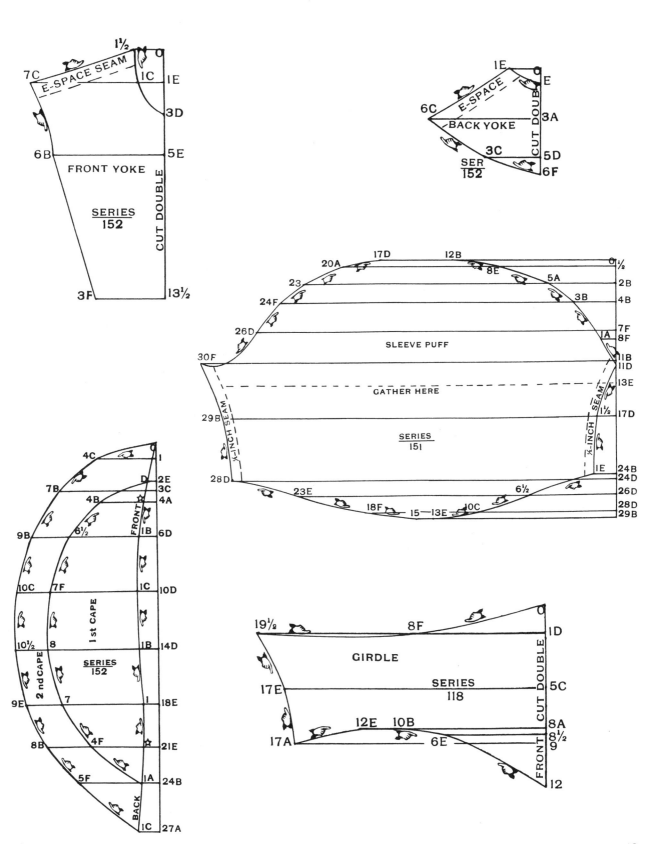

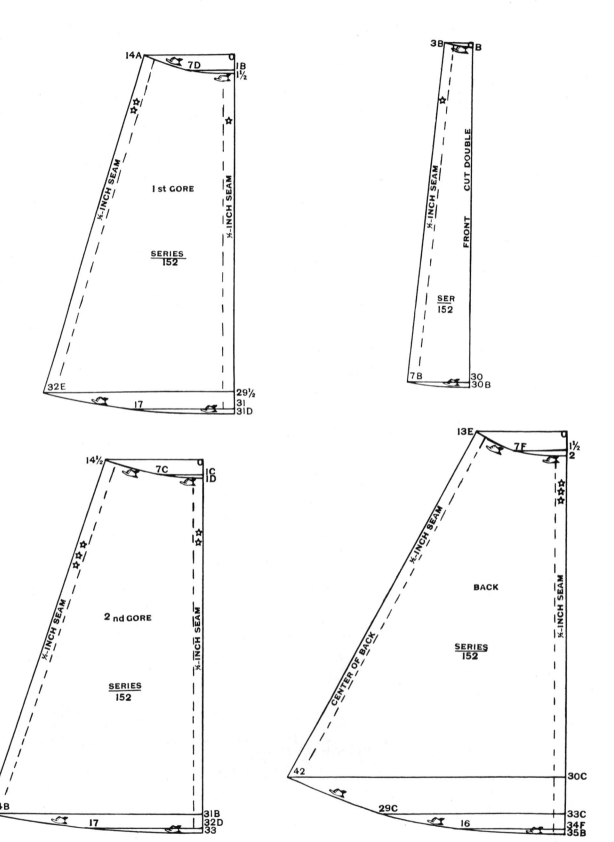

Visiting Costume

Five measures are taken for this suit: Bust, length of waist, length of sleeve, around the waist, and length of skirt. It is drafted in ten pieces: Jacket back, front, vest front, collar, belt, peplum, sleeve, cuff, and circular skirt drafted in two pieces for convenience.

To Draft. Select bust and length of waist scales for jacket back, front, vest front, collar, belt, and peplum. For sleeve and cuff, use bust and length of sleeve scales. For skirt, use waist and length of skirt scales.

To Make. If blouse back is desired, gather on lower lines. But if not, cut at waistline on back of pattern and first dip line on front. Make vest and

sew to canvas of jacket front before putting in jacket lining. Notice star at 2 1/2 in diagram for peplum. Fold to center of back, making an inverted pleat. Finish jacket and peplum with belt. Make and finish sleeve in the usual way.

To make skirt, join skirt pattern according to stars before cutting out goods. Mark, and baste dotted lines together, making six deep tucks on each side of skirt (as shown in diagram). Stitch to desired depth. Press well if made from suitings.

Dark green velvet was used for this garment, with a delicate shade of ecru guipure lace for collar, cuffs, and reveres, and ecru broadcloth for vest. Broadcloth, cheviot, or any of the winter woolens would be appropriate.

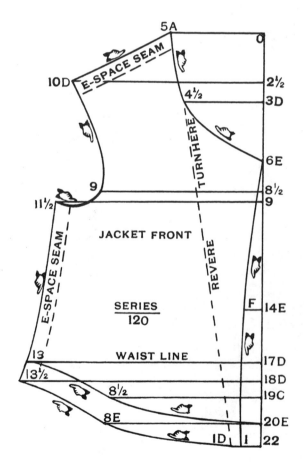

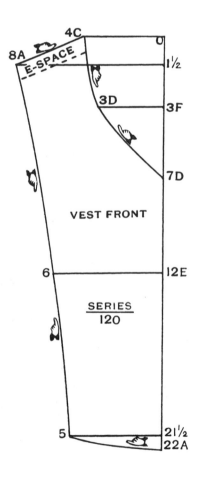

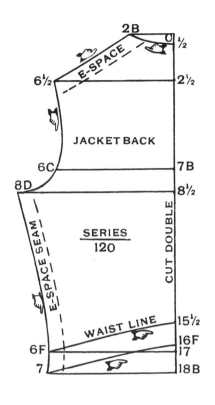

JACKET BACK

E-SPACE

SERIES
120

CUT DOUBLE

E-SPACE SEAM

WAIST LINE

2B
0 ½
6½
2½
6C 7B
8D 8½
6F 15½
16F
17
7 18B

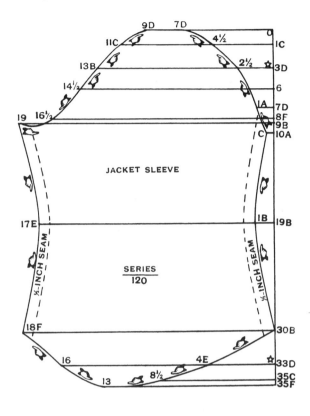

JACKET SLEEVE

SERIES
120

½-INCH SEAM

½-INCH SEAM

9D 7D
11C 4½ 1C
13B 2½ 3D
14½ 6
19 16½ 1A 7D
8F
9B
C 10A
17E 1B 19B
18F 30B
16 4E 33D
13 8½ 35C
35F

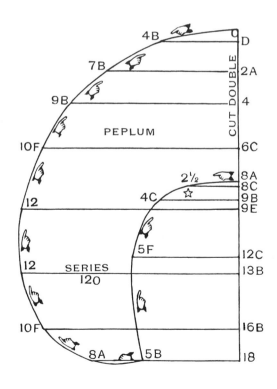

PEPLUM

SERIES
120

CUT DOUBLE

4B D
7B 2A
9B 4
10F 6C
8A
2½ 8C
4C 9B
9E
12
5F
12C
12 13B
SERIES
120
10F 16B
8A 5B 18

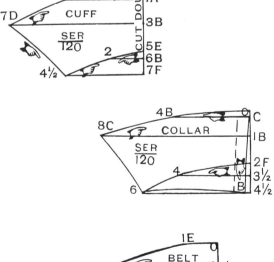

CUFF

SER
120

CUT DOUB

4½ 1A
7D 3B
5E
6B
4½ 2 7F

COLLAR

SER
120

8C 4B C
1B
2F
4 3½
6 B 4½

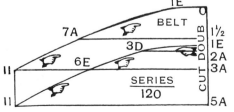

BELT

SERIES
120

CUT DOUB

1E
7A 1½
1E
3D 2A
11 6E 3A
11 5A

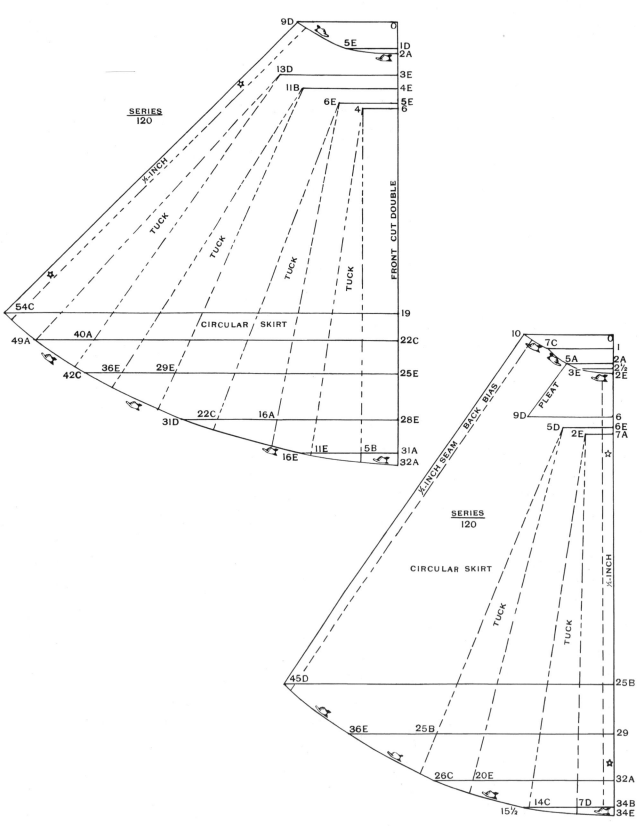

SERIES
120

¼-INCH

TUCK

TUCK

TUCK

TUCK

FRONT CUT DOUBLE

CIRCULAR SKIRT

9D   5E   0
                       1D
                       2A
            13D   3E
       11B   4E
         6E   5E
              4   6

54C
                       19
49A   40A   22C
42C   36E   29E   25E
       31D 22C 16A   28E
             16E 11E 5B 31A
                           32A

¼-INCH SEAM   BACK BIAS

SERIES
120

CIRCULAR SKIRT

PLEAT

TUCK

TUCK

¼-INCH

10   7C   0
                 1
        5A   2A
        3E   2½
                 2E
9D   6
      5D   2E   6E
                 7A

45D   25B

      36E   25B 29

      26C   20E 32A
         14C 7D 34B
      15½   34E

Ladies' Street Costume

Five measures are taken for this garment: Bust, length of waist, length of sleeve, around the waist, and length of skirt. It is drafted in 15 pieces: Back and front of waist, back and front of jacket, back and front of bolero effect, jacket sleeve, shirtwaist sleeve, and a 13-gore skirt (7 pieces).

To Draft. Select bust and length of waist scales for waist back and front, jacket back and front, and bolero effect. For sleeve and jacket sleeve, use bust and length of sleeve scales. For skirt, use waist and length of skirt scales.

Two extra drafts are given with this suit, back and front of bolero effect or bretelles, which may be used in place of the jacket.

To Make. Join shoulder and underarm seams of waist. Gather to fit waist measure. Gather sleeve to cuff and armhole. Join shoulder and underarm seams of jacket. Gather jacket sleeve from points 9C to 14C to fit armhole.

Join shoulder and underarm seams of bretelles. Fasten lower part to girdle. The same sleeve may be used and sewn in armhole with shirtwaist sleeve.

Join skirt according to stars with 1/2-inch seams. Stitch and press seam flat 1 inch below extension. Stitch 3/8 inch from seam. The extension below will produce a ripple effect, like illustration. It may be pressed in pleats if so desired.

Black etamine was used for skirt and jacket, with white batiste waist trimmed with lace.

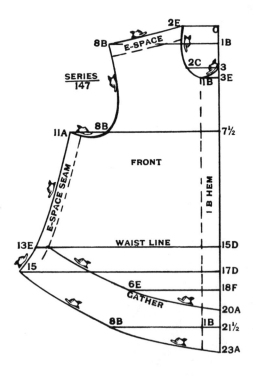

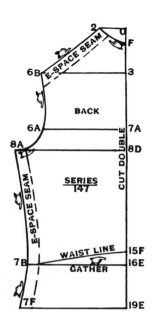

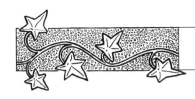
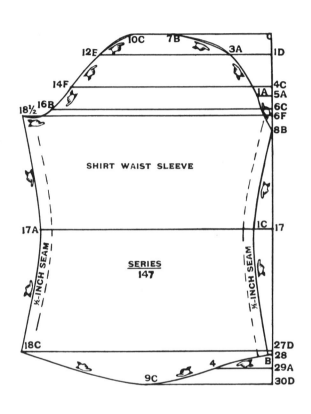

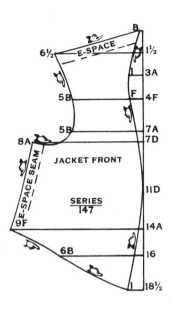

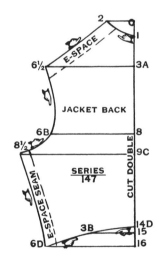

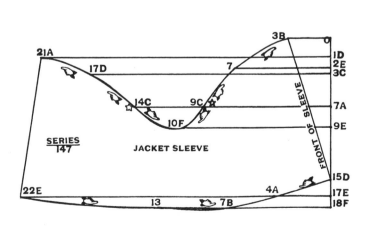

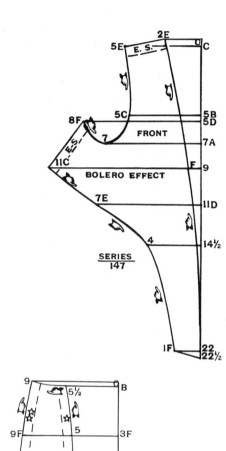

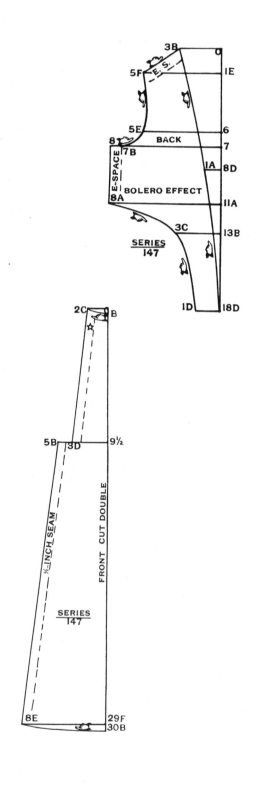

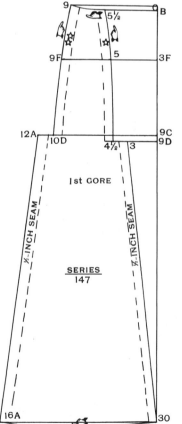

2E
5E E. S. C
5C 5B
8F 5D
7 FRONT 7A
E. S. F 9
11C BOLERO EFFECT
7E 11D
4 14½
SERIES
147
1F 22
22½

3B
5F E. S. 1E
5E 6
8 BACK 7
7B 1A 8D
E-SPACE
8A BOLERO EFFECT 11A
3C 13B
SERIES
147
1D 18D

9 B
5½
9F 5 3F
12A 9C
10D 4½ 3 9D
1st GORE
½-INCH SEAM
½-INCH SEAM
SERIES
147
16A 30

2C B
5B 3D 9½
½-INCH SEAM
FRONT CUT DOUBLE
SERIES
147
8E 29F
30B

52

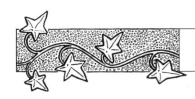

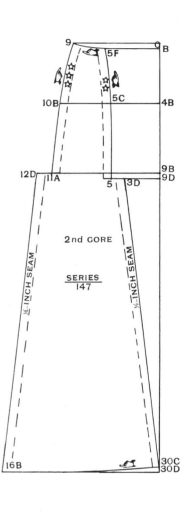

B

9 · 5F

10B · 5C · 4B

12D · 11A · 5 · 3D · 9B · 9D

2nd GORE

SERIES
147

½-INCH SEAM · ½-INCH SEAM

16B · 30C · 30D

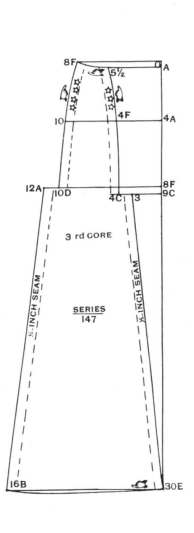

8F · 5½ · A

10 · 4F · 4A

12A · 10D · 4C · 3 · 8F · 9C

3 rd GORE

SERIES
147

½-INCH SEAM · ½-INCH SEAM

16B · 30E

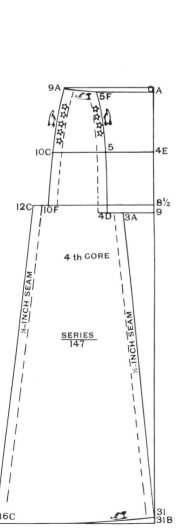

9A · 5F · A

10C · 5 · 4E

12C · 10F · 4D · 3A · 8½ · 9

4 th GORE

½-INCH SEAM · ½-INCH SEAM

SERIES
147

16C · 31 · 31B

53

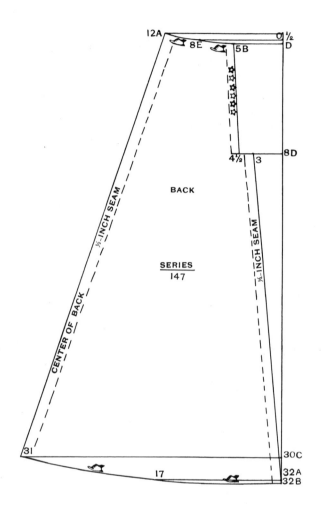

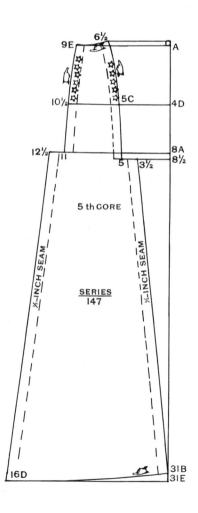

Ladies' Empire Gown

Three measures are taken for this garment: Bust, full length, and sleeve. It is drafted in six pieces: Back and front yoke, two skirt pieces, collar, and sleeve.

To Draft. Take full-length measure from bone in neck to desired length of garment. Take half that number and copy all points on baseline with scale corresponding with that number. Use bust scale for all crosslines. For example: Bust 34, full length 60. Use scale 34 for all crosslines and scale 30 for baseline of yokes, collar, and two skirt portions. For sleeve, use bust and length of sleeve scales.

White china silk was used for this garment, with knife pleating of the same for ruffles, and collar of bruges lace.

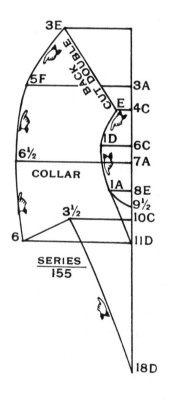

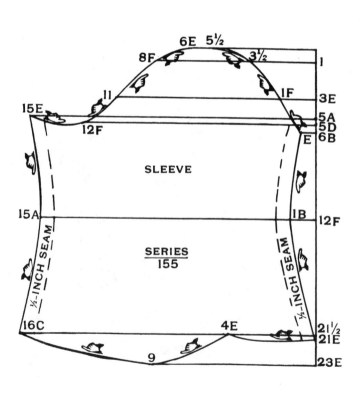

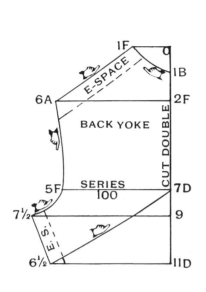

BACK YOKE

SERIES 100

CUT DOUBLE

E-SPACE

E. S.

1F · 0 · 1B · 2F · 6A · 5F · 7D · 9 · 7½ · 6½ · 11D

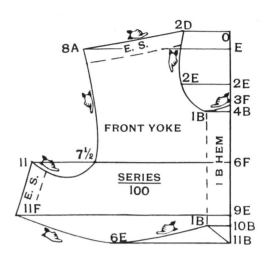

FRONT YOKE

SERIES 100

E. S.

I B HEM

2D · 0 · E · 8A · 2E · 2E · 3F · 4B · 1B · 7½ · 11 · 6F · 11F · 9E · 1B · 10B · 6E · 11B

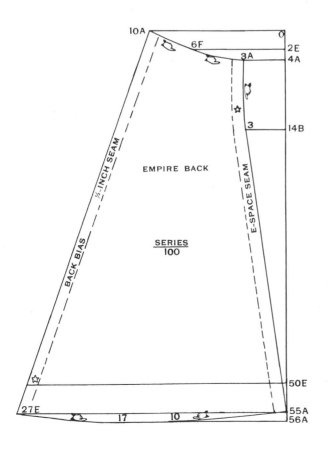

EMPIRE BACK

SERIES 100

½-INCH SEAM

BACK BIAS

E-SPACE SEAM

10A · 0 · 6F · 2E · 3A · 4A · 3 · 14B · 50E · 27E · 17 · 10 · 55A · 56A

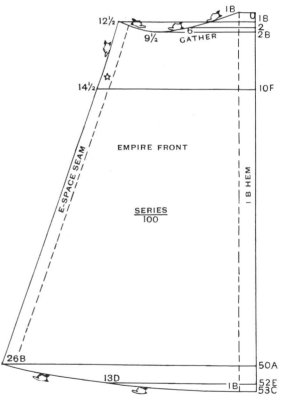

EMPIRE FRONT

SERIES 100

E-SPACE SEAM

I B HEM

GATHER

12½ · 1B · 0 · 1B · 9½ · 6 · 2 · 2B · 14½ · 10F · 26B · 50A · 13D · 52E · 1B · 53C

A Dressy Separate Waist

Four measures are taken for this waist: Bust, length of waist, around the waist, and length of sleeve. It is drafted in nine pieces: Back and front lining, upper back and front, back and front yoke, sleeve lining (two pieces), and sleeve puff.

To Draft. Select bust and length of waist scales for tight lining, upper back and front, and two yoke portions. For sleeve lining and sleeve puff, use bust and length of sleeve scales.

This waist may be made with or without tight lining. Use the first lining draft for medium and slender forms given with the "Using the American Garment Cutter System" instructions.

To Make with Lining. Take up darts in front. Gather upper back and front to fit yokes. In upper front gather from 2D. Notice stars in front and front yoke. Baste all to lining. Join shoulder and under-arm seams. Join seams of sleeve and arrange sleeve puff to same.

A pale shade of pink Liberty satin was used to develop this waist. The yoke and lower part of sleeves are covered with valenciennes insertion and bias folds of satin, with a wide band of lace in each shoulder to match lace down front of waist.

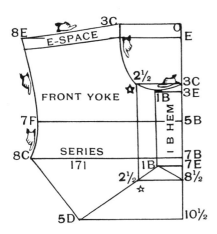

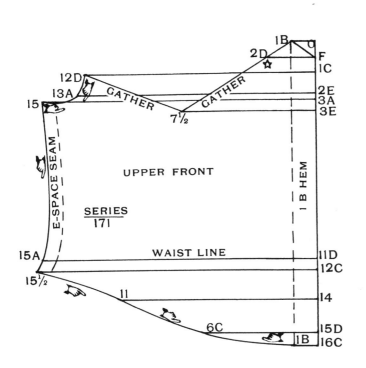

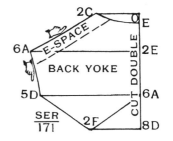

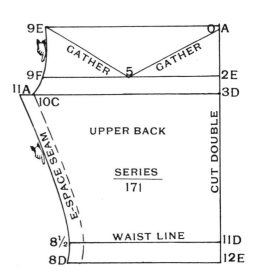

59

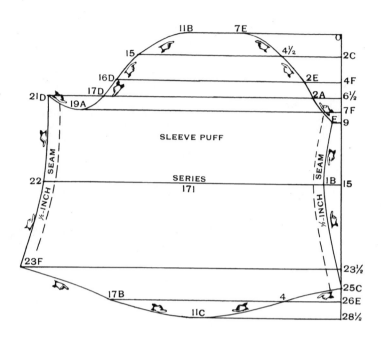

SLEEVE PUFF

SERIES 171

½-INCH SEAM

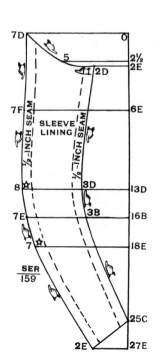

SLEEVE LINING

½-INCH SEAM

SER 159

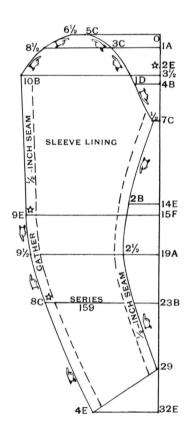

SLEEVE LINING

½-INCH SEAM

GATHER

SERIES 159

Ladies' Evening Waist

Ladies' Evening Waist

Four measures are taken for this waist: Bust, length of waist, around the waist, and sleeve. It is drafted in seven pieces: Back and front of tight lining, full front, lining for full front, back, chemisette, and sleeve puff.

To Draft. Select bust and length of waist scales for tight lining, full front, front lining, upper back, and chemisette. For sleeve puff, use bust and length of sleeve scales.

Use the first lining draft for medium and slender forms given with the "Using the American Garment Cutter System" instructions.

To Make. Gather full front between stars (notice diagrams). Sew to lining for full front. Take up dart in lining front. Baste upper fronts to lining. Also baste upper back to lining back. Join shoulder and underarm seams. Gather upper fronts and back to fit waist measure. Gather lower part of sleeve puff into small band to fit arm.

Silver-gray peau de crepe was used to make this attractive waist, with material of the same tucked for chemisette. Irish crochet insertion and princess lace were used for trimming.

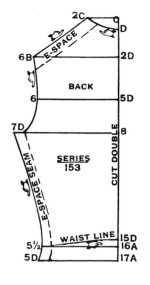

2C
D
6B E-SPACE 2D
BACK
6 5D
7D 8
SERIES
153
CUT DOUBLE
E-SPACE SEAM
WAIST LINE 15D
5½ 16A
5D 17A

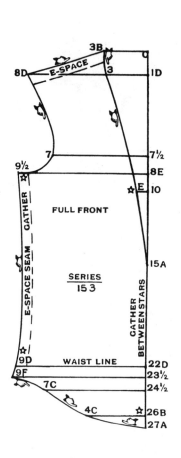

3B
8D E-SPACE 3
1D
7 7½
9½ 8E
E 10
FULL FRONT
E-SPACE SEAM GATHER
SERIES
153
GATHER BETWEEN STARS
15A
9D WAIST LINE 22D
9F 23½
7C 24½
4C 26B
27A

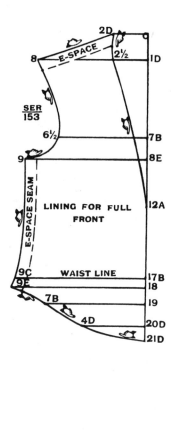

2D
8 E-SPACE 2½ 1D
SER
153
6½ 7B
9 8E
12A
LINING FOR FULL
FRONT
E-SPACE SEAM
9C WAIST LINE 17B
9E 18
7B 19
4D 20D
21D

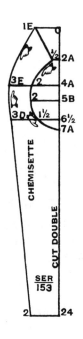

1E
½ 2A
3E 2 4A
2 5B
3D 1½ 6½
7A
CHEMISETTE
CUT DOUBLE
SER
153
2 24

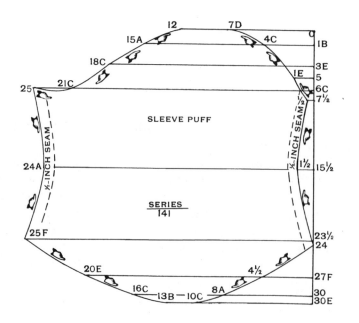

12 7D
15A 4C 1B
18C 3E
1E 5
21C 6C
25 7½
SLEEVE PUFF
24A 1½ 15½
⅛-INCH SEAM
SERIES
141
25F 23½
24
20E 4½ 27F
16C 8A 30
13B—10C 30E

A Dressy Shirtwaist

Three measures are taken for this waist: Bust, length of waist, and length of sleeve. It is drafted in four pieces: Back and front of waist, chemisette, and sleeve.

To Draft. Select bust and length of waist scales for back and front of waist and chemisette. For sleeve, use bust and length of sleeve scales.

Before drawing line for shoulder seam on front of pattern, fold dotted lines to heavy lines making two backward-turning tucks. Then curve from point 2 at neck to 11A, at armhole, and cut on that line.

Cut out on dotted line on front of pattern for vest front or chemisette.

To Make. Fold tucks as directed and stitch. Join shoulder and underarm seams. Gather back and front to fit waist measure. To make sleeve, cut on heavy line from star to star. Sew back seam of sleeve and gather extra material to fit space allowed.

One of the many beautiful figured taffeta silks was used for this design, with lace for collar and chemisette.

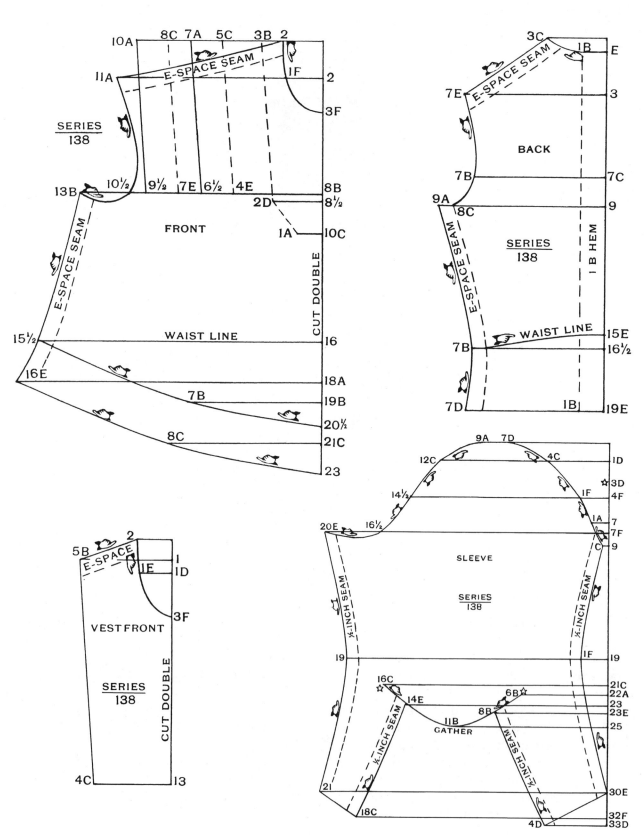

Ladies' Dressing Sack

Three measures are taken for this garment: Bust, length of waist, and length of sleeve. It is drafted in six pieces: Back and front waist, collar, sleeve, and peplum (two pieces).

To Draft. Select bust and length of waist scales for back and front of waist, collar, and peplum. For sleeve, use bust and length of sleeve scales.

To Make. Fold front on dotted lines and stitch tucks 1/4 inch from fold, making five backward-turning tucks. Join shoulder and underarm seams.

Gather to fit waist measure. Join pattern of peplum. Before cutting goods sew to waist and finish with belt. Make sleeve in the usual way.

Any of the soft materials are suitable for a garment of this kind. Desirable reproductions are obtainable from messlinette, crepe weaves, foulard, pongee, albatross, cashmere, lawn, swiss, or dimity.

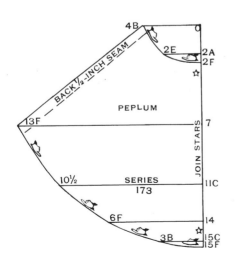

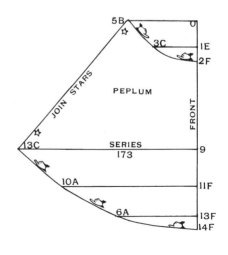

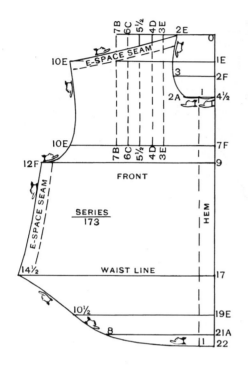

FRONT

SERIES
173

WAIST LINE

HEM

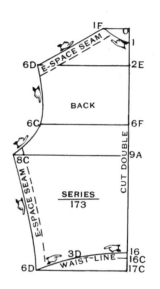

BACK

SERIES
173

CUT DOUBLE

WAIST-LINE

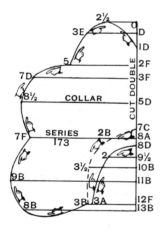

COLLAR

SERIES
173

CUT DOUBLE

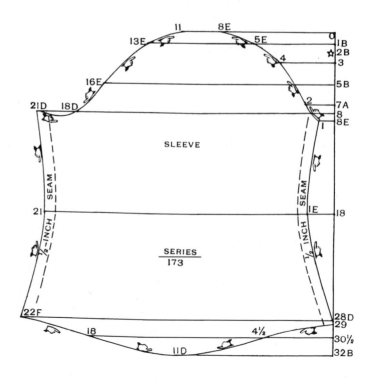

SLEEVE

SERIES
173

66

Seamless Corset Cover

Two measures are taken for this garment: Bust and length of waist. It is drafted in two pieces: Waist and peplum.

To Draft and Make. Select bust and length of waist scales for waist and peplum. Fold muslin on true bias. Place center of back on fold and cut double. Gather upper and lower part of waist to fit bust and waist. Join peplum to waist.

The material required is 1 1/4 yards 36 inches wide and 4 yards lace.

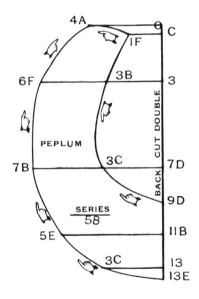

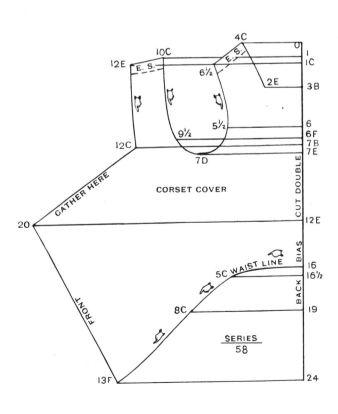

Ladies' Corset Cover

Two measures are required for this waist: Bust and length of waist. It is drafted in two pieces: Back and front.

To Draft and Make. Select bust and length of waist scales. Join shoulder and underarm seams. Gather to fit bust and waist.

To make waist like illustration for medium form, use 1 yard material 36 inches wide, 2 1/2 yards insertion, 4 yards lace, 3 yards beading, and 2 1/2 yards ribbon.

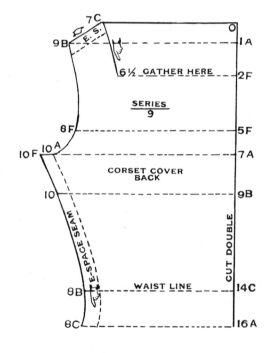

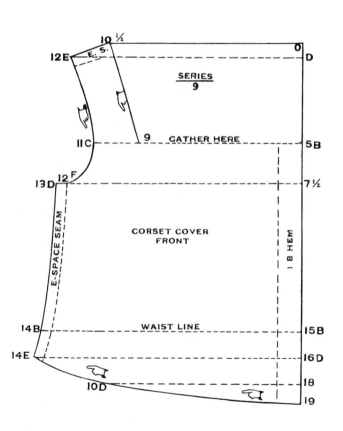

January 1907 American Modiste

The main feature to be noted is the insistence of both fashion and good form upon absolute fitness of costume for the time and place where it is worn. The varying occupations and social functions that fill the day and evening call for gowning distinctly appropriate to each.

The beauty of fur applied to cloth cannot be overestimated. Often one could utilize the good pieces of a partially worn neck fur or muff for trimming a cloth or velvet costume or wrap.

The new skirt fits the hips perfectly, and the line that marks the release of the fullness necessary at the foot may be set high or low according to fancy. The severe tailor-mades follow unpretentious lines and have few pleats, while for dressy toilettes as much elaboration as one wishes may be lavished upon the skirt.

The best-looking walking skirt for the city clears the ground by about 1 1/2 to 2 inches, while the rainy-day skirt is 1 inch or perhaps 2 inches shorter. Trains are the rule, not only on evening gowns but on all ceremonious toilettes, and the skirts are very long on the sides and front.

For evening models and dinner gowns, stiff as well as soft fabrics will be worn. In the firm materials beautiful designs of flowered taffeta and satin duchesse promise to be exceedingly popular, and moirés of varying shades will be seen. Favor will be given the old-fashioned peau de soie and surah; bengaline as well as silk-warp poplin will be much used for winter frocks. Chiffon cloth is a durable as well as fine material, having all the effects so desirable in costumes designed for evening wear.

In thinking out a dress one will generally find the collar a stumbling block. Whenever possible one falls back on lace, and lace will be much used for neckwear this season. Very thin pieces of featherbone are generally used for stiffening.

Much has been said of the pinafore or jumper style of waist. While this is a very youthful style, it is not confined to young girls. Women of mature years are also affecting the guimpe style. Very beautiful and costly models are shown with rich hand embroidery, in color. A great many of these are being made in the black taffetas and black satins, to be worn with black skirts.

The separate waist is always an all-absorbing problem. The lingerie styles of all kinds will be worn throughout the winter. It is fashion's fancy to have the laces on waists, or even the entire lace waist, dyed to match the suit for which the waist is designed. There is war being waged between silk and lingerie blouses, while over and above them both flannel makes an appeal to at least one or two hooks in the wardrobe of the woman who knows the relief of turning from overelaboration. Net waists over plaid silk linings are fancies which can be carried out in ways that one would not have dreamed of.

Of braiding we also see much, especially in gowns of a more dressy order, where occasionally the entire foot is thus trimmed to the height of 1/2 yard or so.

Ladies' Evening Gown

Five measures are taken for this gown: Bust, length of waist, length of sleeve, around the waist, and length of skirt. It is drafted in ten pieces: Back and front lining, upper back and front, girdle, sleeve puff, and full gathered skirt in seven gores (four pieces).

To Draft. Select bust and length of waist scales for tight lining and upper back and front. For girdle, use waist and length of waist scales. For sleeve puff, use bust and length of sleeve scales. For skirt, use waist and length of skirt scales.

To make waist like illustration the lining will have to be cut away to yoke depth.

To Make. Gather upper back and front to fit lining. Join shoulder and underarm seams. Gather lower part of waist to fit waist measure. Finish in the usual way. Gather sleeve puff to fit arm and armhole.

Join skirt according to stars and gather to fit waist measure. Finish bottom in the usual way.

Cream-colored crepe de chine was used for this garment, with narrow ruffles of the same material to trim skirt, and double ruffle around yoke. Material required for medium form, 14 yards 27 inches wide. Chantilly embroidery and ribbon are used to decorate waist and skirt.

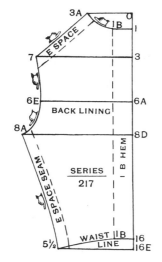

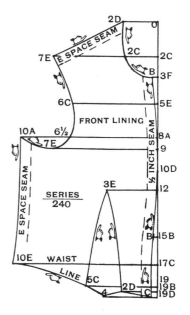

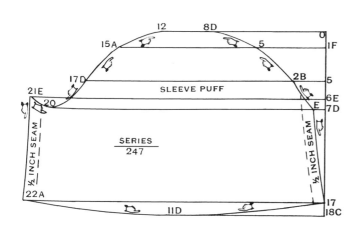

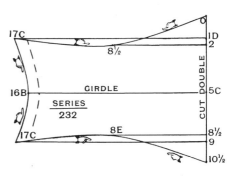

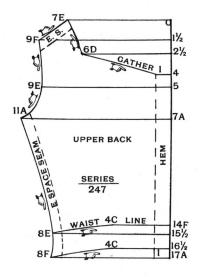

UPPER BACK

SERIES
247

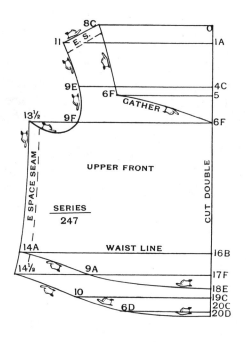

UPPER FRONT

SERIES
247

WAIST LINE

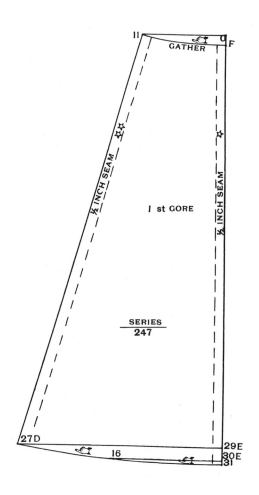

GATHER

1 st GORE

SERIES
247

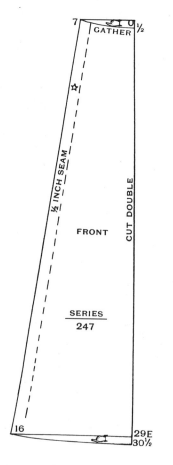

GATHER

FRONT

SERIES
247

Ladies' Evening Gown

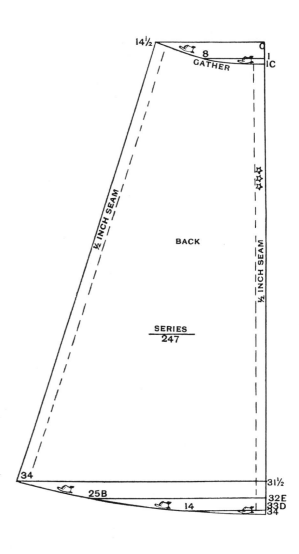

14½   8   0
         GATHER   1
                   IC

½ INCH SEAM

BACK

½ INCH SEAM

SERIES
247

34   31½
      25B   32E
         14   33D
                    34

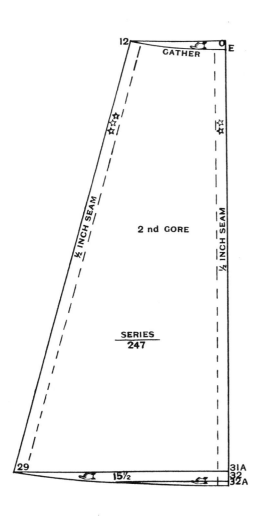

12   0 E
   GATHER

½ INCH SEAM

2 nd GORE

½ INCH SEAM

SERIES
247

29   31A
   15½   32
             32A

Ladies' Separate Waist

Three measures are taken for this waist: Bust, length of waist, and length of sleeve. It is drafted in six pieces: Back and front of waist, back and front yoke, sleeve puff, and cuff.

To Draft. Select bust and length of waist scales for back and front of waist and two yoke portions. For sleeve and cuff, use bust and length of sleeve scales.

Before making curved line on top of waist pattern, fold pattern on dotted lines and make tucks 1/2 inch deep. Then curve as directed and cut on that line.

To Make. Fold waist sections on dotted lines and stitch tucks 1/2 inch deep, making seven tucks on each side of front and five on each side of back.

Join yokes to waist with 1/2-inch seam. Close shoulder and underarm seams. Finish lower part of waist as desired.

Join sleeve puff and cuff separately. Then place seam of sleeve even with single star in top of cuff, and single star of sleeve even with seam of cuff. Finish in the usual way.

One of the many beautiful pressed stripe velvets was used for this waist. Yokes and collar are made of velvet trimmed with insertion. The front is finished with stole effect of insertion. Material required for medium form, 4 yards 20 inches wide.

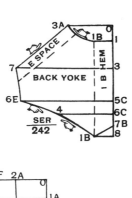

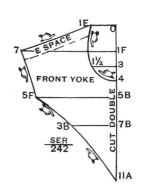

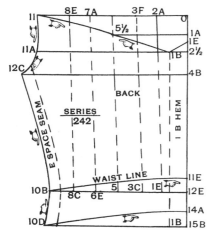

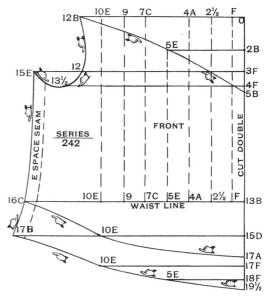

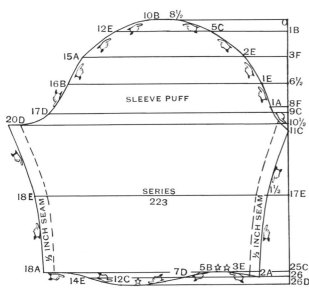

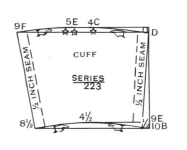

Ladies' Reception Gown

Five measures are taken for this costume: Bust, length of waist, length of sleeve, around the waist, and length of skirt. It is drafted in 18 pieces: Back and front lining, upper back and front, 2 yoke pieces, sleeve lining (2 pieces), sleeve puff, girdle, skirt yoke lining (4 pieces), and a 7-gore empire skirt drafted in 4 pieces.

To Draft. Select bust and length of waist scales for back and front lining, upper back and front, and two yoke portions. For girdle, use waist and length of waist scales. For sleeve lining and puff, use bust and length of sleeve scales. For skirt and skirt yokes, use waist and length of skirt scales.

To Make. Join front of linings in 1/2-inch seam and sew darts. Tuck goods for yoke before cutting. Sew to lining. Gather upper back and front to fit lining. Then join shoulder and underarm seams. To make sleeve like illustration, cut off lower part of sleeve lining. Gather sleeve puff to fit lining.

Join skirt according to stars. If empire skirt is desired use yoke portions and gather skirt to fit yoke. (If the empire extension is not wanted, cut off the upper part at waistline and do not use yoke portions.) Gather skirt at top and on dotted line below waistline. Gather back gore to point 7A. Then fold the remaining material in an inverted pleat at center back.

White peau de cygne was used to develop this garment, with lace insertion and heavy lace trimming. Material required for medium form, 12 yards 27 inches wide.

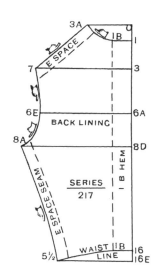
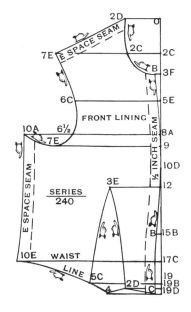

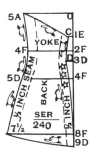

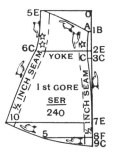

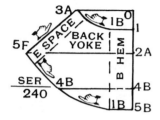

3A
1B
5F
E SPACE
BACK YOKE
B HEM
1
2A
4B
5B
1B
SER 240
4B

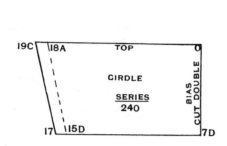

19C
18A
TOP
GIRDLE
SERIES 240
BIAS CUT DOUBLE
17
15D
7D

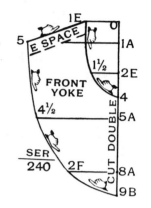

1E
5
E SPACE
FRONT YOKE
1A
2E
4
5A
8A
9B
1½
4½
SER 240
2F
CUT DOUBLE

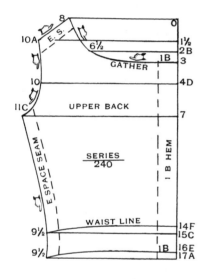

8
10A
E. S.
6½
1B
GATHER
1½
2B
3
10
4D
11C
UPPER BACK
7
E SPACE SEAM
SERIES 240
B HEM
9½
WAIST LINE
14F
15C
16E
17A
9½
1B

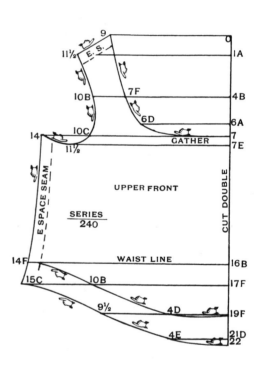

9
11½
E. S.
1A
10B
7F
4B
6D
6A
10C
14
11½
GATHER
7
7E
E SPACE SEAM
UPPER FRONT
SERIES 240
CUT DOUBLE
14F
WAIST LINE
16B
15C
10B
17F
9½
4D
19F
4E
21D
22

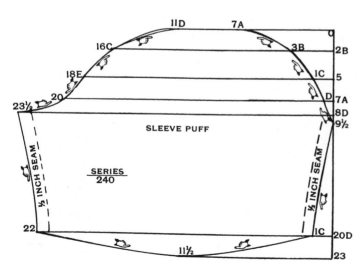

11D
7A
16C
3B
2B
18E
1C
5
20
D
7A
23½
8D
9½
SLEEVE PUFF
½ INCH SEAM
½ INCH SEAM
SERIES 240
22
1C
20D
11½
23

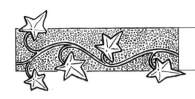

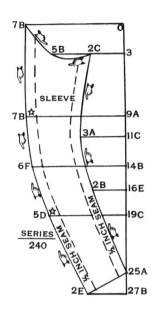

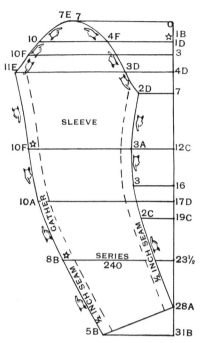

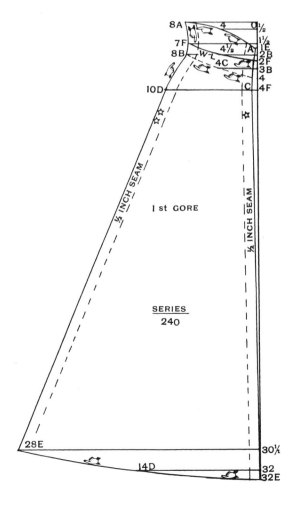

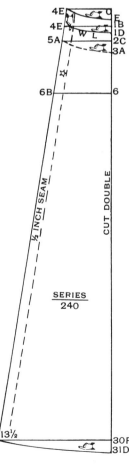

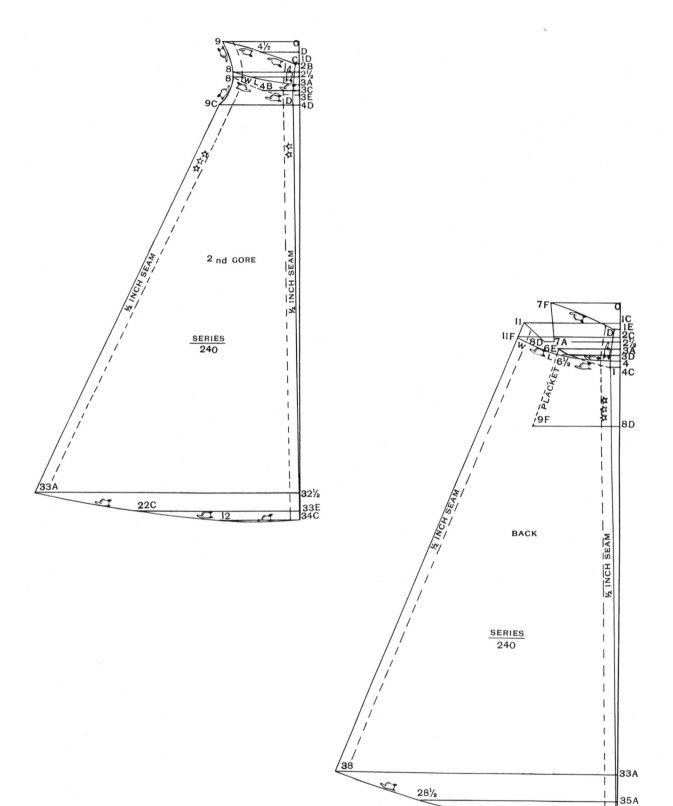

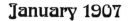
Ladies' Auto Fur Coat

Four measures are taken for this coat: Bust, length of waist, full length, and length of sleeve. It is drafted in 12 pieces: Back, front, underarm gore, 3 styles of collar, pocket, cuffs, and 2 styles of sleeve drafted in 3 pieces.

To Draft. Select bust and length of waist scales for coat back, front, and underarm gore. Draft to waistline. Then subtract length of waist measure from full-length measure. This will give desired scale for baseline from waistline down. For example: Bust 35, length of waist 15, full length 52. Use scale 30 and copy points on baseline to waistline. Then use scale 37 from waistline to bottom of coat. Use bust scale for all crosslines. For collars and pocket, use bust and length of waist scales. For sleeves and cuffs, use bust and length of sleeve scales.

To Make. For coat like illustration cut revere off on dotted line and use cape collar. Use coat sleeve and fur coat cuff. Join the different seams of coat and fold extension in back at dotted line over to heavy line in underarm gore.

If you prefer to make a cloth coat, use shawl or coat collar and either of the two sleeves. To make fancy sleeve, cut points out on heavy line and turn goods 1/2 inch. Then fold over to dotted line and stitch, thus making a deep tuck in lower part of sleeve. Top of sleeve may be gathered or pleated; to make pleats fold stars to Os. Sleeve may be finished with or without cuff. If cuff is desired place star in cuff even with seam of sleeve.

The diagram is suitable for any coat materials. Black karakul was used to develop coat like illustration. It is perhaps the most popular fur for day wear, and has a very attractive moiré surface.

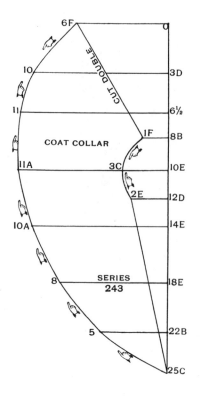

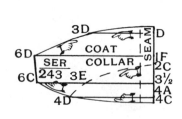

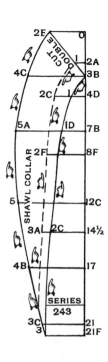

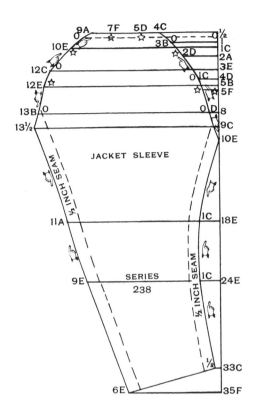

JACKET SLEEVE

½ INCH SEAM

SERIES 238

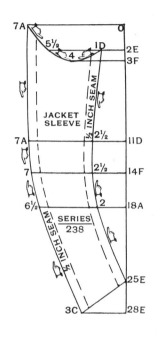

JACKET SLEEVE

½ INCH SEAM

SERIES 238

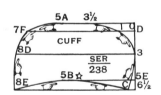

CUFF

SER 238

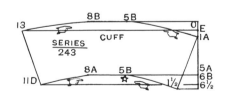

CUFF

SERIES 243

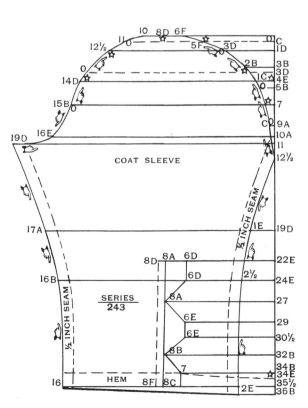

COAT SLEEVE

½ INCH SEAM

SERIES 243

½ INCH SEAM

HEM

83

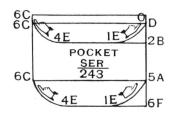

POCKET

SER

243

6C
6C
O D
4E   IE
2 B
6C
5A
4E   IE
6F

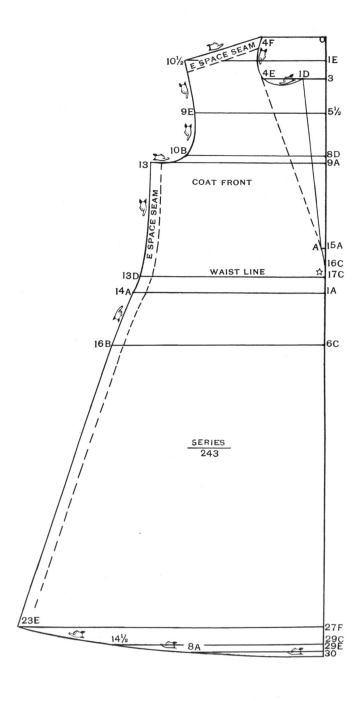

10½   E SPACE SEAM   4F
O
1E
4E   ID   3
9E   5½
10B   8D
9A
13
COAT FRONT

E SPACE SEAM

A   15A
16C
13D   WAIST LINE   ☆ 17C
14A   1A

16B   6C

SERIES
243

23E   27F
14½   29C
8A   29E
30

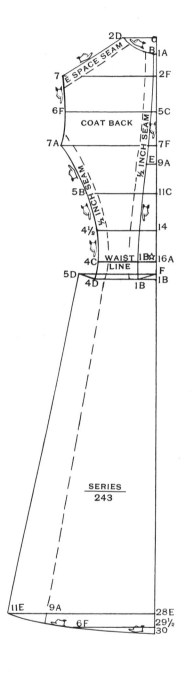

COAT BACK

WAIST LINE

½ INCH SEAM

E SPACE SEAM

SERIES
243

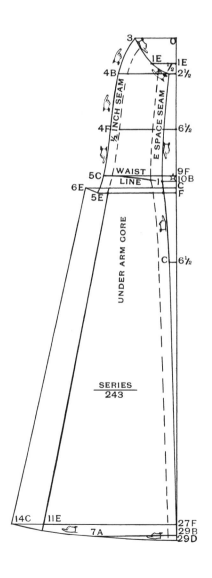

UNDER ARM GORE

WAIST LINE

½ INCH SEAM

E SPACE SEAM

SERIES
243

Ladies' Dinner Gown

Ladies' Dinner Gown

Five measures are taken for this garment: Bust, length of waist, around the waist, length of sleeve, and length of skirt. It is drafted in 17 pieces: Blouse back and front, jumper waist back and front, sleeve lining (2 pieces), sleeve cap, sleeve puff, and an 11-gore skirt (9 pieces).

To Draft. Select bust and length of waist scales for blouse and jumper waists. For sleeve lining, sleeve puff, and sleeve cap, use bust and length of sleeve scales. For skirt and flounce sections, use waist and length of skirt scales.

When drafting pattern for jumper waist, fold back and front on dotted lines to heavy lines. Then make curve for shoulder and cut out on that line.

To prove up length of skirt, measure from top of skirt to star, then from top of flounce to bottom of skirt.

To Make. Join shoulder and underarm seams of blouse. Face sleeve lining to cuff depth. Join seams. Sew seam of sleeve puff and arrange on lining like illustration. Sew to blouse waist.

For jumper waist, fold goods dotted lines to heavy lines and stitch as shown in diagram. The resulting pleat over shoulder seams may be stitched to yoke depth (in the illustration it is plain). Join shoulder and underarm seams. Jumper waist is cut low under arm to show blouse waist. Jumper waist may be finished with or without sleeve cap. If sleeve cap is used, gather and sew to waist. Back closing is given in diagram for blouse and jumper waists.

Join the different sections of the flounce according to stars. Pleat by folding dotted lines to heavy lines, making three backward-turning pleats at each gore. Join upper part of skirt according to stars by folding dotted line to heavy line on each gore. Fold dotted line in front to center of front. Fold dotted line in back seam of fourth gore to heavy line in back. Join flounce to upper part of skirt and stitch to position.

Brown velvet was used for the skirt and jumper waist, trimmed with soutache and one of the many woven braids. Material required for medium form, 12 yards 27 inches wide. Allover lace was used for blouse waist, 4 yards 27 inches wide.

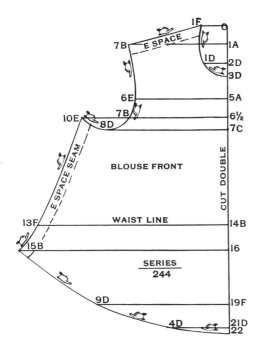

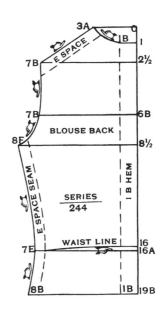

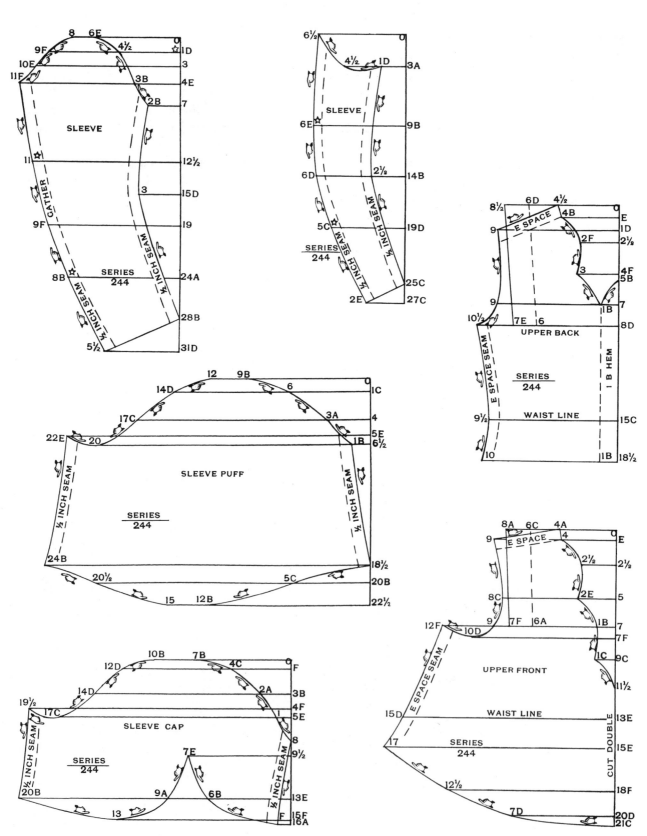

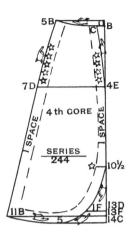

4th GORE

SERIES
244

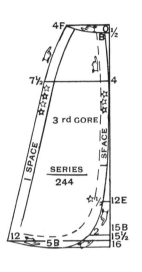

3rd GORE

SERIES
244

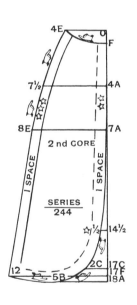

2nd GORE

SERIES
244

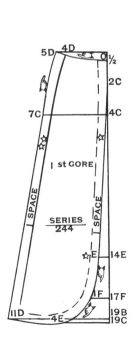

1st GORE

SERIES
244

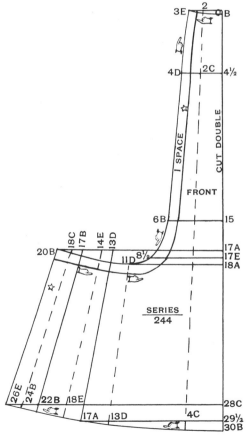

FRONT

CUT DOUBLE

SERIES
244

89

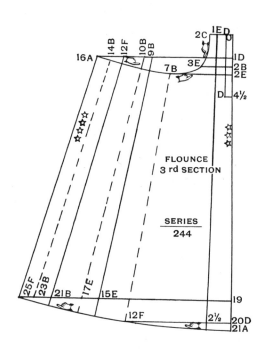

FLOUNCE
3 rd SECTION

SERIES
244

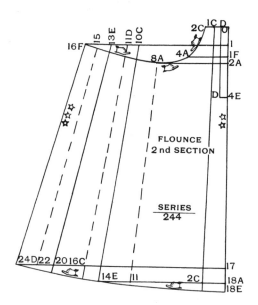

FLOUNCE
2nd SECTION

SERIES
244

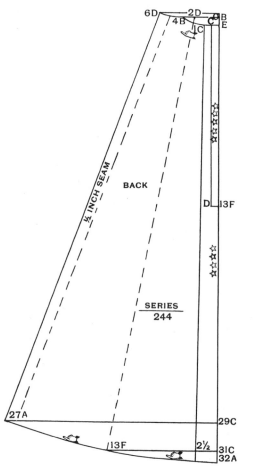

BACK

½ INCH SEAM

SERIES
244

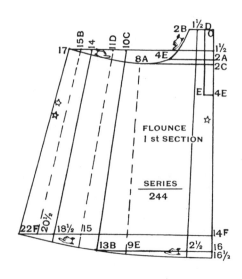

FLOUNCE
1 st SECTION

SERIES
244

Advanced Styles in Tailored Waists

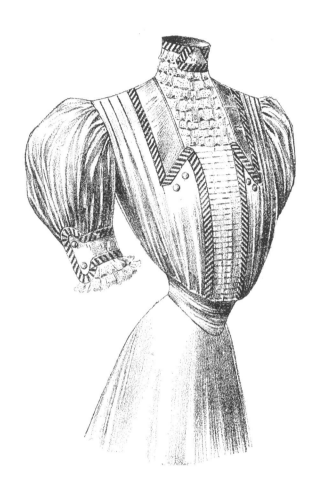

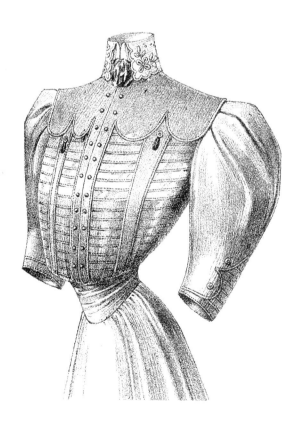

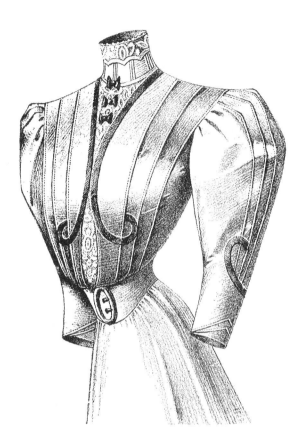

The popularity of white and light striped flannels steadily increases. They are popularly dubbed flannel, though the material usually is a hard finish, lightly woven cloth, something on the order of a fine canvas cloth. All degrees of tailoring ability are permissible, as they are made in every way, from the trimmed Eton coat and pony jacket to the severest tailor suit.

The long coat, the three-quarter length, tight-fitting, and single-breasted style, with the corner curved away in front to a longer depth at the back, is a favorite. But even tailors dislike to venture on it. It is particularly difficult to fit when the pleats are omitted in the back and the single smooth middle back form substituted.

The season's high novelty is tussah, a soft firm silk on the order of poplin or pongee. It will be used for suits, coats, and costumes. For tailored suits, serge will be much used, and English and Scottish tweeds in mixtures, plaids, or stripes. Chiffon broadcloth is to be worn for early spring and panamas will also have a vogue. Plain and novelty silks will be employed for dressy and semidressy effects, as well as for separate coats. Voile is as much liked as ever before. It admits of pleated skirts being artistically draped.

Many shades of brown are being made into suit models, as they are serviceable tints for day use.

Nearly all, even the plainest tailored suits, have velvet collars, particularly where the goods is mixed. For instance, a soft gray velvet is put on a cloth of mixed and almost invisible plaid in blue-gray. Sometimes velvet cuffs are added. Most distinctive of all in both coats and suit costumes are the elaborate effects in braiding.

The separate silk coat will again be worn with all manner of costumes.

A good deal may be said about the trimmings used upon spring gowns. Skirts are trimmed with three or four quite wide folds, piped at the top, and either of the same width or in graduated sizes. Greek key patterns, in narrow folds in several rows, and also in wide folds which run far up the skirt and are put on singly, are very chic indeed. Braids are used in the same fashion, and there is quite a fancy for running a soutache braid along the edge of the wide braid, with an interval of about 1/8 inch between them. The most fashionable braids are those of flat weave and plain or simple edges. The handsomest of the elaborate linen suits that are reckoned sufficiently elegant to be worn to dressy functions are "embroidered" in fine soutache braiding, the braid used edgewise, in intricate patterns known as "vermicelli." Many of these have small crochet buttons introduced into their designs, several gross sometimes consumed on a single costume.

Checks and blocks—real checkerboard styles—are much to the fore in spring gowns of silk, and will be even more seen in handsome cotton gowns. Large, even block checks of black and white, brown and white, and green and white, are a fad that will surely be modishly endorsed. In rough silks of the rajah order the blocks formed of lines of contrasting color are probably most liked. The trimmings of costumes made of them usually match the color of their stripe. It is to be a season of all kinds of stripes. If there is a striped silk to be made up a prettier mode could not be chosen than to make it with a bias seam up the front, the stripes forming a "V" design.

Cotton goods grow more and more beautiful. Lovely soft pastel shades are the ones most used, and combinations bespeak the artist's brush. The

embroidered swisses are exceptionally beautiful and many of them show colored effects on a white plaided ground.

Net and lace waists seemingly grow more prominent. The ecru and butter color tones afford variation from the numerous models in white. The idea of a silk waist to be worn over a lingerie guimpe seems to be one of the most popular fancies of the season.

A great deal of velvet ribbon enters into the trimming of all descriptions of toilettes, but especially those designed for evening wear. It is always either self-colored or black, and is used a great deal to trim lace and net waists.

A Dressy Street Costume

Five measures are taken for this garment: Bust, length of waist, around the waist, length of sleeve, and length of skirt. It is drafted in 12 pieces: Front, side front, front underarm, back, side back, back underarm, vest front, 2 sleeve pieces, and a straight kilt skirt drafted in 3 pieces.

To Draft. Select bust and length of waist scales for backs, fronts, underarm gores, and vest front of jacket. For sleeve, use bust and length of sleeve scales. For skirt, use waist and length of skirt scales.

In drafting skirt pattern you will notice the letter B in four different places in the three skirt sections. Copy those down from top line with length of skirt scale.

To Make. Join the different parts of the jacket together by folding dotted lines to heavy lines, and stitch 3/8 inch from fold. Upper part of side front

and side back cannot be stitched until the sleeve is stitched in, as the shoulder extends over top of sleeve. Fold front to dotted line of vest front and stitch to position. Join the two sleeve sections by folding dotted line in small section to heavy line in large section. Gather lower part and sew to cuff of small section, and stitch 3/8 inch from fold.

Join the three sections of the skirt pattern according to stars and dotted lines before cutting goods. Fold dotted lines to heavy lines, making 12 backward-turning pleats on each side of skirt. Stitch to any desired depth and press well.

This diagram is made especially for plaid and striped materials. The material used for this garment was a brown and white shadow plaid. Material required for medium form, 6 yards 50 inches wide.

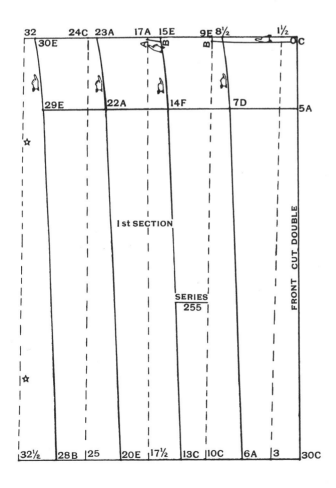

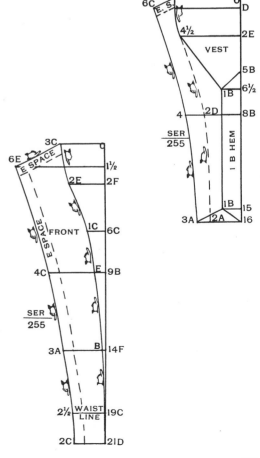

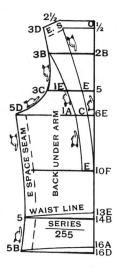
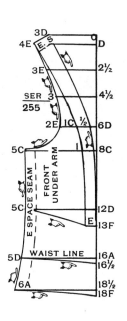
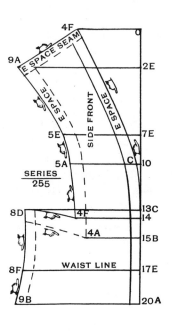
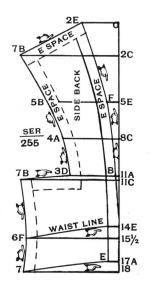
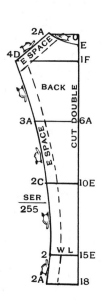
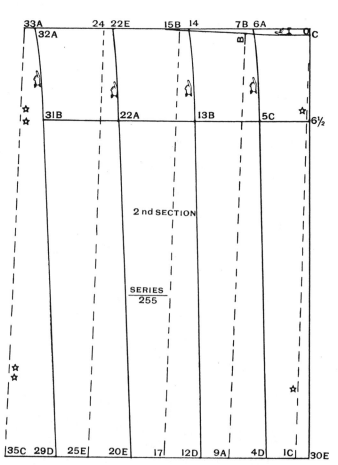

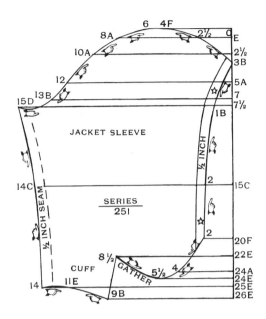

6 4F
8A
10A
2½
3B
12
5A
13B
7
15D
7½
1B
JACKET SLEEVE
½ INCH
14C
15C
½ INCH SEAM
SERIES
251
2
20F
22E
8½
24A
CUFF
GATHER
5½ 4
24E
14 11E
25E
9B
26E
0E
2½

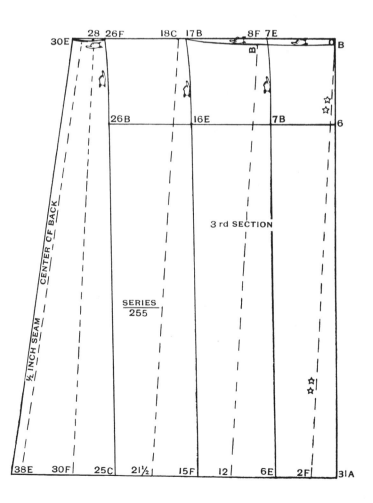

28 26F   18C 17B   8F 7E
30E   B
B   B
26B   16E   7B   6
CENTER OF BACK
3rd SECTION
½ INCH SEAM
SERIES
255
38E   30F   25C   21½   15F   12   6E   2F   31A

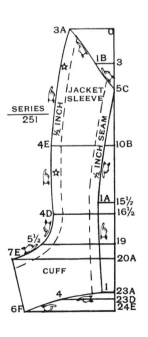

3A   0
1B   3
JACKET
SLEEVE
5C
SERIES
251
½ INCH
½ INCH SEAM
4E   10B
1A   15½
4D   16½
5½   19
7E   20A
CUFF
4   1   23A
23D
6F   24E

Spring Costume

Spring Costume

Five measures are taken for this garment: Bust, length of waist, around the waist, length of sleeve, and length of skirt. It is drafted in 14 pieces: Jacket back, side back, front, side front, front facing, collar, cuff, 2 sleeve portions, and a 9-gore ripple skirt drafted in 5 pieces.

To Draft. Select bust and length of waist scales for jacket back, side back, front, side front, front facing, and collar. For sleeve and cuff, use bust and length of sleeve scales. For skirt, use waist and length of skirt scales.

To Make. Join back with 1/2-inch seam. Then fold dotted line in back to heavy line in side back. Follow same directions with front and side front.

Stitch 3/8 inch from edge. Join shoulder and underarm seams. Face fronts with front facing. Sew collar to position. Join seams in sleeve. Make cuff. Arrange cuff on sleeve with star in cuff even with inseam of sleeve. Sew sleeve to jacket.

Join skirt according to stars. Stitch and press well. No diagram is given for the straps on skirt, as they are cut any desired width. Finish top and bottom in the usual way.

The material used for this skirt was one of the many pretty light striped flannels. To make like illustration would require, for medium form, 7 1/2 yards 48 inches wide.

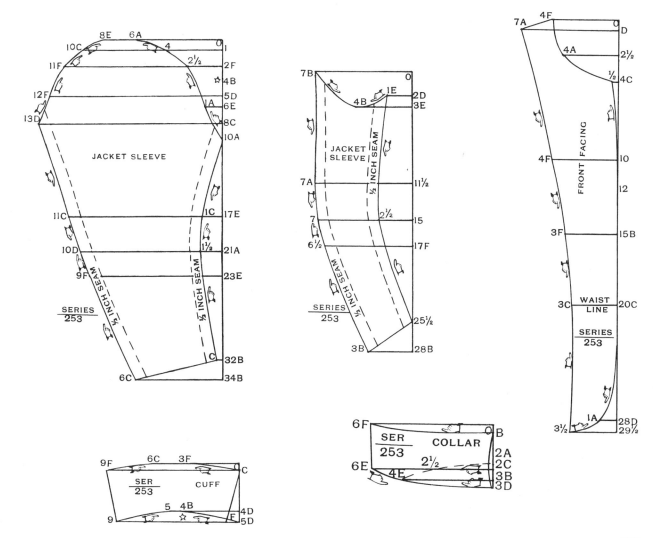

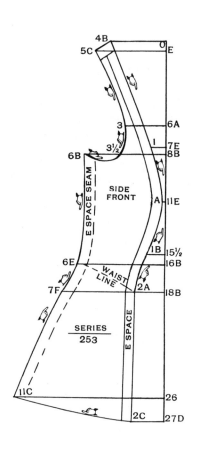

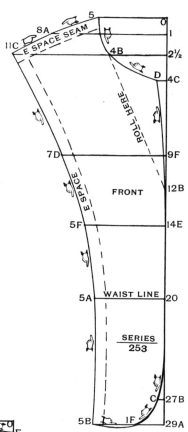

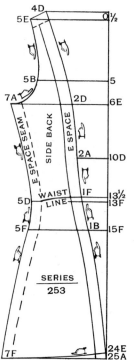

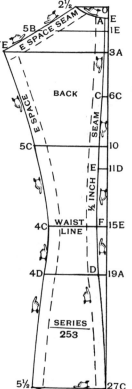

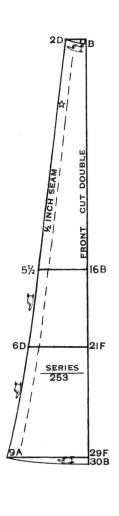

2D | B
½ INCH SEAM
FRONT CUT DOUBLE
5½ | 16B
6D | 21F
SERIES
253
9A | 29F
30B

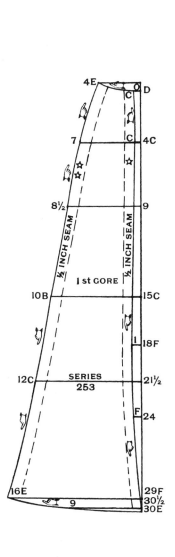

4E | O D
| C
7 | C | 4C
8½ | 9
½ INCH SEAM
½ INCH SEAM
1 st GORE
10B | 15C
| 18F
12C | SERIES
253 | 21½
| F | 24
16E | 29F
9 | 30½
30E

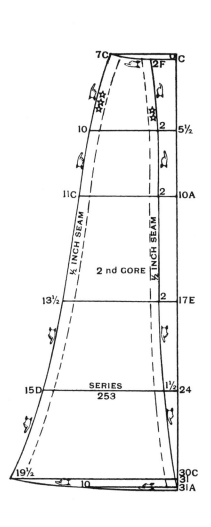

7C | 2F C
10 | 2 | 5½
11C | 2 | 10A
½ INCH SEAM
½ INCH SEAM
2 nd GORE
13½ | 2 | 17E
15D | SERIES
253 | 1½ | 24
19½ | 30C
31
10 | 31A

105

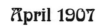

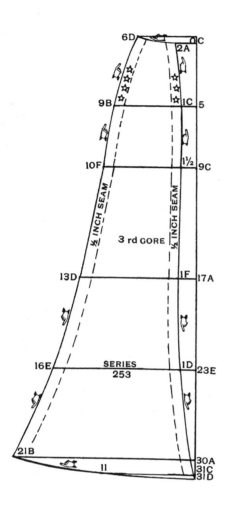

6D 0C
2A
9B 1C 5
10F 1½ 9C
½ INCH SEAM
½ INCH SEAM
3 rd GORE
13D 1F 17A
16E 1D 23E
SERIES
253
21B 30A
31C
11 31D

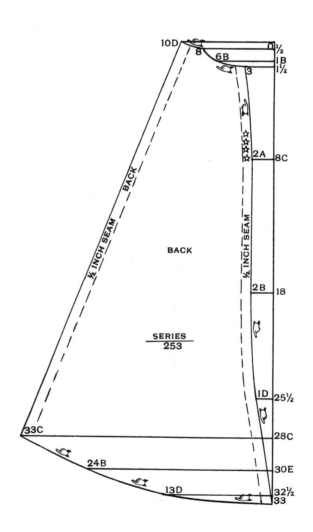

10D 0 ½
8 6B 1B
3 1½
½ INCH SEAM BACK
½ INCH SEAM
2A 8C
BACK
2B 18
SERIES
253
1D 25½
33C 28C
24B 30E
13D 32½
33

Ladies' Reception Gown

Five measures are taken for this gown: Bust, length of waist, around the waist, length of sleeve, and length of skirt. It is drafted in 12 pieces: Back and front lining, upper back and front, 2 yoke pieces, sleeve puff, sleeve ruffle, and a 7-gore tucked skirt drafted in 4 pieces.

To Draft. Select bust and length of waist scales for front and back lining, upper back and front, two yoke portions, and sleeve ruffle. For sleeve puff, use bust and length of sleeve scales. For skirt, use waist and length of skirt scales.

When making pattern for upper back and front, fold dotted line to heavy line before making curve for shoulder. Then cut out on that line.

To Make. Join front lining and take up darts. Baste yokes to lining. Fold dotted line to heavy line in upper back and front. Stitch to any desired depth. Join lining and outside shoulder seams separately.

Join underarm seams. Gather to fit waist measure. Join seam in sleeve and gather to fit arm and armhole. Gather top of sleeve ruffle and sew under tuck in waist.

Join skirt according to stars by folding dotted line to heavy. Stitch 1/2 inch from fold, making nine 1/2-inch tucks on each side of skirt. Fold last tuck to center of back. Ease extra fullness into skirt band. Join lower part of skirt in 1/2-inch seams.

A pretty shade of gray silk was the material used for this garment, with a darker shade of silk ribbon 1 inch wide to trim. Bottom of skirt has several rows of bias folds, finished at top with velvet band. Body part of skirt is ornamented with silk embroidery. Sixteen yards of silk 20 inches wide will be required for medium form.

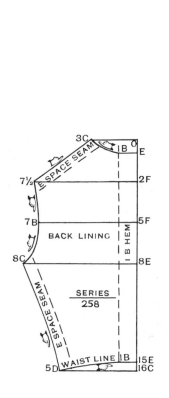

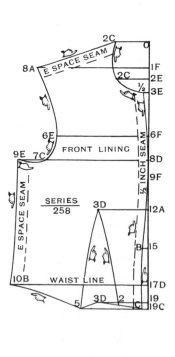

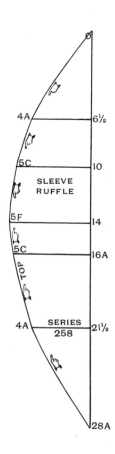

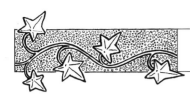

Back Yoke
3½ IB E
6C E SPACE
BACK YOKE IB HEM 2A
SER 258 4½ 4F
2D IB 5F
6B

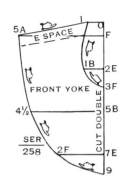

5A E SPACE F
IB 2E
FRONT YOKE 3F
4½ CUT DOUBLE 5B
SER 258 2F 7E
9

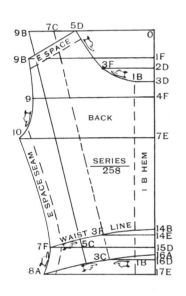

7C 5D 0
9B
E SPACE
9B IF
3F 2D
IB 3D
9 4F
BACK 7E
10
SERIES 258
E SPACE SEAM IB HEM
WAIST 3F LINE 14B
14E
7F 5C 15D
16A
3C IB 16D
8A 17E

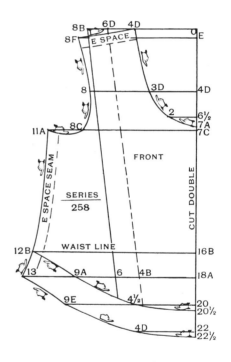

8B 6D 4D
8F 0 E
E SPACE
8 3D 4D
8 2 6½
7A
8C 7C
11A
E SPACE SEAM FRONT CUT DOUBLE
SERIES 258
12B WAIST LINE 16B
13 9A 6 4B 18A
9E 4½ 20 20½
4D 22 22½

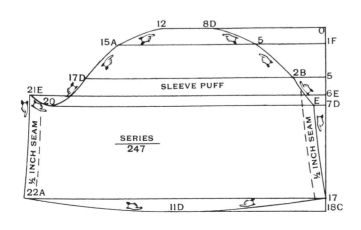

12 8D 0
15A 5 IF
17D 2B 5
21E SLEEVE PUFF 6E
20 E 7D
½ INCH SEAM ½ INCH SEAM
SERIES 247
22A 17
11D 18C

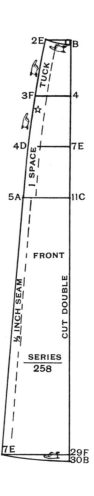

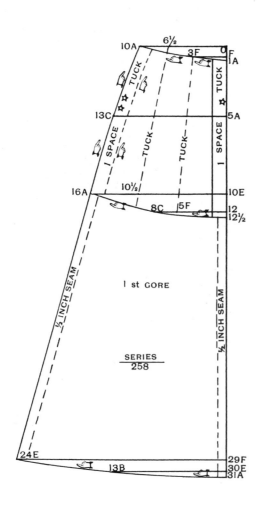

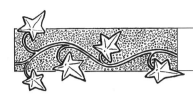

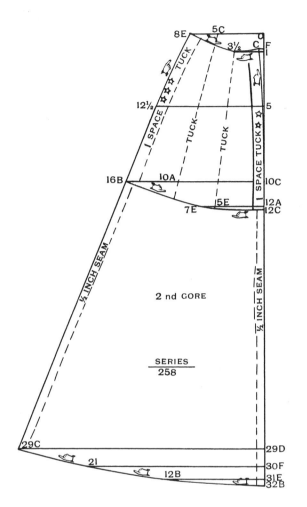

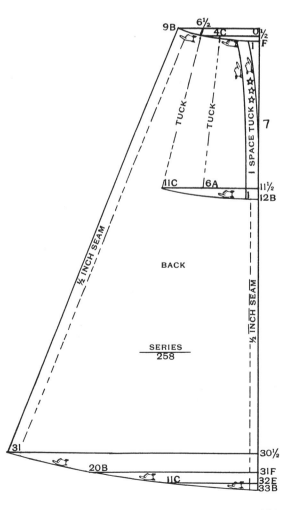

July 1907 American Modiste

Pinafore or jumper waists for summer wear are made in fanciful form, with all manner of sheer guimpes and pretty lace and embroidery trimmings. There is still another feature that highly recommends the jumper styles, and that is their economic value in remodeling dresses and waists of past seasons.

Waists, especially those of a separate order, have such elaborate front trimmings that their closing at the back is a very generally accepted rule. But whatever may be their mode of fastening, it is concealed beneath a fold of the material or some other arrangement.

The Marie Antoinette and the Beau Brummel are the leading styles in tailored waists. There is a charm and daintiness about the frilled fronts of these models which is making them very popular. These waists always button in the front and are designed to be worn with the stiffly laundered linen collar. They have sleeves with either the frilled trimmed cuffs or the straight shirt cuffs stiffly starched.

We will see skirts that touch the ground, skirts of round length, skirts with slight trains, but nothing really short except for morning and general utility wear. For tailor-mades the weight at the bottom is obtained by bias bands or folds of the material itself, or if the body of the skirt is cut on the bias of the striped cloth, then the bands are cut on the straight. There are many clever and new arrangements of these bands and application of the striped materials.

White linen coats and skirts trimmed with narrow irish crochet insertion and hand embroidery are made up upon very simple lines with loose, collarless, short-sleeved coats and plainly gored skirts. The heavy openwork insertion outlines all the seams and a very narrow corresponding edge finishes the borders of the coat. Soutache braiding plays an important part in the ornamentation of the somewhat elaborate linen coat and skirt costume, and is a trifle newer than hand embroidery. Often the two are combined.

The old-time foulards, which are again in vogue, take very kindly to the Japanese styles of the season.

Ladies' Jumper Suit

113

Ladies' Jumper Suit

Five measures are taken for this suit: Bust, length of waist, around the waist, length of sleeve, and length of skirt. It is drafted in 11 pieces: Back and front of guimpe blouse waist, peplum, jumper drafted in 1 piece, sleeve puff, cuff, and a 9-gore side-pleated skirt drafted in 5 pieces.

To Draft. Select bust and length of waist scales for back and front of waist and jumper. For peplum, use waist and length of skirt scales. For sleeve, use bust and length of sleeve scales. For skirt, use waist and length of skirt scales.

Notice diagram for sleeve, as there are two in one. For deep cuff and elbow puff, cut on dotted lines for elbow sleeve. For full-length shirtwaist sleeve, cut sleeve puff full length and cut cuff off on dotted line, using lower part of cuff.

To Make. Join shoulder and underarm seams of blouse waist. Gather lower part of waist and sew peplum to same. Gather sleeve puff to cuff and join in one seam.

For jumper, make two backward-turning tucks by folding dotted lines together and stitch to position. Join sleeve and underarm seam as directed. Gather to fit waist measure.

Join skirt according to stars by folding dotted lines to heavy lines, making ten side pleats on each side of skirt. Stitch to any desired depth. Press thoroughly.

The material used for this garment is a blue and white checked foulard with coin spots, trimmed with a dark shade of blue velvet. Material required for medium form, 14 yards 21 inches wide. The blouse waist is made of allover lace, 3 1/2 yards.

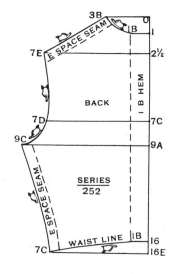

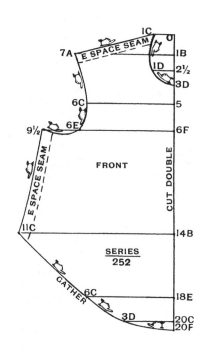

Ladies' Jumper Suit

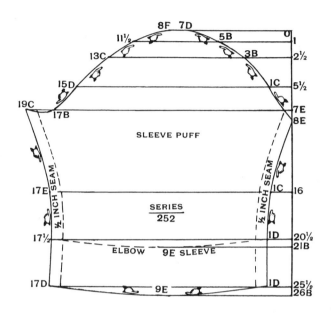

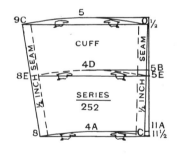

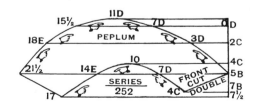

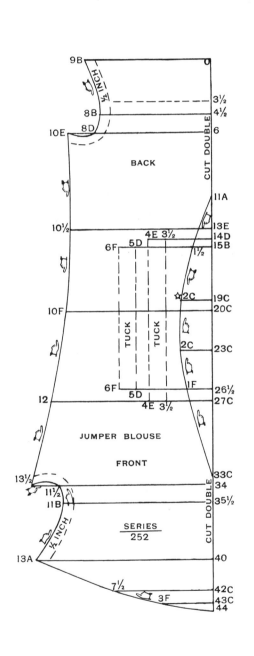

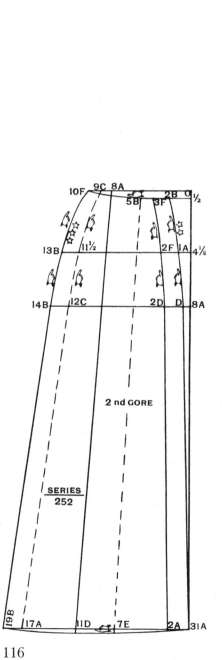

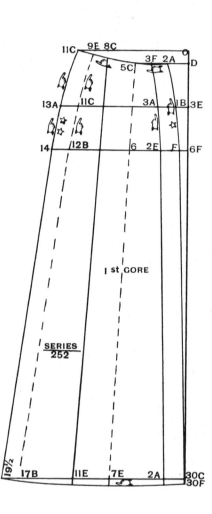

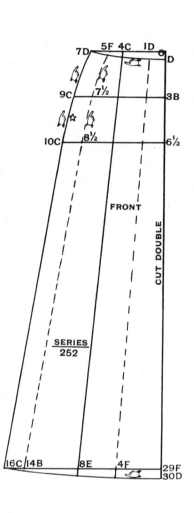

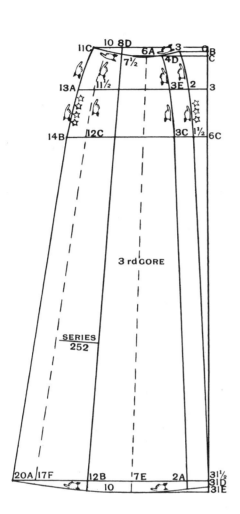

3 rd GORE

SERIES
252

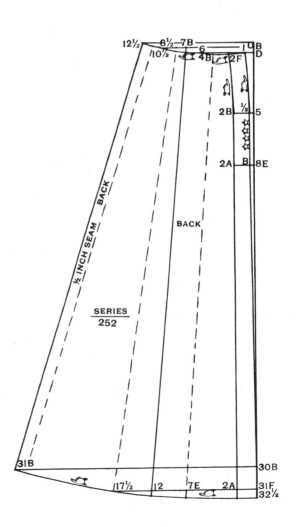

½ INCH SEAM BACK

BACK

SERIES
252

117

Ladies' Visiting Gown

Five measures are taken for this suit: Bust, length of waist, around the waist, length of sleeve, and length of skirt. It is drafted in 14 pieces: Back and front lining of jacket, upper back and front, collar, sleeve lining (2 pieces), jacket sleeve, cuff, and a 9-gore tucked skirt drafted in 5 pieces.

To Draft. Select bust and length of waist scales for jacket back and front lining, upper back, front, and collar. For sleeve lining, jacket sleeve, and cuff, use bust and length of sleeve scales. For skirt, use waist and length of skirt scales.

To Make. Cover back and front lining of jacket from seam to dotted line with material. Then stitch upper back and front to linings as far as armhole. Join shoulder seams of lining and upper back and front separately. Cover fronts of lining to dotted line for vest and turn upper front back like illustration. Join collar and roll on dotted lines.

Sleeve may be made with sleeve lining or cut lining the same size as the sleeve puff. If made with lining, join lining and puff separately. Gather lower part into band and place center of cuff even with seam of sleeve.

Join skirt according to stars. Make three backward-turning tucks at each seam by folding dotted lines to heavy lines. The last dotted line on each gore folds to first heavy line on joining gore. Stitch to any desired depth. Press folds to bottom of skirt.

One of the many pretty shades of bright brown broadcloth was used for this suit, with oriental embroidery for vest. Trimmings of fancy silk braid, soutache, and buttons. Material required for medium form, 6 1/2 yards 48 inches wide.

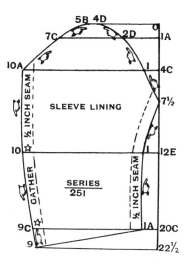

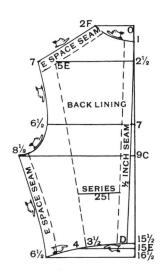

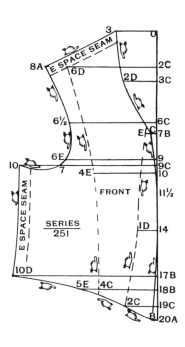

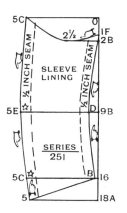

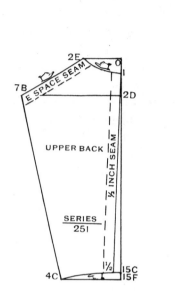

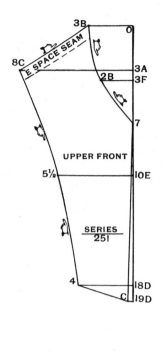

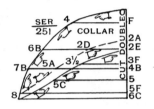

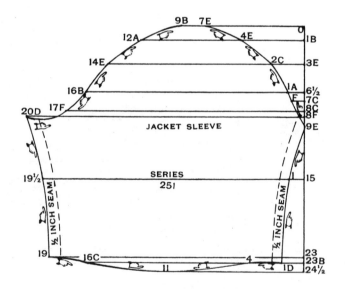

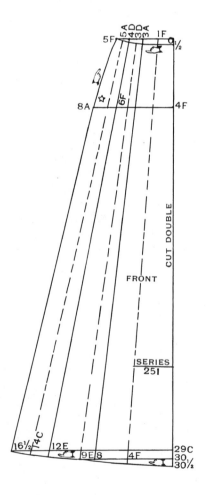

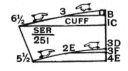

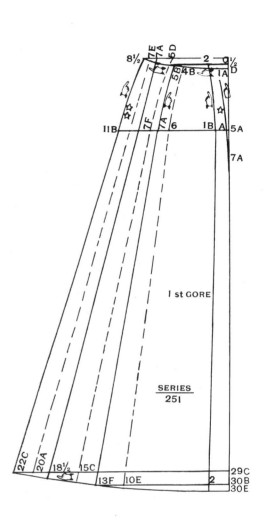

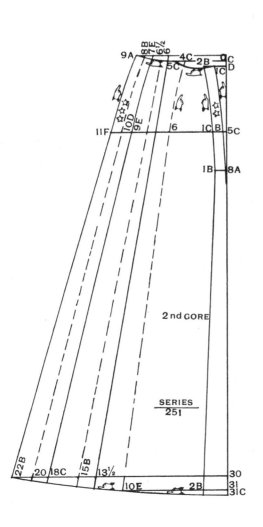

1st GORE

SERIES
251

2nd GORE

SERIES
251

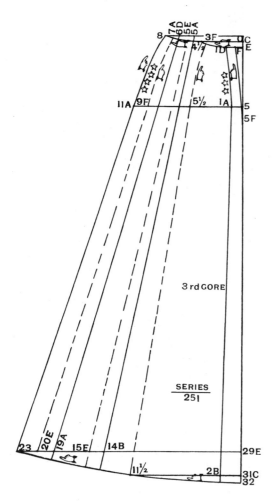

3 rd GORE

SERIES
251

8 7A 6D 5E 5A 3F C
E
4½ 1D F
11A 9F 5½ 1A 5
5F
23 20E 19A 15E 14B 29E
11½ 2B 31C
32

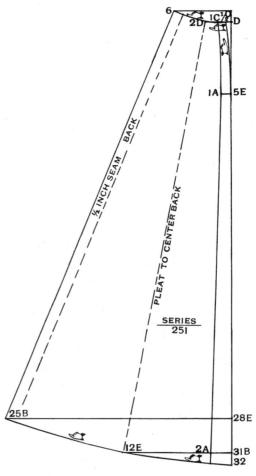

6 1C ½ D
2D
½ INCH SEAM BACK
PLEAT TO CENTER BACK
1A 5E
SERIES
251
25B 28E
12E 2A 31B
32

122

Ladies' Afternoon Gown

Five measures are taken for this gown: Bust, length of waist, around the waist, length of sleeve, and length of skirt. It is drafted in 11 pieces: Back and front of blouse waist, sleeve puff, jumper blouse back and front (drafted in 1 piece), girdle, and a 10-gore skirt (drafted in 6 pieces).

To Draft. Select bust and length of waist scales for blouse back and front and jumper blouse. For sleeve puff, use bust and length of sleeve scales. For girdle, use waist and length of waist scales. For skirt, use waist and length of skirt scales.

To Make. Join fronts with 1/2-inch seam. Face one side of back and hem the other. Join underarm seams and gather to fit waist measure. Cut girdle on bias fold of material.

Join skirt according to stars by folding first dotted line in front to heavy line, and first dotted line in first gore to the same heavy line in front. Fold second dotted line in first gore to the next heavy line. This completes the first box pleat. Follow the same directions throughout the skirt, making four box pleats on each side of skirt and one at center back and center front. Fit skirt. Stitch pleats to any desired depth and press thoroughly. Then finish lower part of skirt with 1/2-inch seams.

Blue and white novelty silk was used for this gown. Blue velvet ribbon was used to trim skirt and jumper blouse.

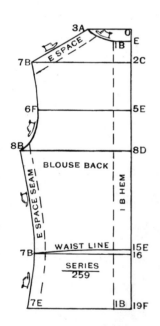

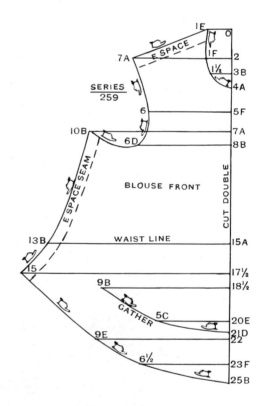

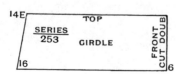

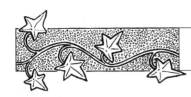

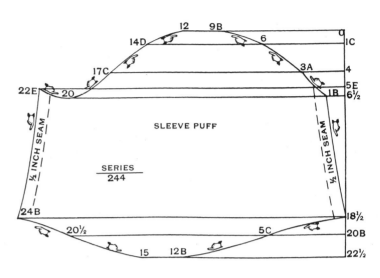

SLEEVE PUFF

SERIES
244

12 9B
14D
17C   6   1C
22E   20   3A   4
                    5E
                    6½
½ INCH SEAM   1B
                    ½ INCH SEAM
24B   20½   5C   18½
        15   12B   20B
                        22½

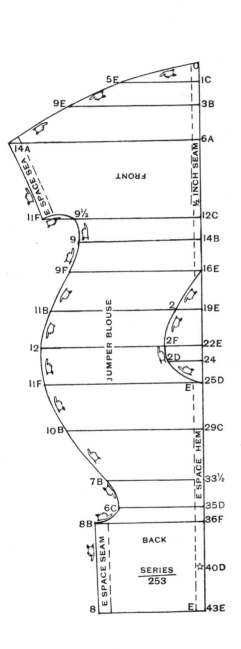

5E   1C
9E   3B
14A   6A
E SPACE SEAM
FRONT   ½ INCH SEAM
11F   9½   12C
    9   14B
9F   16E
JUMPER BLOUSE   2   19E
11B   2F   22E
12   2D   24
11F   25D
        E1
        E SPACE HEM
10B   29C
7B   33½
6C   35D
8B   36F
E SPACE SEAM
BACK   40D
SERIES
253
8   43E

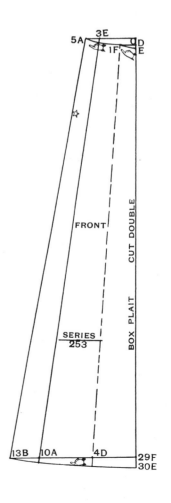

5A   3E
        1F   D
            E
FRONT   CUT DOUBLE
BOX PLAIT
SERIES
253
13B   10A   4D   29F
                        30E

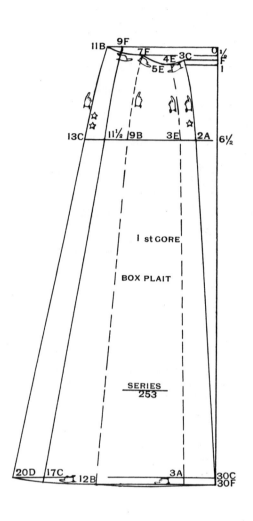

1 st GORE

BOX PLAIT

SERIES
253

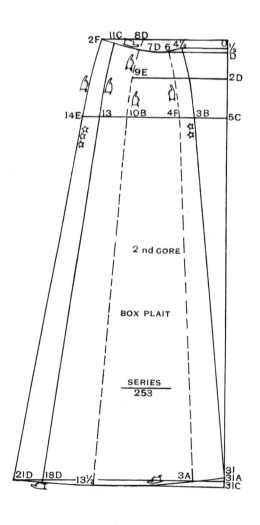

2 nd GORE

BOX PLAIT

SERIES
253

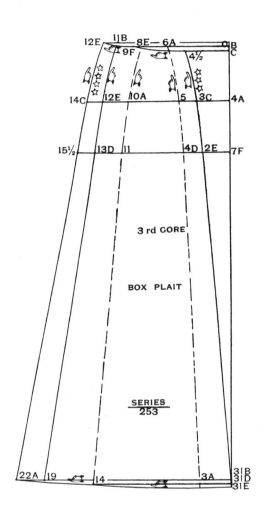

3 rd GORE

BOX PLAIT

SERIES
253

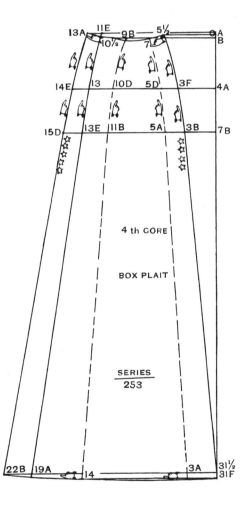

4 th GORE

BOX PLAIT

SERIES
253

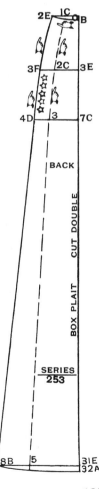

BACK

BOX PLAIT   CUT DOUBLE

SERIES
253

Ladies' Jumper Blouse

Four measures are taken for this waist: Bust, length of waist, around the waist, and length of sleeve. It is drafted in seven pieces: Guimpe blouse back, front, sleeve puff, and collar, and jumper blouse back, front, and sleeve.

To Draft. Select bust and length of waist scales for guimpe blouse back and front, jumper back and front, and kimono sleeve. For guimpe blouse sleeve, use bust and length of sleeve scales.

The illustration does not do this waist justice, as the kimono sleeve is pictured too wide.

Before cutting shoulders of jumper blouse pattern, fold dotted lines to heavy lines making two backward-turning tucks in back and front of waist. Then curve shoulder line and cut on that line.

To Make. First make the guimpe blouse by joining shoulder and underarm seams. Finish neck with collar. Gather lower part to fit waist measure.

Fold jumper goods on dotted line to heavy line and stitch to yoke depth. Join shoulder and underarm seams. Cut kimono sleeve double. Join with 1/2-inch seam under arm. Then join to jumper blouse. Second tuck will fold over upper part of sleeve. Gather lower part of blouse to fit waist measure.

The guimpe is made of net, trimmed with val lace. Material required for medium form, 4 yards 21 inches wide. The jumper is a pretty shade of brown silk, trimmed with insertion and val lace. Material required for medium form, 2 1/4 yards 19 inches wide.

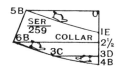

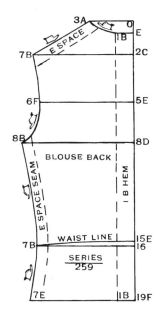

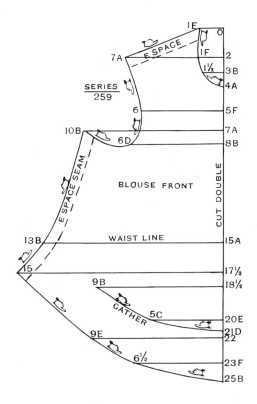

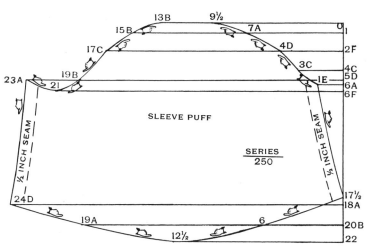

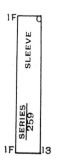

1F

SLEEVE

SERIES
259

1F   13

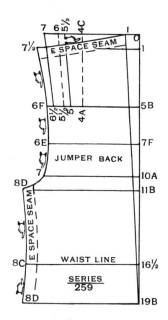

7   6½   5½   4C   I
7½   E SPACE SEAM   I   O

6F   5B
6½ 5½ 5 4A
6E   7F

JUMPER BACK

7   10A
8D   11B

E SPACE SEAM

8C   WAIST LINE   16½

SERIES
259

8D   19B

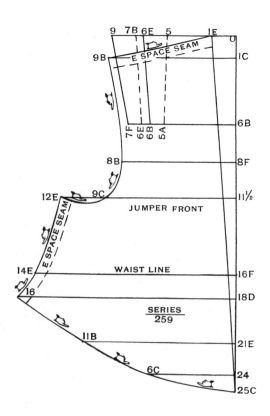

9   7B 6E   5   IE
9B   E SPACE SEAM   IC

7F 6E 6B 5A   6B

8B   8F

12E   9C   11½

JUMPER FRONT

E SPACE SEAM

14E   WAIST LINE   16F
16   18D

SERIES
259

11B   21E

6C   24
25C

Ladies' Street Suit

Five measures are taken for this suit: Bust, length of waist, around the waist, length of sleeve, and length of skirt. It is drafted in 15 pieces: Jacket back, side back, front, side front, vest front, jacket trimming, girdle (2 pieces), sleeve, cuff, and a 9-gore skirt drafted in 5 pieces.

To Draft. Select bust and length of waist scales for jacket back, front, side back, side front, vest front, and trimming. For sleeve and cuff, use bust and length of sleeve scales. For girdle, use waist and length of waist scales. For skirt, use waist and length of skirt scales.

To Make. The illustration does not use the jacket trimming. Should you want the broad shoulder effect, use it, and join inseam with side front and side back.

Baste vest front and front together, then join to side front. Follow same directions with back. Then join shoulder and underarm seams.

Gather sleeve into small band. Then close seams. Place center of cuff even with inseam of sleeve. Gather to fit armhole.

Join front and underarm seams of girdle, and close in back. Bone all seams with featherbone.

Join skirt according to stars. Stitch and press well. Finish top and bottom in the usual way.

White cheviot was the material used for this suit. Venice lace medallions and white velvet ribbon were used to trim skirt and jacket. Material required for medium form, 6 yards 48 inches wide.

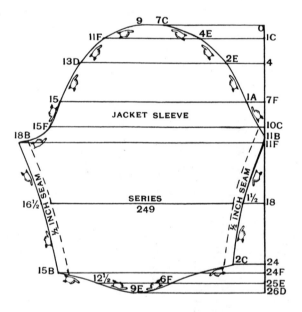

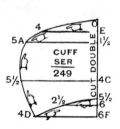

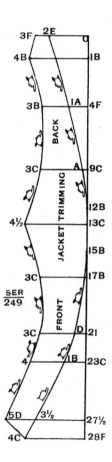

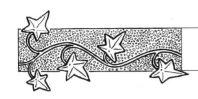

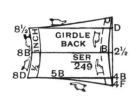

GIRDLE BACK

8½
8B
8D
INCH
D
B 2½
SER 249
5B
4B
4F

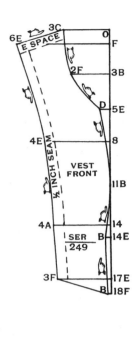

6E 3C O F
E SPACE
2F 3B
D
2A 5E
4E 8
½ INCH SEAM
VEST FRONT
11B
4A SER 249 B 14
14E
3F 17E
B 18F

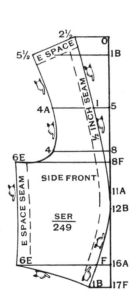

2½ O
5½ E SPACE 1B
½ INCH SEAM
4A 5
4 8
6E 8F
E SPACE SEAM
SIDE FRONT
SER 249
11A
12B
6E F 16A
1B 17F

5D 2C O E
E SPACE
2A 2E
1B 5
4 B 7B
½ INCH SEAM
FRONT
9½
SER 249 11C
3B A 13D
3A
B 18½
19C

1A O
4A E SPACE 1½
½ INCH SEAM
3C
3D 5½
6 7A
SIDE BACK
E SPACE SEAM
SERIES 249
9½
4F B 13D
14½

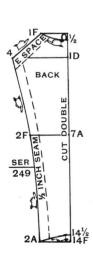

1F
4 E SPACE 1½
BACK 1D
CUT DOUBLE
2F 7A
SER 249
½ INCH SEAM
2A 14½
14F

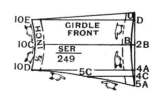

10E O D
GIRDLE FRONT
10C B 2B
SER 249
10D 5C 4A
½ INCH 4C
5A

133

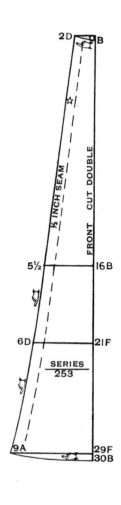

2D B

½ INCH SEAM

FRONT CUT DOUBLE

5½ 16B

6D 21F

SERIES
253

9A 29F
30B

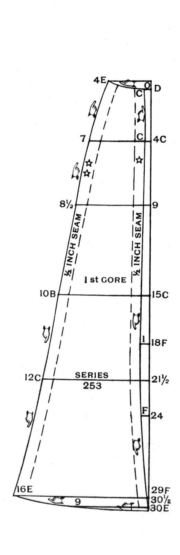

4E D
C

7 C 4C

½ INCH SEAM ½ INCH SEAM

8½ 9

1st GORE

10B 15C

18F

SERIES
253

12C 21½

F 24

16E 29F
30½
9 30E

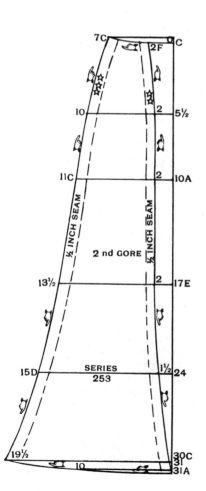

7C 2F C

10 2 5½

11C 2 10A

½ INCH SEAM ½ INCH SEAM

2nd GORE

13½ 2 17E

SERIES
253

15D 1½ 24

19½ 30C
31
10 31A

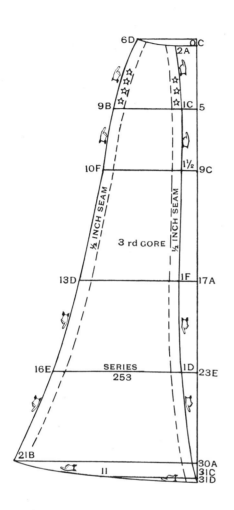

6D 0C
2A
9B 1C 5
10F 1½ 9C
½ INCH SEAM ½ INCH SEAM
3 rd GORE
13D 1F 17A
16E SERIES 1D 23E
253
21B 30A
11 31C
31D

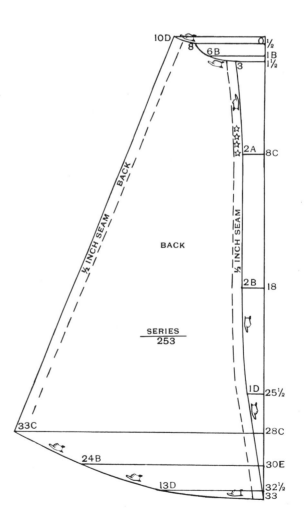

10D 0 ½
8 1B
6B 1½
3
2A 8C
½ INCH SEAM BACK ½ INCH SEAM
BACK
2B 18
SERIES
253
1D 25½
33C 28C
24B 30E
13D 32½
33

Ladies' Chemise

Two measures are taken for this garment: Bust and full length. It is drafted in two pieces: Back and front.

To Draft and Make. Select bust and full-length scales for back and front. Neck may be made round or square (notice dotted lines). Join under-arm seams. Finish neck with band or beading.

This garment may be made very fancy, and is taking the place of the corset cover and short skirt.

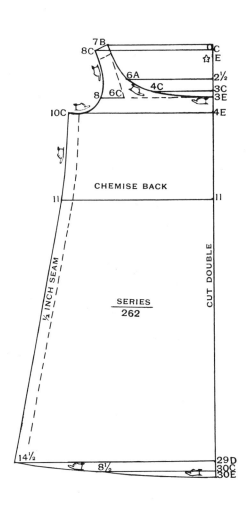

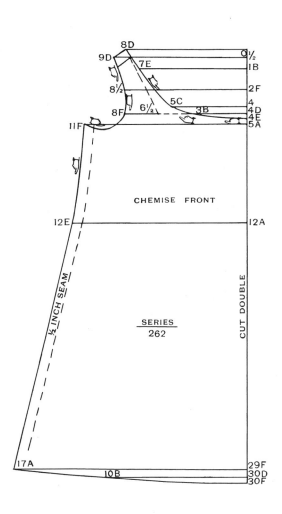

October 1907 American Modiste

Combinations of materials are decidedly the thing this season. For example, take the use of trimming hems of broadcloth, velvet, or silk on skirts of various materials. The fashion designers have made an extremely clever use of this fancy and are putting broad hems of plain material, often contrasting in color and always in texture, at the foot of dressy skirts.

Broadcloth with or without fur lining is to enjoy another season of coat utility. Black will undoubtedly prove the most popular color for average wear, with white and pastel tints for carriage use.

For absolute comfort and all-round practical purposes, such as railway traveling, automobiling, and stormy weather in town, the medium long, loosely fitting box type coats are to be commended. They may be absolutely plain and finished all round with rows of stitching, or they may have braided collars and cuffs and pocket flaps.

Jacket coats in most instances have seams either lapped or clearly outlined by heavy rows of stitching. Binding braids are being applied both to suit jackets and to separate wraps. This fancy extends to many of the new fur coats, and especially to the new plushes that so closely imitate fur and are to be so much worn this winter. The demand was largely for the black binding braids, but recently there has developed a call for binding braids in matching tones. Some very handsome cord ornaments with pendant edges are shown. These are especially for separate wraps, and are of interwoven cords and braids, with ball-fringe edges and handmade pendants.

Thin, soft, crushable materials are the most fashionable for waists and gowns.

In wearing separate waists there are two or three rules that the well-dressed woman never transgresses. The first is, if the waist is not white it must be of the same color as the skirt. Second, the white waist must be either of lace, taffeta, embroidered batiste, or fine lingerie materials mixed with a profusion of lace or embroidery. This is speaking, of course, of the dressy type of waists. For general wear linen, flannel, woolen plaids or checks, albatross, or piqué are used. Many waists made of dyed nets and laces are shown this fall to be worn with costumes of the same shade. These are all in the fashionable colorings, such as navy, brown, mulberry, and dark red. They are usually touched up with some other color or trimmed with metallic braids in either gilt or silver. Japanese or oriental embroidery also help to brighten up many of these dyed lace waists.

The strictly tailored pleated skirt shows scarcely any trimming. In most instances several rows of stitching above the hem is deemed quite sufficient, although occasionally a narrow row of hercules or fancy silk braid is used in lieu of stitching, or a waving line of soutache. Many novel variations in the spacing and placing of pleats are shown in the new skirts and some extremely smart fabrics are used. Among the most novel of these are bordered materials, which are very stylish indeed when made up in pleated effects.

For materials, serge is the heavy goods first noticed, and to be greatly used, blue the color most popular and brown and black following. Quite a new fabric for skirts is striped broadcloth, and some in tartan designs of fine, almost invisible, cross stripes of blues, greens, and browns. Broadcloth will be worn extensively this winter, both in the plain colors and the new striped effects. For plain tailor-made suits, hand-finished worsteds of all sorts will be the thing. As usual, cheviot will be worn a great deal, so will serge, and for fall, panama. English tweed is also being favored for suits. Among the fashionable materials of last winter, velvet may almost be said to have occupied the first place. The general opinion prevails that its vogue for this fall and winter will be equal if not even greater.

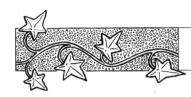 

Ladies' Traveling Suit

Five measures are taken for this suit: Bust, length of waist, around the waist, length of sleeve, and length of skirt. It is drafted in ten pieces: Jacket back, front, side front, vest, sleeve, and a nine-gore inverted pleated skirt drafted in five pieces.

To Draft. Select bust and length of waist scales for jacket back, front, side front, and vest. For sleeve, use bust and length of sleeve scales. For skirt, use waist and length of skirt scales.

The difference between the waist and hip measure is 16 inches.

Pleat back and front of jacket pattern by folding dotted lines to heavy lines. Then make curve line for shoulder and cut out pattern on that line.

To make like illustration, join front of pattern to vest front and cut goods in one piece.

To Make. Fold dotted lines to heavy lines, making three backward-turning tucks on each side of back. Follow same directions with front by folding last dotted line on front to second heavy line on side front. Stitch tucks 3/8 inch from fold. Join shoulder and underarm seams. To make sleeve, fold goods on dotted lines and stitch 1/2 inch from fold. Join seams and gather to fit armhole.

To make skirt, join according to stars. Then fold first dotted line to heavy line, also first dotted line in first gore to same heavy line on front. Follow same directions throughout the skirt. Stitch pleats to any desired depth. Finish lower part of skirt with 1/2-inch seams.

One of the checked novelties was used for this garment, with soutache braid and bias bands of the same material for trimming. Material required for medium form, 8 yards 48 inches wide.

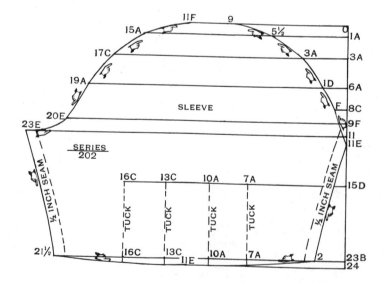

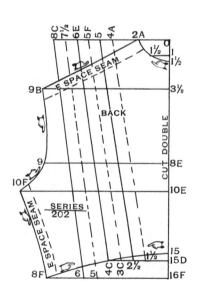

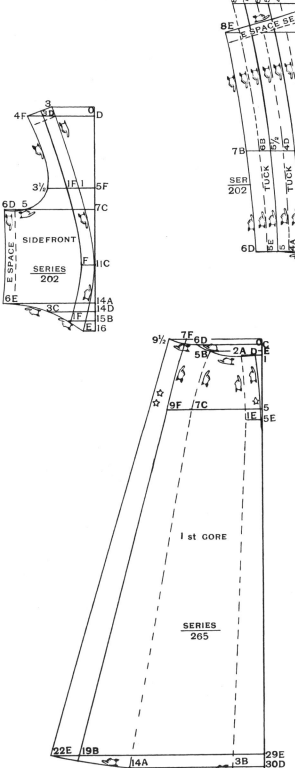

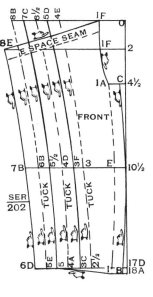

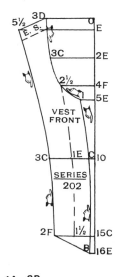

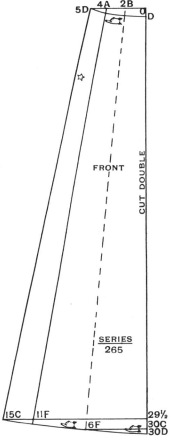

141

October 1907

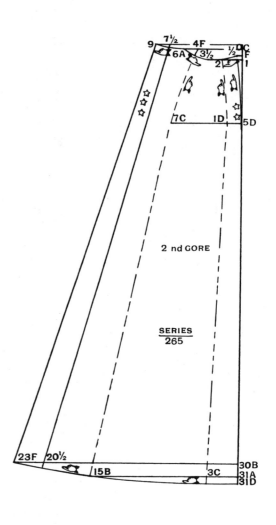

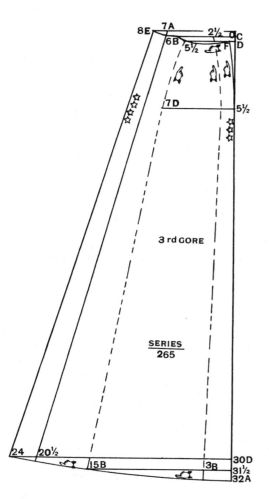

142

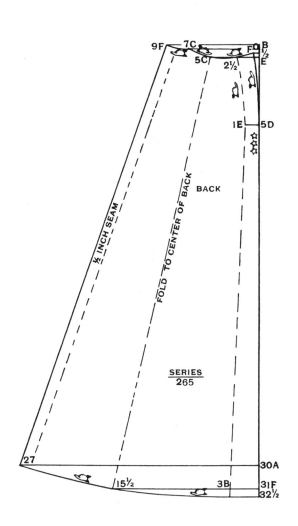

Ladies' Reception Gown

Five measures are taken for this gown: Bust, length of waist, around the waist, length of sleeve, and length of skirt. It is drafted in 15 pieces: Blouse back and front, sleeve puff, jumper, sleeve facing, oversleeve, plain 7-gore foundation skirt with habit back (4 pieces), and overskirt (5 pieces).

To Draft. Select bust and length of waist scales for blouse back, front, jumper, and sleeve facing. For sleeve puff and oversleeve, use bust and length of sleeve scales. For skirt and overskirt, use waist and length of skirt scales.

The difference between the waist and hip measure is 18 inches.

To Make. Join shoulder and underarm seams of blouse. Gather sleeve into a narrow band and sew to armhole. Gather waist to fit waist measure. If possible make jumper with back and front cut double. Fold dotted line to heavy line and stitch. Use sleeve facing on outside of armhole.

Join skirt according to stars. Finish top and bottom in the usual way. Right and left side of overskirt are not cut the same. There is one gore for the right side and two for the left, as shown in illustration. The back is cut double as it is made with habit back. Make a box pleat on each side of front by folding first dotted line to heavy line on front and second dotted line to heavy line on right side gore and left side gore. Box pleats may be stitched or not as desired. Join other sections according to stars. Close overskirt at left side.

The material used for this gown is a dark blue taffeta, with net oversleeve and blouse. The overskirt and jumper are trimmed with narrow braiding. Material required for medium form, 14 yards 27 inches wide.

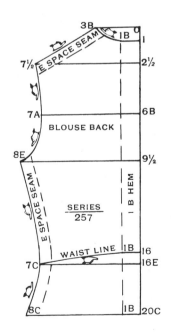

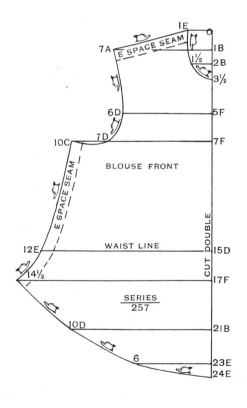

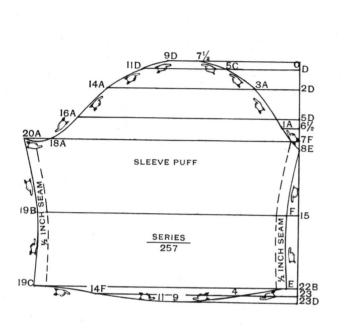

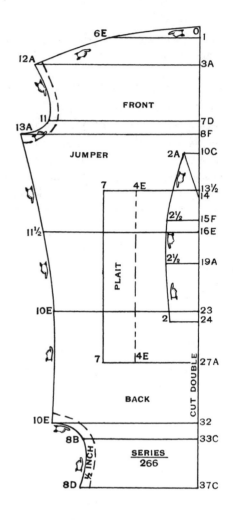

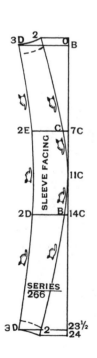

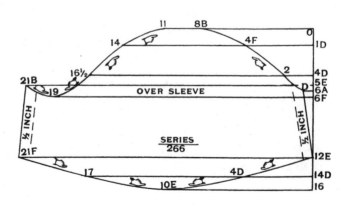

146

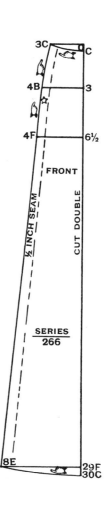

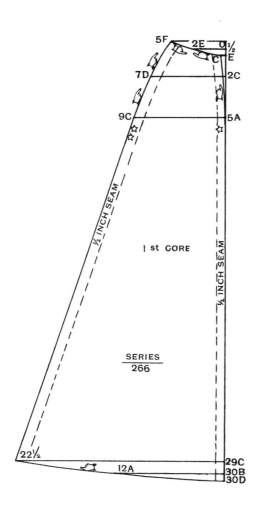

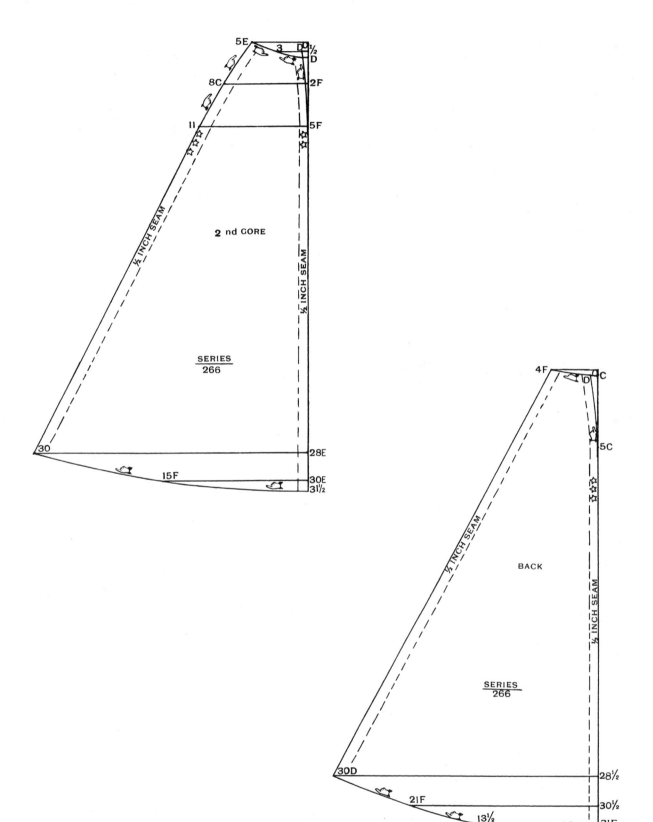

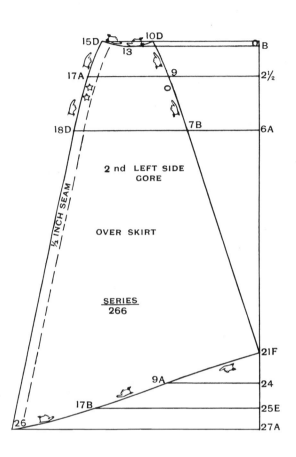

2 nd LEFT SIDE GORE

OVER SKIRT

SERIES
266

½ INCH SEAM

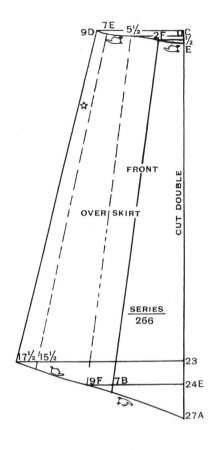

FRONT

OVER SKIRT

CUT DOUBLE

SERIES
266

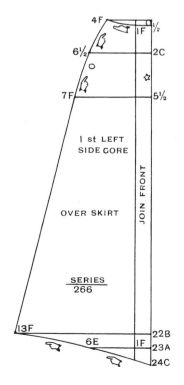

1 st LEFT
SIDE GORE

OVER SKIRT

JOIN FRONT

SERIES
266

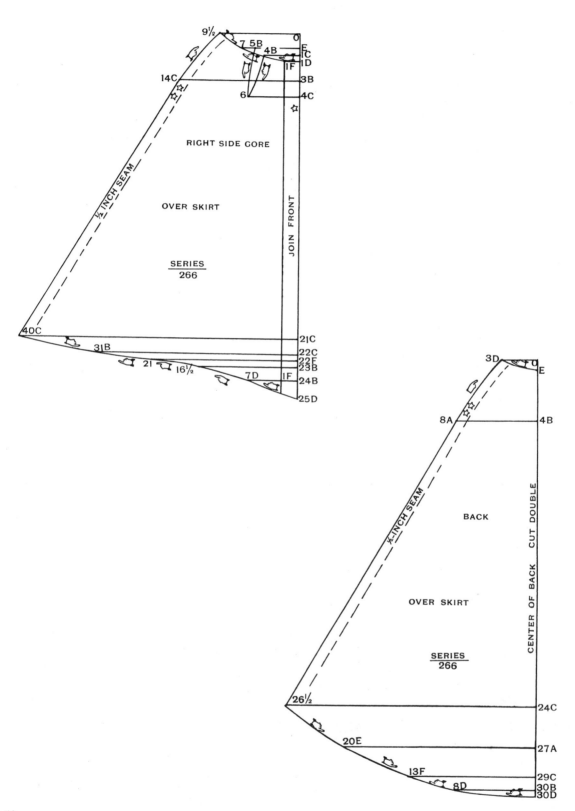

Dressy Tailor-Made Suit

Five measures are taken for this suit: Bust, length of waist, around the waist, length of sleeve, and length of skirt. It is drafted in 12 pieces: Jacket back, front, side back, side front, collar, pocket lap, sleeve (2 pieces), and a 7-gore french flare skirt (4 pieces).

To Draft. Select bust and length of waist scales for jacket back, front, side back, side front, pocket lap, and collar. For sleeve, use bust and length of sleeve scales. For skirt, use waist and length of skirt scales.

The difference between the waist and hip measure is 17 inches.

To Make. Join jacket front and side front, back and side back, with 1/2-inch seams. Stitch, press, and finish with welt seams. Join shoulder and underarm seams. Join seams of sleeve and finish back seam at wrist with lap and buttons.

Join skirt according to stars by folding dotted lines to heavy lines. Then stitch 3/8 inch from fold. Finish top and bottom in the usual way. The skirt trimming is one of the new ideas. Three folds cut on straight of goods, trimmed at lower edge with bias band, decorate lower part of skirt.

Material required for medium form, 9 yards 50 inches wide.

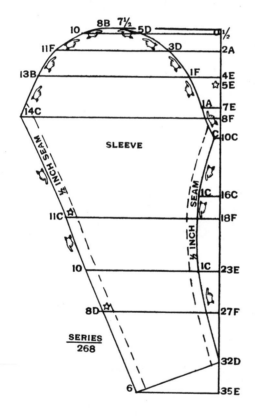

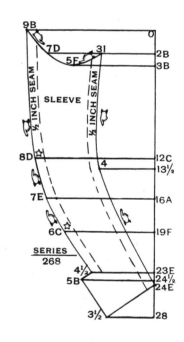

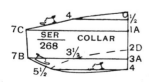

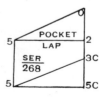

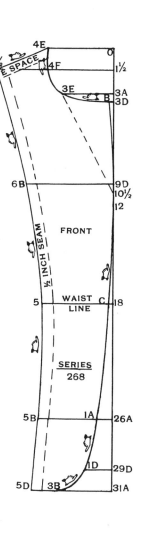

4E
8½ E SPACE | 4F
O
1½
3E | B | 3A
3D
6B
9D
10½
12
FRONT
½ INCH SEAM
5 | WAIST LINE | C | 18
SERIES
268
5B | 1A | 26A
1D | 29D
5D | 3B | 31A

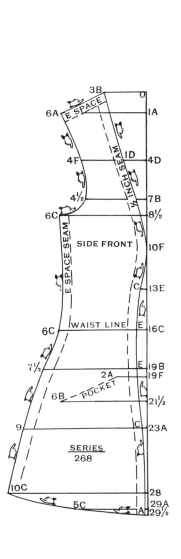

3B
6A | E SPACE
O
1A
4F | 1D | 4D
4½
6C | 7B
8½
E SPACE SEAM | SIDE FRONT | 10F
C | 13E
6C | WAIST LINE | E | 16C
7½ | E | 19B
2A | 19F
6B | POCKET
21½
9 | C | 23A
SERIES
268
10C | 28
5C | 29A
A | 29½

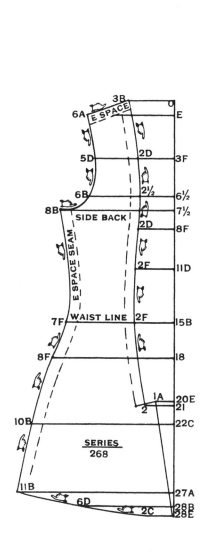

3B
6A | E SPACE
O | E
5D | 2D | 3F
6B | 2½ | 6½
8B | 7½
SIDE BACK | 2D | 8F
E SPACE SEAM | 2F | 11D
7F | WAIST LINE | 2F | 15B
8F | 18
1A | 20E
2 | 21
10B | 22C
SERIES
268
11B | 27A
6D | 28B
2C | 28E

153

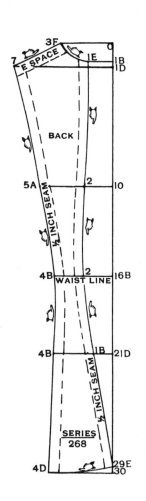

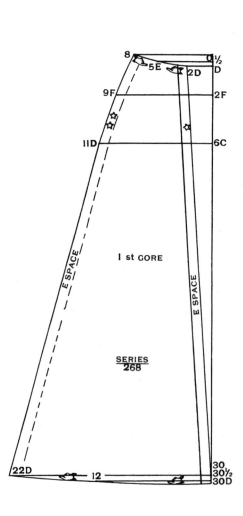

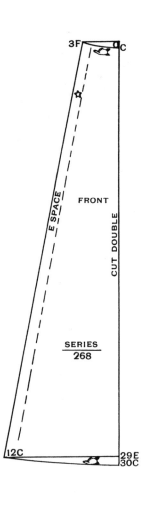

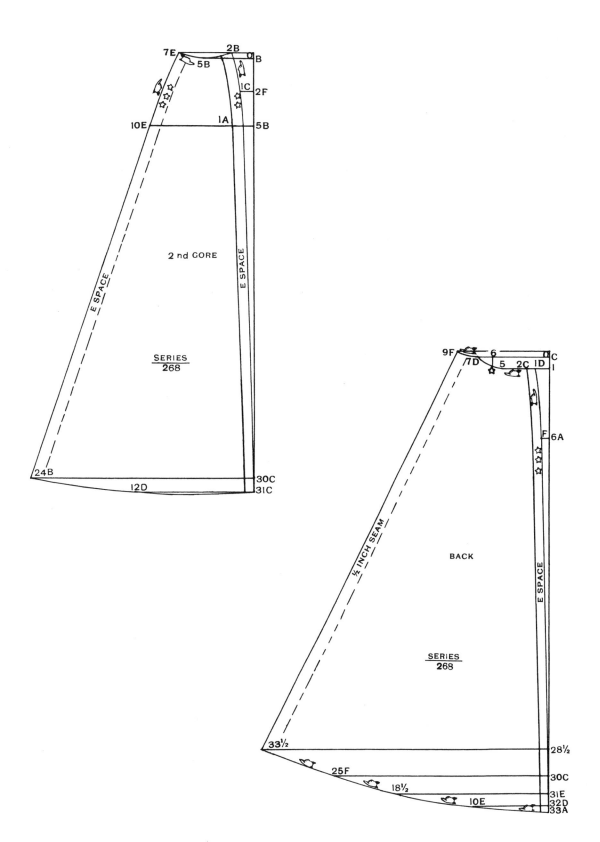

2nd GORE

SERIES
268

BACK

SERIES
268

Ladies' Auto Coat

Four measures are taken for this coat: Bust, length of waist, full length, and sleeve. It is drafted in six pieces: Back and front of coat, cape, collar, sleeve, and cuff.

To Draft. Select bust and length of waist scales for cape, collar, and back and front of coat to waistline. Then subtract length of waist measure from full-length measure. This will give desired scale for baseline from waistline down. Use bust scale for all crosslines.

This sleeve must be drafted with length of waist scale (for baseline) and length of sleeve scale (for crosslines). To prove up length of sleeve, measure on line out from 12E, from 1 to 31.

For cuff, use bust and length of sleeve scales.

To Make. Join shoulder and back seam of coat. Stitch and press well. Sleeve is sewn to coat from point 15 1/2 on front to point 13E on back. Place stars on sleeve even with stars on coat, and stitch 1/2-inch seam. Join the side edges of the body and sleeve in a seam.

Notice where cape diagram says "cut open." Cut back and front open to points 5F and 6C. Pleat or gather extra fullness of cape to fit points. Place star on cape even with shoulder seam. Stitch with a flat seam to dotted lines on coat.

Finish sleeve with cuff; place star even with seam. Join collar to neck, meeting at center of front.

This coat and sleeve are decidedly new and comfortable, and may be worn over any gown with comfort. Material required for medium form, 4 yards 50 inches wide.

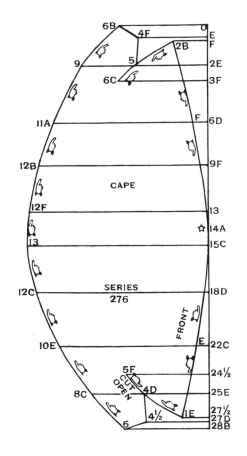

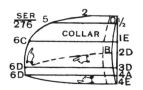

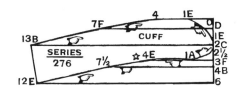

October 1907

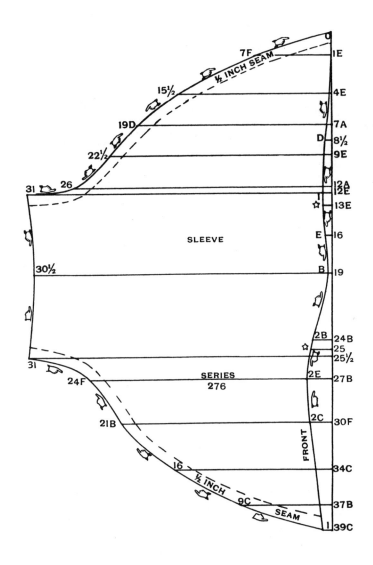

SLEEVE

SERIES 276

FRONT

158

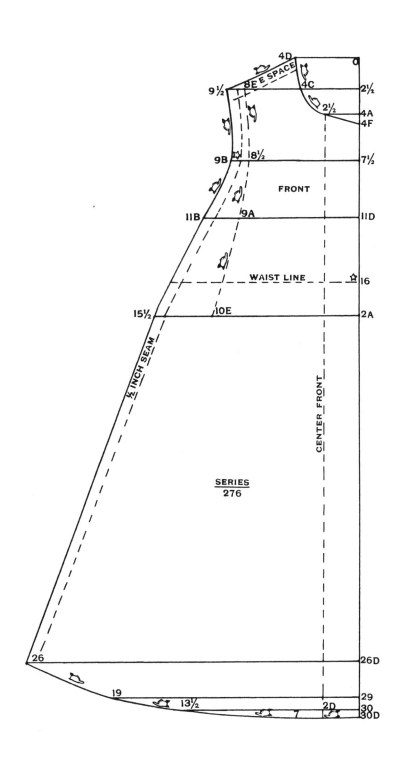

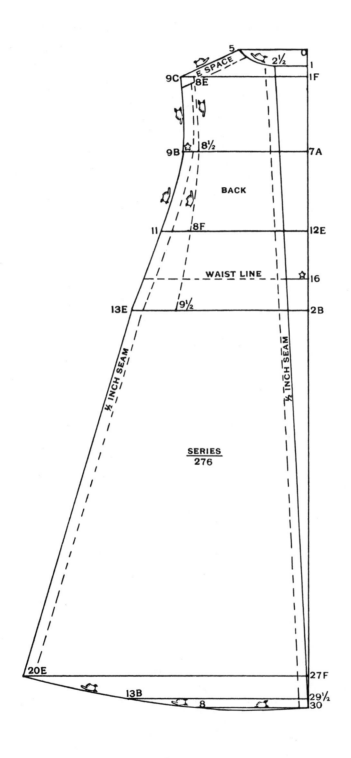

October 1907

Japanese Robe

Four measures are taken for this garment: Bust, length of waist, full length, and length of sleeve. It is drafted in four pieces: Back and front of skirt portion, yoke, and sleeve.

To Draft. This garment can be either short or full length. Select bust and length of waist scales for yoke, and back and front of kimono to waistline. Then subtract length of waist measure from full length. This will give desired scale for baseline

from waistline down. Use bust scale for all crosslines. For sleeve, use bust and length of sleeve scales.

To Make. Gather back and front of skirt. Join to back and front of yoke. Close underarm seams. No diagram is given for collar and front facing. Cut material 5 inches wide. Sew to fronts and yoke. Fold in center and sew to outside. Face sleeves and gather to fit armhole.

Material required for medium form, 7 1/2 yards 27 inches wide.

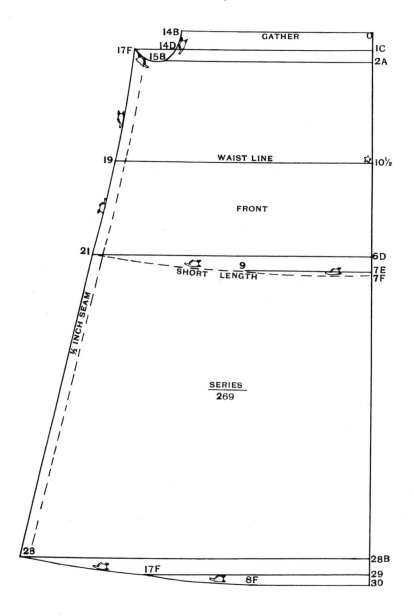

162

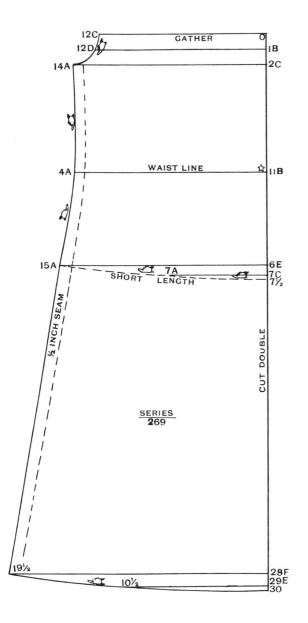

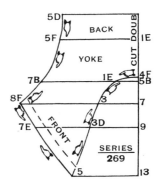

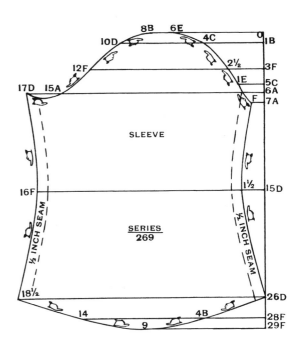

Ladies' Separate Waist

Four measures are taken for this waist: Bust, length of waist, around the waist, and length of sleeve. It is drafted in nine pieces: Back and front lining, upper back and front, two yoke pieces, sleeve cap, sleeve puff, and collar.

To Draft. Select bust and length of waist scales for back and front lining, upper back and front, two yoke pieces, sleeve cap, and collar. For sleeve puff, use bust and length of sleeve scales.

This waist may be made with or without lining, as desired.

Fold tucks in pattern 1/2 inch deep. Then make curved line for shoulder and cut out on that line.

To Make. Fold first two short tucks on dotted line and stitch 1/2 inch from fold. Join shoulder seam. Then fold third tuck on dotted line and place sleeve cap under it, point 13B, 1 inch in front of shoulder seam. Stitch tuck as illustrated.

Join collar to waist. Close underarm seam. Gather to fit waist measure. Join yoke and finish with straight collar. Close seam of sleeve. Gather to fit arm and armhole.

The materials used for this waist were prune-colored chiffon taffeta, white batiste for the yoke and sleeve puff, and allover lace for the collar.

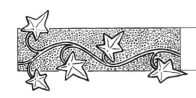

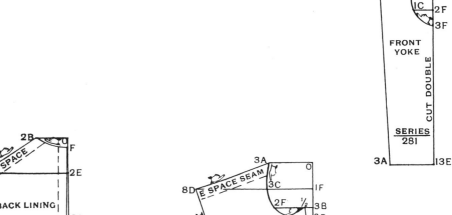

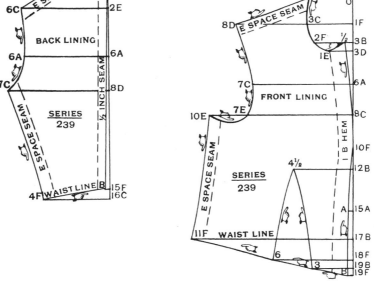

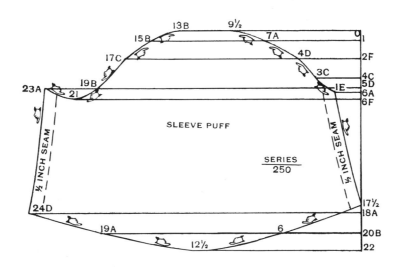

165

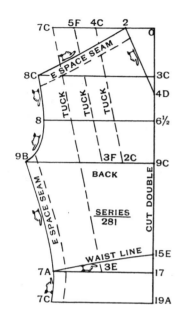

7C 5F 4C 2 0

8C E SPACE SEAM 3C

4D

TUCK TUCK TUCK

8 6½

9B 3F 2C 9C

BACK

E SPACE SEAM CUT DOUBLE

SERIES
281

WAIST LINE 15E

7A 3E 17

7C 19A

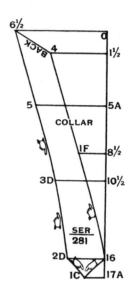

6½ 0

BACK 4 1½

5 5A

COLLAR

1F 8½

3D 10½

SER
281

2D 16

1C 17A

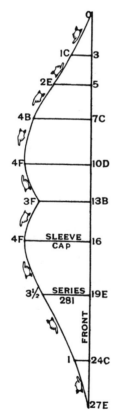

0

1C 3

2E 5

4B 7C

4F 10D

3F 13B

4F 16
SLEEVE
CAP

SERIES 19E
281

3½ 19E

FRONT

1 24C

27E

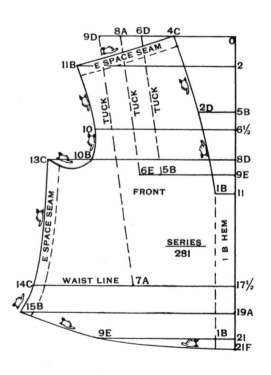

9D 8A 6D 4C 0

11B E SPACE SEAM 2

TUCK TUCK TUCK 2D 5B

10 6½

13C 10B 8D

6E 5B 9E

FRONT 1B 11

E SPACE SEAM 1 B HEM

SERIES
281

14C WAIST LINE 7A 17½

15B 19A

9E 1B 21

21F

One-Piece Corset Cover

Three measures are taken for this garment: Bust, length of waist, and around the waist. It is drafted in three pieces: Back and front (one piece), sleeve, and belt.

To Draft and Make. Select bust and length of waist scales for back/front and sleeve. For belt, use bust and waist measure scales.

Join underarm seam. Gather waist between stars. Place star on belt even with underarm seam and arrange gathers to fit same. Close seam of sleeve. Place seam even with star at 9B and sew to armhole.

This diagram is made especially for corset cover embroidery, with a narrow embroidery for sleeve. Use straight edge of sleeve for outside. Material required for medium form, 1 1/2 yards of flouncing.

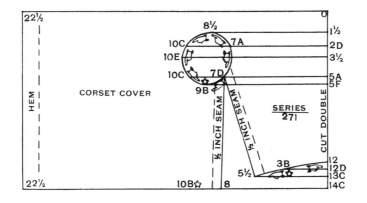

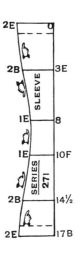

January 1908 American Modiste

Perhaps the greatest novelty is the development of the long vest of fancy material. Silk or satin embroidered by hand is used for these vests, but cloth and velvet are also used embroidered in gold or silver or braided soutache. Many of the smartest black suits are made with these waistcoats, which are quite narrow, giving merely a suggestion of color rather than appearing as a conspicuous part of the coat.

Some of the Chinese cloaks are very gorgeous in coloring, too much so perhaps for the conservative woman. The most attractive of all these models are the coats of soft heavy black satin, lined with color and embroidered in oriental blues, yellows, and greens, with the lovely dull blues predominating. Chiffon broadcloth is chosen for the material nine times out of ten.

The separate coat seems to be creeping into favor. Jackets of velvet with skirts of broadcloth of the same shade are much seen in Paris.

Almost all the blouses of sheer material must have a silk lining. The girl who cannot afford this expense will find at the lining counter many cotton goods with silk luster to them that really answer every purpose. A good quantity of silk mull will make a suitable lining for a chiffon waist, but care must be taken to secure a firm piece and not to have the lining fit very snug.

It will be quite correct to have sleeves made of different material from the waist.

Lace; gauze; plain, figured, and polka-dotted nets; punted chiffons; and a host of attractive silk materials are used this season for evening dresses. A trimming novelty especially smart consists of velvet ribbon the width of baby ribbon, and of soutache of little more than half that width. Silk fringe, the joy of our grandmothers, has come into the glory of its own again on evening wraps. It is used in all kinds of ways, particularly as an edging for the fichulike arrangement seen on many cloaks and as a finish for the edges of lace and chiffon stoles. Braids of all kinds are used, rarely one kind alone.

Dressy Redingote

Five measures are taken for this suit: Bust, length of waist, around the waist, length of sleeve, and length of skirt. It is drafted in 17 pieces: Jacket lining back, front, and side back; jacket back and front; belt; collar; cuff; sleeve (2 pieces); skirt for coat (2 pieces); and a 9-gore pleated skirt (5 pieces).

To Draft. Select bust and length of waist scales for jacket back, front, and side back; jacket back and front; and collar. For belt, use waist and length of waist scales. For sleeve and cuff, use bust and length of sleeve scales. For coat skirt, use waist and desired length of skirt scales. For skirt, use waist and length of skirt scales.

The difference between the waist and hip measure is 16 inches.

To Make. Join the three sections of jacket lining and take up darts. Cover lining 1 inch beyond dotted line for vest.

Fold dotted lines together on back of jacket and stitch to waistline. Fold dotted lines together on front of jacket and stitch as far as directed. A tuck (which the illustration does not show) covers the top of the sleeve.

Close shoulder and underarm seams. Gather or pleat to fit waist measure and sew to belt.

Coat part of skirt may be cut in one piece by joining pattern at side seam. Then take up dart over hips to fit waist measure. Join to jacket belt.

Close seams of sleeve and ease in extra fullness on upper part at elbow. When cuff is used, place star on cuff even with inseam of sleeve.

Join skirt according to stars by folding first dotted line on front to first heavy line, also first dotted line on first gore to same heavy line. Follow same directions throughout the skirt, making an inverted pleat at each gore.

Broadcloth was the material used for this suit, with one of the many pretty braided designs for trimming.

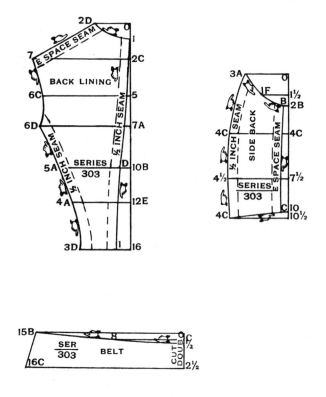

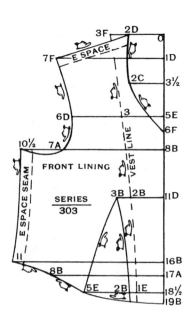

Dressy Redingote

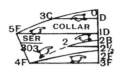

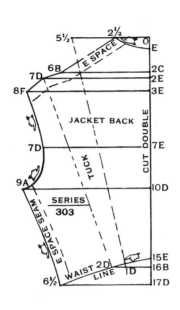

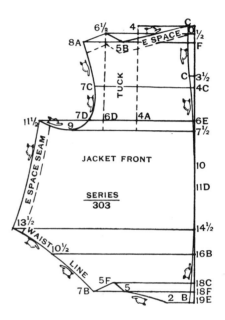

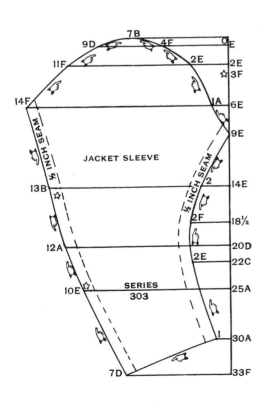

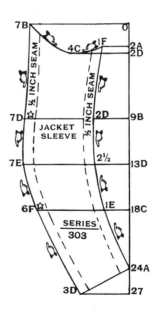

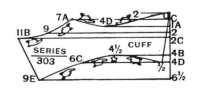

171

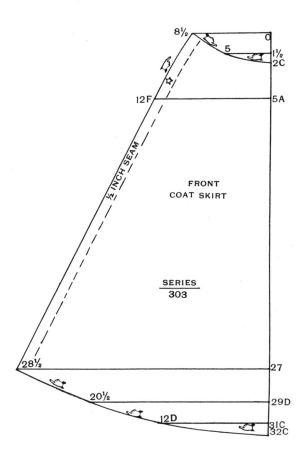

8½   5   0
1½
2C
12F   5A

½ INCH SEAM

FRONT
COAT SKIRT

SERIES
303

28½   27
20½   29D
12D   31C
32C

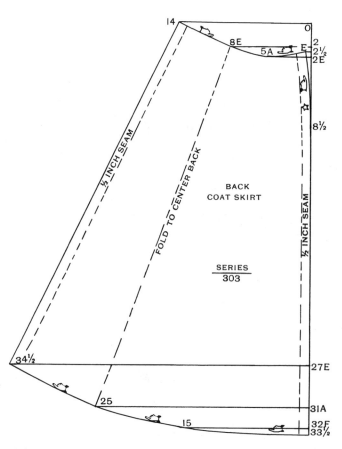

14   0
8E   2
5A   E   2½
2E
8½

½ INCH SEAM

FOLD TO CENTER BACK

BACK
COAT SKIRT

½ INCH SEAM

SERIES
303

34½   27E
25   31A
15   32F
33½

172

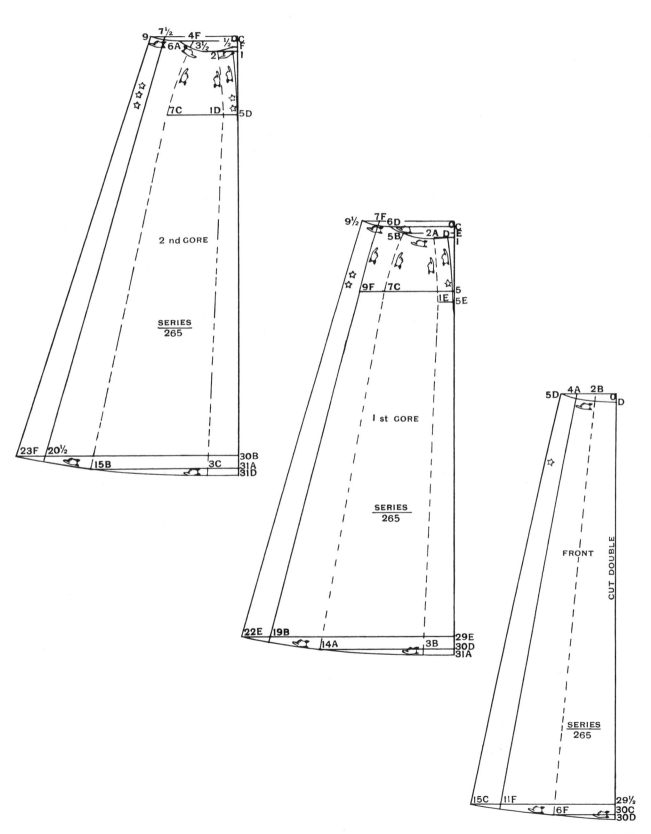

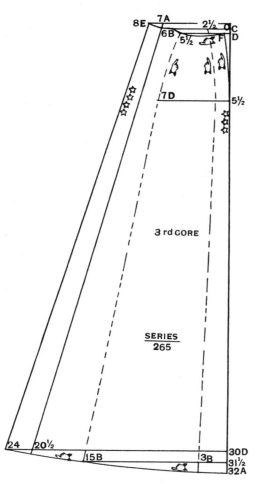

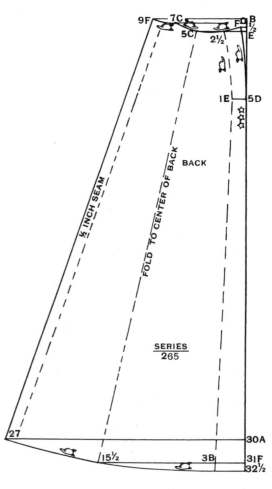

A Stylish Street Suit

Six measures are taken for this suit: Bust, length of waist, full length, around the waist, length of sleeve, and length of skirt. It is drafted in 16 pieces: Coat back, front, side back, side front, underarm, 2 collars, sleeve (2 pieces), cuff, and an 11-gore flared skirt (6 pieces).

To Draft. Select bust and length of waist scales for coat back, front, side back, side front, and underarm. Gore to waistline. Then subtract length of waist measure from full-length measure. This will give desired scale for baseline from waistline to bottom of coat. Use bust scale for all crosslines. For collars, use bust and length of waist scales. For sleeve and cuff, use bust and length of sleeve scales.

If flat collar is desired, cut revere off on dotted line.

The difference between the waist and hip measure of skirt is 18 inches.

To Make. Join the different parts of coat, matching waistlines. Fold dotted line on skirt part of side back to dotted line on back. Press to position. Close under part of pleat with 1/2-inch seam. Finish center of back open.

Join back seam of sleeve. Ease in extra fullness on upper part of elbow. Shrink out fullness and press into shape. Join cuff to sleeve with star on cuff even with inseam of sleeve.

Join skirt according to stars. Stitch and press.

Eight yards of 50-inch material is required for this suit. This is one of the new flare skirts and is suitable for most materials.

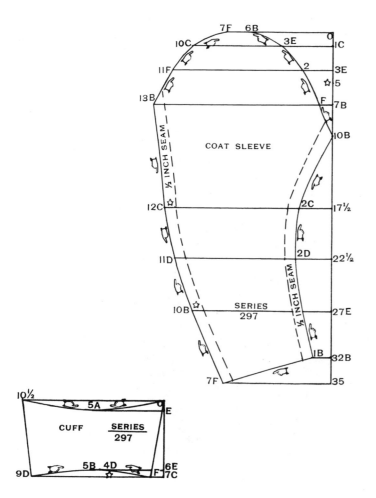

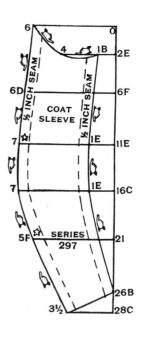

A Stylish Street Suit

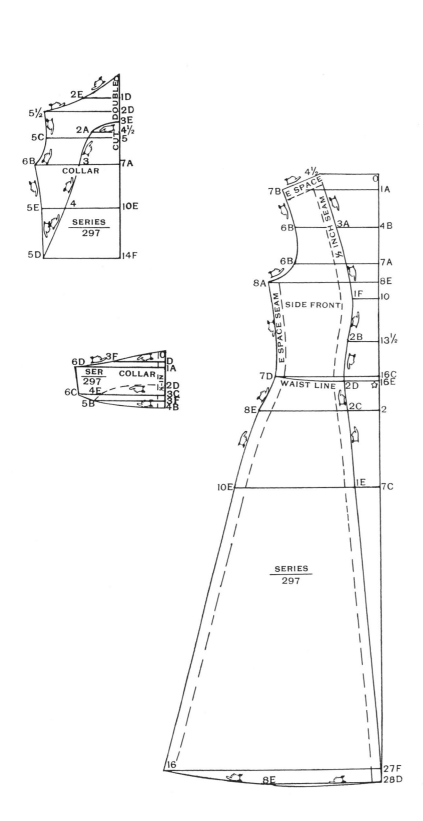

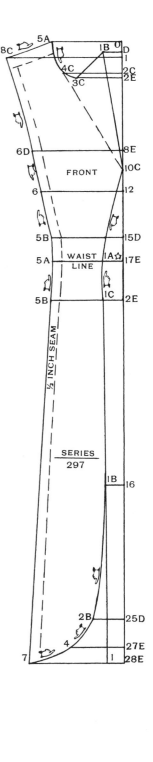

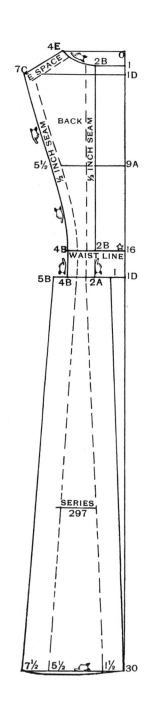
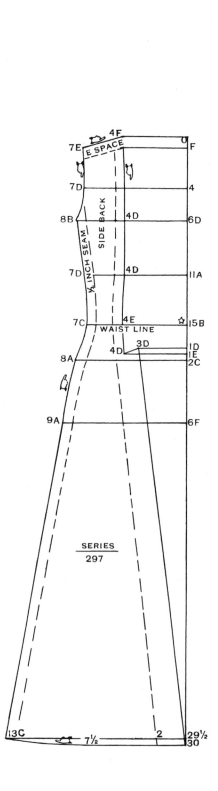
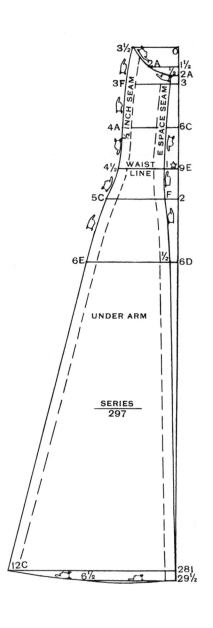

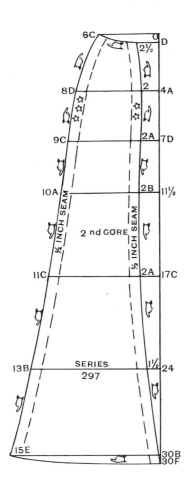

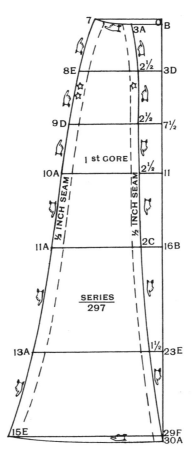

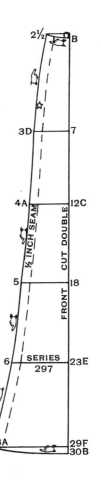

179

January 1908

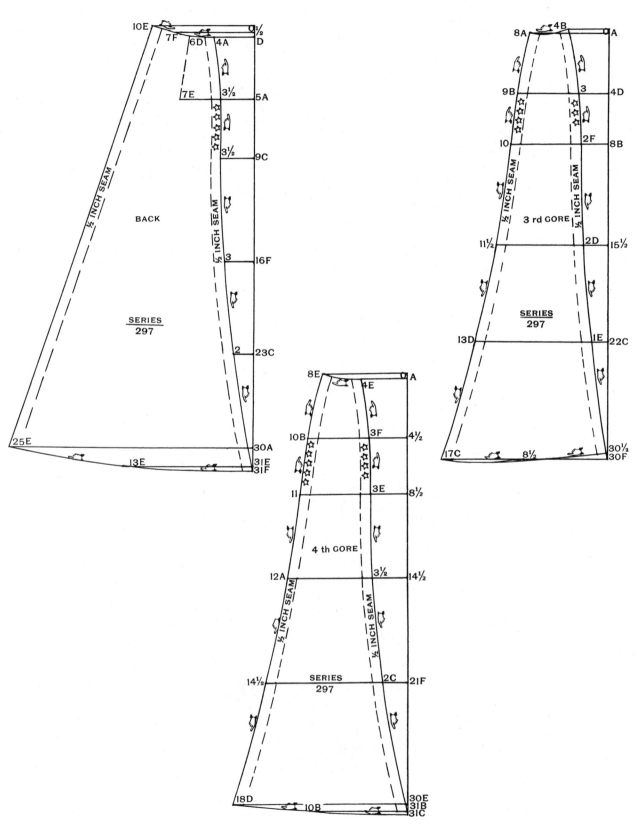

180

Ladies' Evening Dress

Five measures are taken for this dress: Bust, length of waist, around the waist, length of sleeve, and length of skirt. It is drafted in 12 pieces: Back and front lining, upper back and front, 2 yoke pieces, bretelle, sleeve puff, and a 7-gore gathered skirt drafted in 4 pieces.

To Draft. Select bust and length of waist scales for back and front lining, upper back and front, 2 yoke portions, and bretelle. For sleeve puff, use bust and length of sleeve scales. For skirt, use waist and length of skirt scales.

Two yoke portions are given for high-necked dress.

To Make. Join front lining and take up darts. Gather upper back and front to fit lining and arrange on same. Join shoulder and underarm seams. Then gather to fit waist measure. Join seam of sleeve puff. Gather to fit arm and armhole.

Join skirt according to stars. Gather top to fit waist measure. Finish bottom in the usual way.

Black point d'esprit was the material used for this gown, trimmed with black velvet and taffeta. Skirt is trimmed with bias fold of taffeta gathered at one edge and arranged on skirt in zigzag shape. Material required for medium form, 12 yards 27 inches wide.

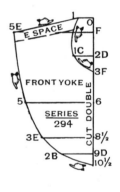

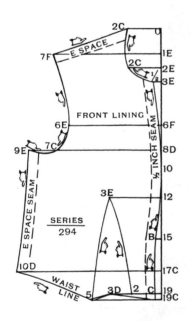

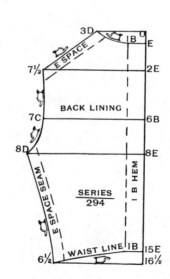

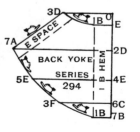

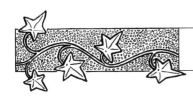

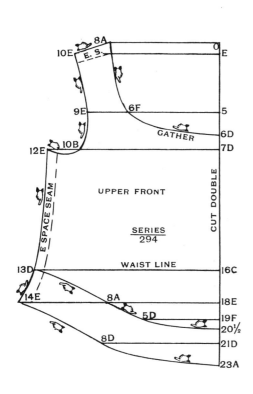

UPPER FRONT

SERIES
294

E SPACE SEAM

E. S.

GATHER

WAIST LINE

CUT DOUBLE

8A
10E
0 E
9E 6F
5
6D
7D
12E 10B
13D
14E 8A
5D 16C
18E
19F
20½
21D
23A

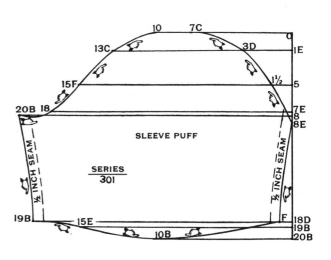

SLEEVE PUFF

SERIES
301

½ INCH SEAM

½ INCH SEAM

10 7C
13C 3D 1E
15F 1½ 5
20B 18 7E
8
8E
19B 15E F 18D
10B 19B
20B

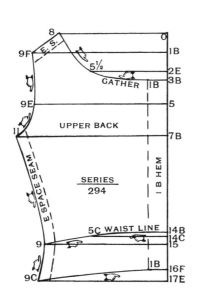

UPPER BACK

SERIES
294

E SPACE SEAM

E. S.

GATHER

WAIST LINE

I B HEM

8 0
9F 1B
5½ 2E
3B
1B
9E 5
11 7B
5C 14B
9 14C
15
1B 16F
9C 17E

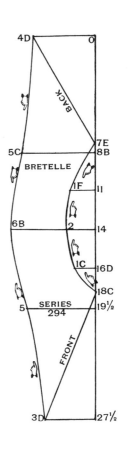

BACK

BRETELLE

FRONT

SERIES
294

4D 0
7E
5C 8B
1F 11
6B 2 14
1C 16D
18C
5 19½
3D 27½

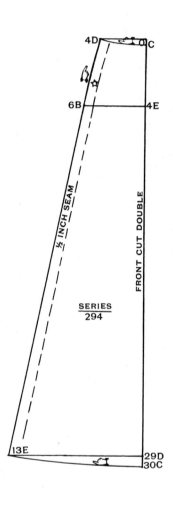

4D   0C

6B   4E

½ INCH SEAM

FRONT CUT DOUBLE

SERIES
294

13E   29D
       30C

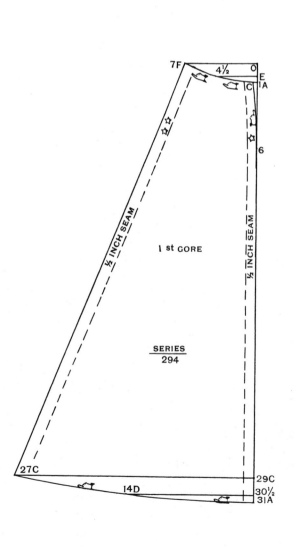

7F   4½   0
           E
     C 1A

6

½ INCH SEAM

½ INCH SEAM

1 st GORE

SERIES
294

27C   29C
    14D   30½
          31A

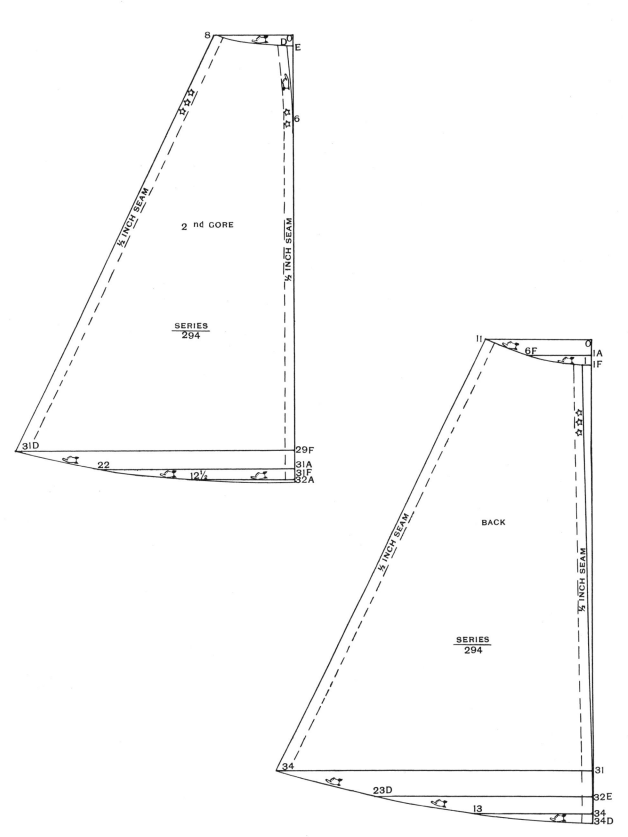

2 nd GORE

½ INCH SEAM

½ INCH SEAM

SERIES
294

8

D
E

6

31D

29F
31A
22
12½
31F
32A

BACK

½ INCH SEAM

½ INCH SEAM

SERIES
294

11

6F

O
1A
1F

34

31

23D

32E

13

34
34D

185

Dainty Waist

Four measures are taken for this waist: Bust, length of waist, around the waist, and length of sleeve. It is drafted in nine pieces: Lining back, front, and underarm; blouse back and front; belt; sleeve lining (two pieces); and sleeve puff.

To Draft. Select bust and length of waist scales for lining back, front, and underarm, and blouse back and front. For belt, use waist and length of waist scales. For sleeve lining and sleeve puff, use bust and length of sleeve scales.

This waist may be made with or without tight lining.

To make short sleeve with lining, cut lining off on dotted lines.

To Make. Make lining and outside separately. Join seam in front of lining and take up darts. Join underarm to back and front. Close shoulder seams.

Tuck material for waist and sleeve before cutting. Join blouse back and front at shoulder and underarm seams. Gather to fit waist measure. To make long sleeve, face lower part of lining 1 inch above dotted line for cuff.

The materials used for this waist are cluny lace and net.

186

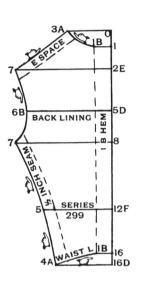

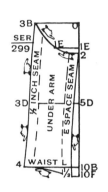

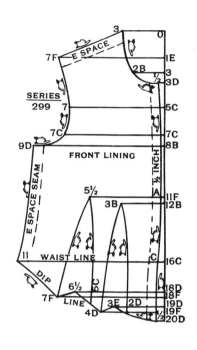

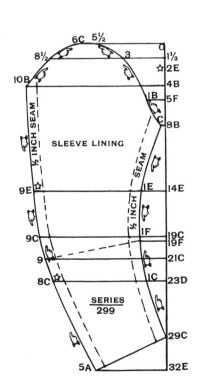

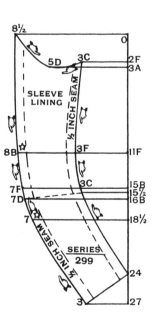

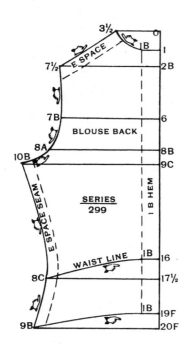

BLOUSE BACK

SERIES
299

E SPACE

E SPACE SEAM

1 B HEM

WAIT LINE

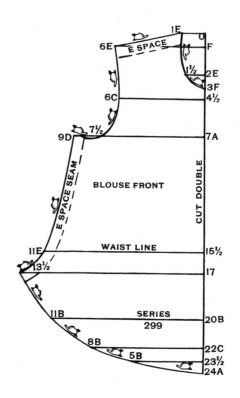

BLOUSE FRONT

CUT DOUBLE

E SPACE

E SPACE SEAM

WAIST LINE

SERIES
299

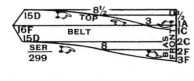

TOP
BELT
SER
299

BIAS
FRONT

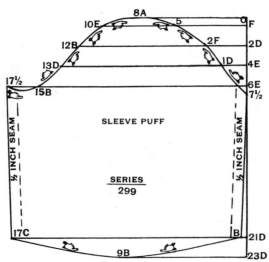

SLEEVE PUFF

SERIES
299

½ INCH SEAM

½ INCH SEAM

April 1908 American Modiste

Neither coat nor collar is made to fasten, as they must exhibit a certain expanse of shawl-shaped waistcoat, and above all a high stock swathing the throat up to the ears and filling in the opening of the vest with an extremely voluminous jabot. The embroidered waistcoat is to have considerable influence on the spring costume. Light cloth and light watered silk will be called to its service. Its most attractive shape will be that which we associate with the cavalier coat and the lace cravat and the sleeve ruffle. Waistcoats are also made of fanciful brocade, and some of tapestry are novel, while the oriental embroideries are not banished from recognition.

As to fabrics, mixed weaves reign this spring in all cloths. Combinations of two dull tones are quite a feature, and gray united with almost any shade will be a popular combination in design and will also be featured in trimmings. Stripes are used both up and down and across. The vogue for rough silks continues in all its force. There is no doubt that this will be one of the most popular materials for spring and summer suits, and for tailor-made shirtwaist dresses. It is also proving very popular for evening auto coats.

Some very fascinating waists are shown in irish lace, combined with valenciennes. Then there are beautiful colored laces—filet, guipure, etc. The embroidered filets will appear in a more general way in spring fashions. Many of these coarse nets are shown in color with lacy embroidery, which is done with a silk tape or flat silk braid. Among the sheer series of dress fabrics this spring is a new square-mesh net.

All sorts of jabot effects are to be very fashionable in neckwear this spring. These are to be used to finish the necks of dressy gowns and are also worn with embroidered linen collars and plain tailored waists. There are a multitude of natty silk bows, some made with triple loops, others with double loops and a rosette center. The collar-and-cuff set was never more prominent than it is today.

 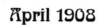

White Linen Suit

Four measures are taken for this garment: Bust, length of waist, around the waist, and length of skirt. It is drafted in 10 pieces: Back and front of waist, collar, cuff, and an 11-gore inverted pleated skirt drafted in 6 pieces.

To Draft. Select bust and length of waist scales for back and front of waist and collar. For cuff, use bust and length of sleeve scales. For skirt, use waist and length of skirt scales.

This is one of the new waists, where sleeve and waist are drafted in one piece, with the seams along the shoulder and top of the sleeve.

The difference between the waist and hip measure is 18 inches.

To Make. Join shoulder and sleeve seams, also underarm and sleeve seams. Gather sleeve to fit arm measure and arrange gathers in narrow band. Join cuff with star even with inseam of sleeve. Gather to fit waist measure.

Join skirt according to stars and stitch seams 1/2-space deep. Then fold dotted line on front to first heavy line on extension. Also fold first dotted line on first gore to same heavy line on front, thus forming a box pleat on each gore and five on each side of skirt. Join the extension in lower part of skirt with 1/2-inch seams. Press pleats well into position.

The material used for this suit is white linen, with waist, collar, cuffs, and skirt worked in eyelet and french embroidery. Material required for medium form, 10 yards 36 inches wide.

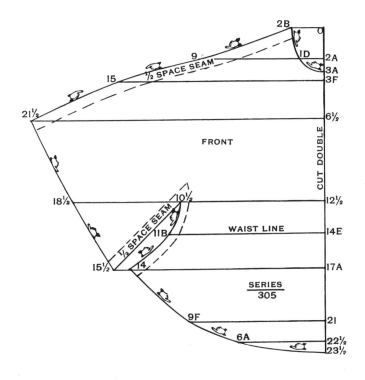

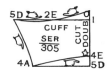

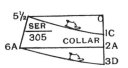

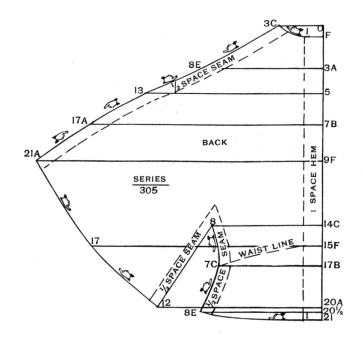

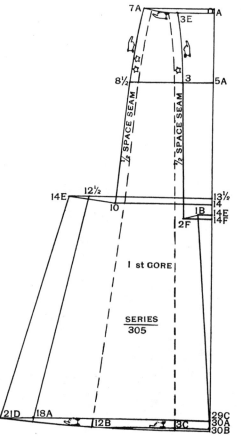

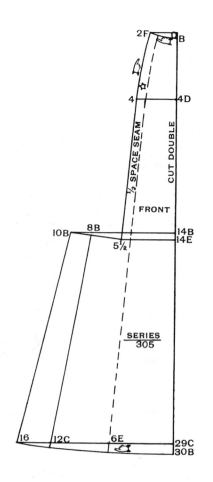

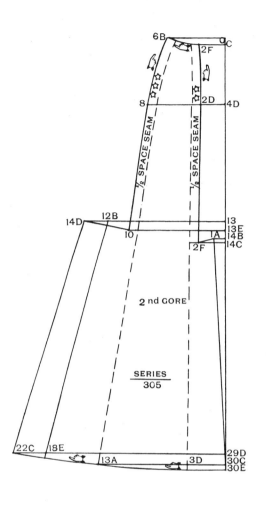

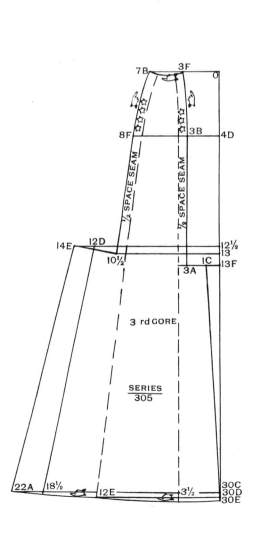

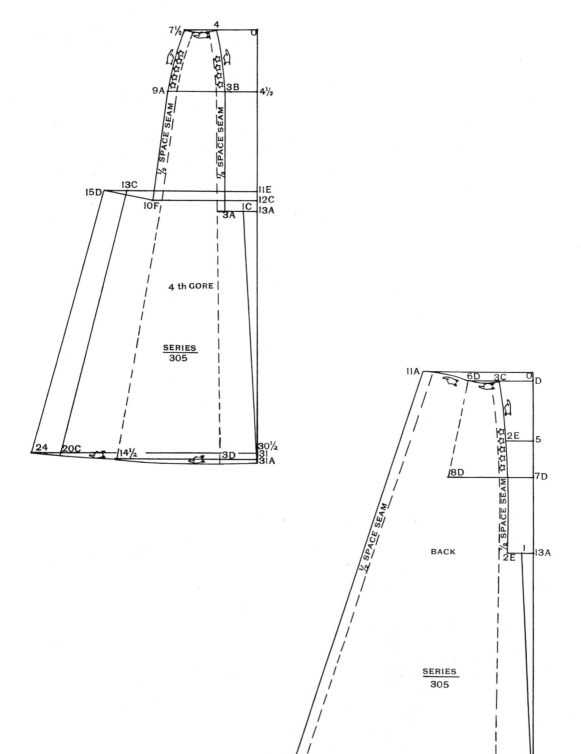

Easter Model

Five measures are taken for this suit: Bust, length of waist, around the waist, length of sleeve, and length of skirt. It is drafted in 20 pieces: Coat back, front, side front, side back, collar, cuff and 2 sleeve portions; vest back, front, and double-breasted portion; 2 collars; and a 13-gore pleated skirt drafted in 7 pieces.

To Draft. Select bust and length of waist scales for all parts of vest, also coat back, front, side front, side back, and collar. For sleeve and cuff, use bust and length of sleeve scales. For skirt, use waist and length of skirt scales.

The difference between the waist and hip measure is 18 inches.

Use coat collar for double-breasted vest. Use round collar when single-breasted vest is desired.

To Make. To make vest like illustration, join small section to front in lining only. Then cut outside in one piece. Join backs to same.

Join the different parts of coat according to the seams given. Finish side back with underlap. Join sleeve. Ease in extra fullness on upper part of sleeve between stars. Join cuff to sleeve; place star even with inseam of sleeve. This coat is cut with a very deep armhole, and there are no gathers at top of sleeve. Ease in extra fullness. Stitch and press thoroughly.

Join skirt according to numbers by folding first dotted line on first gore to heavy line on front, and second dotted line to heavy line on second gore. Follow same directions throughout the skirt.

Materials required for medium form: Vest, 1 yard 42 inches wide. Coat and skirt, 6 1/2 yards 54 inches wide.

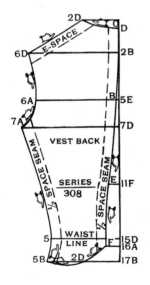

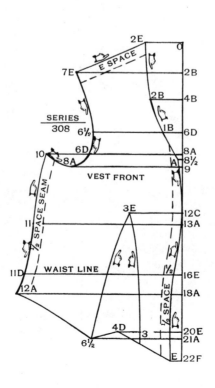

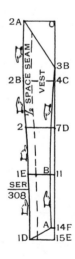

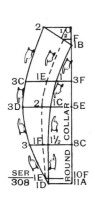

ROUND COLLAR

SER 308

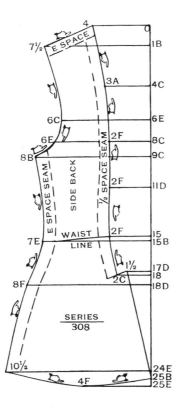

SIDE BACK

E SPACE SEAM

1/2 SPACE SEAM

WAIST LINE

E SPACE

SERIES 308

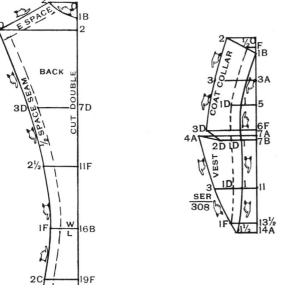

BACK

CUT DOUBLE

1/2 SPACE SEAM

E SPACE

W L

SERIES 308

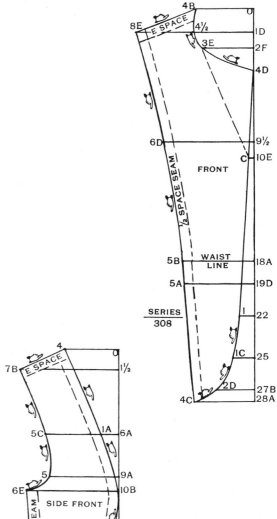

FRONT

1/2 SPACE SEAM

WAIST LINE

E SPACE

SERIES 308

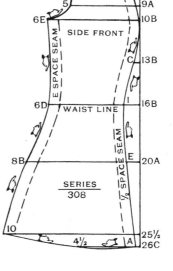

COAT COLLAR

VEST

SER 308

SIDE FRONT

E SPACE SEAM

1/2 SPACE SEAM

WAIST LINE

E SPACE

SERIES 308

COLLAR

SER 308 4

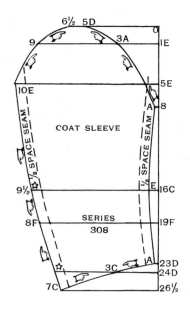

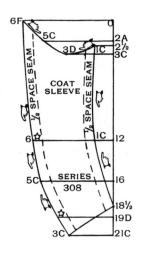

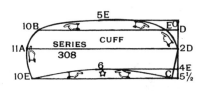

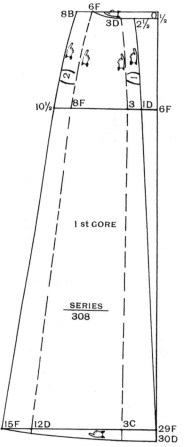

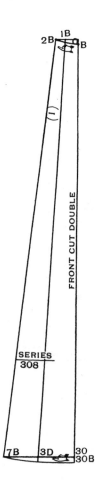

198

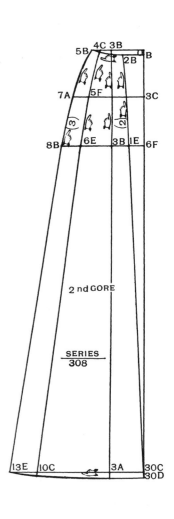

2 nd GORE

SERIES
308

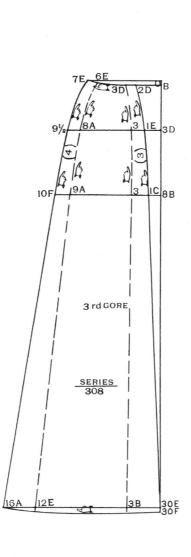

3 rd GORE

SERIES
308

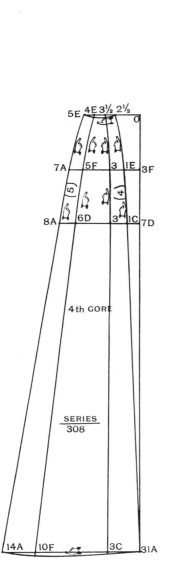

4th GORE

SERIES
308

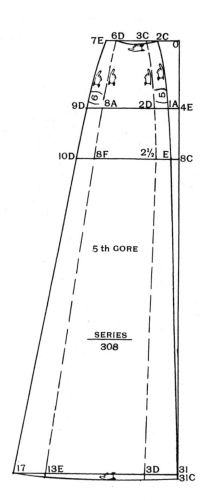

7E 6D 3C 2C 0

9D 8A (6) 2D (5) 1A 4E

10D 8F 2½ E 8C

5 th GORE

SERIES
308

17 13E 3D 31 31C

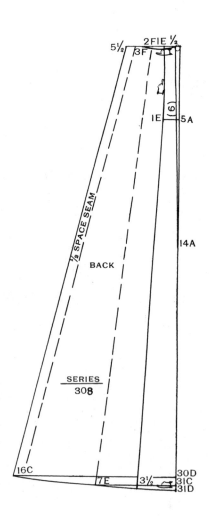

5½ 2F1E ½
3F

1E (6) 5A

½ SPACE SEAM

BACK

14A

SERIES
308

16C 7E 3½ 30D 31C 31D

The Season's Newest Mode

Five measures are taken for this suit: Bust, length of waist, around the waist, length of sleeve, and length of skirt. It is drafted in 16 pieces: Jacket back, front, underarm gore, vest front, collar, back and front belt, back and front peplum, 2 sleeve pieces, cuff, and circular skirt drafted in 4 pieces.

To Draft. Select bust and length of waist scales for jacket back, front, vest front, underarm gore, collar, and back and front peplum. For sleeve and cuff, use bust and length of sleeve scales. For belts, use waist and length of waist scales. For skirt, use waist and length of skirt scales.

The difference between the waist and hip measure is 18 inches.

To Make. Join vest front to jacket front. Fold to dotted line on vest. Place star on vest at point 2F even with star on front of jacket, point 1B. Fold goods on dotted lines on back of jacket and stitch 1/2 space from fold. Join back and front at shoul-

der seams. Also join underarm at shoulder. Then fold back and front on dotted line and sew to underarm gore, having edges and shoulder seam even. Stitch 1 inch from folded edge. This gives the broad shoulder effect. Pleat front of jacket at waist by folding stars to Os, making four small pleats. Make four 1/2-inch tucks in back of peplum. Join peplum to back and front of jacket. Arrange collar on jacket. Finish with belts of braid.

Skirt is made with front gore, side, and back cut in one piece. Join three sections of skirt pattern according to stars, and cut skirt material in one piece. Join front to side with 1/2-space seam. Close center back seam. Finish top and bottom in the usual way.

One of the many novelties in back and white worsted goods was used for this suit, trimmed with wide silk braid. White piqué vest, and black velvet collar. Material required for medium form, 6 yards 54 inches wide.

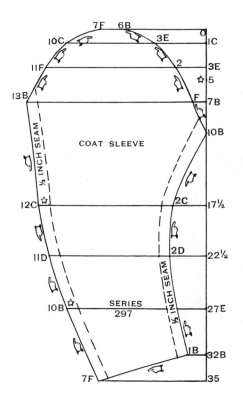

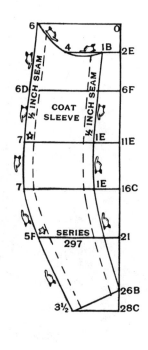

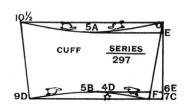

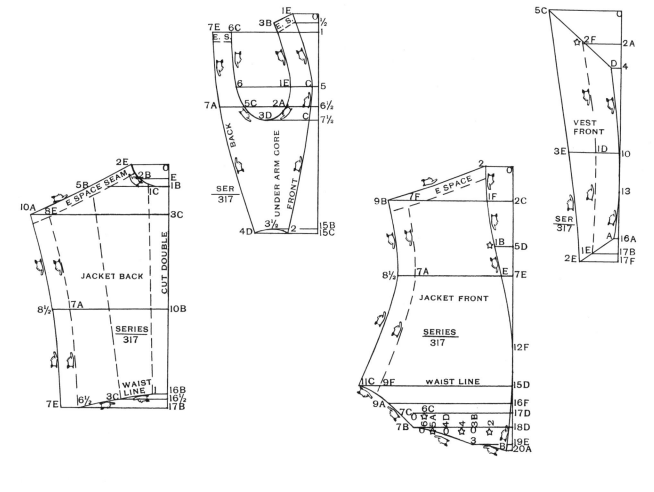

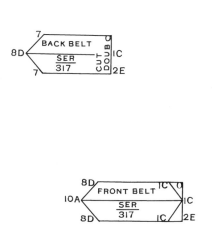

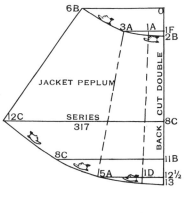

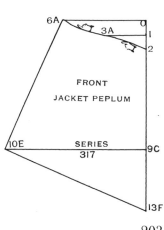

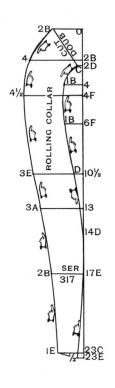
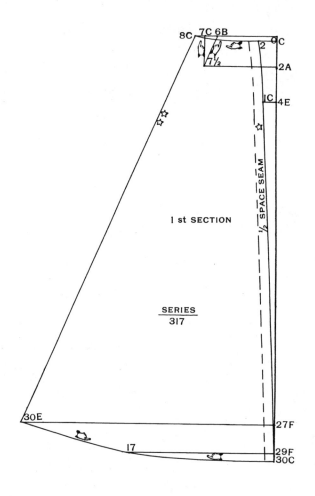
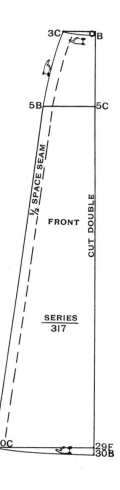

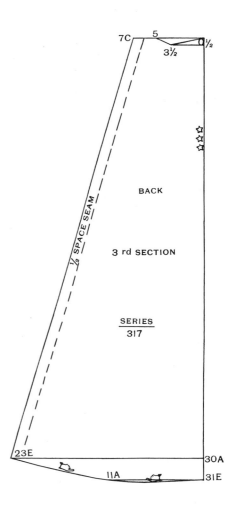

7C 5 ½
3½

BACK

½ SPACE SEAM

3 rd SECTION

SERIES
317

23E   30A
11A   31E

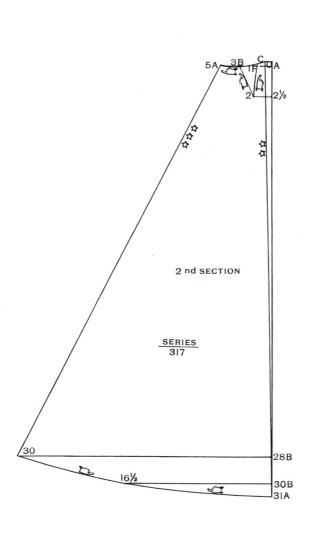

5A 3B C A
1F
2 2½

2 nd SECTION

SERIES
317

30   28B
16½   30B
          31A

Afternoon Toilette

Five measures are taken for this dress: Bust, length of waist, around the waist, length of sleeve, and length of skirt. It is drafted in ten pieces: Back and front of waist, collar, sleeve puff, and a seven-gore tucked skirt with yoke drafted in six pieces.

To Draft. Select bust and length of waist scales for blouse back, front, and collar. For sleeve puff, use bust and length of sleeve scales. For skirt and yoke, use waist and length of skirt scales.

The difference between the waist and hip measure is 18 inches.

To Make. Tuck goods in waist before cutting. Join shoulder and underarm seams. Join seam in sleeve. Gather to fit arm and armhole.

Join skirt with 1/2-space seams. Then fold each dotted line and stitch tuck 1 space deep, making 14 backward-turning tucks on each side of skirt. The last tuck in back of skirt folds to center of back. Join the two yoke sections before cutting material. Then join skirt to yoke. Finish top and bottom of skirt in the usual way.

To trim like illustration, baste insertion on very firm. Cut material away underneath. Turn edges back and stitch.

Figured organdy was the material used for this garment, trimmed with valenciennes insertion.

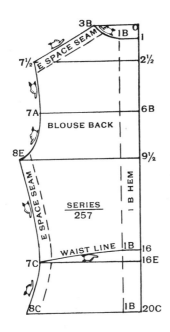

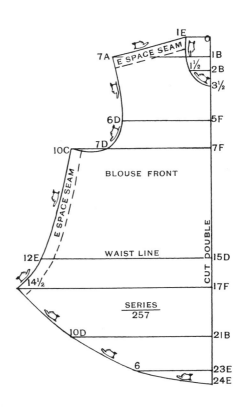

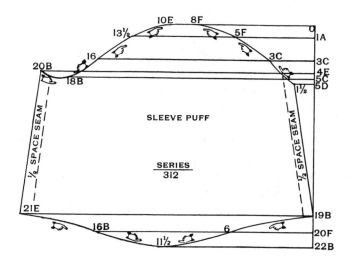

SLEEVE PUFF

SERIES
312

½ SPACE SEAM
½ SPACE SEAM

10E   8F
13½   5F
1A
16   3C
20B   3C
18B   4E
5C
5D   1½
20B
21E
19B
16B   6   20F
11½   22B

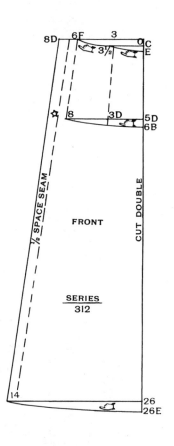

8D   6F   3   C
3½   E
8   3D   5D
6B
½ SPACE SEAM
FRONT
CUT DOUBLE
SERIES
312
14   26
26E

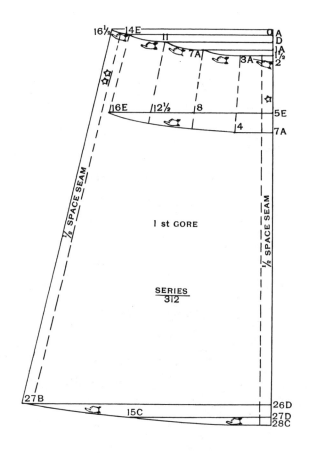

16½   14E
11   A
D
7A   1A
1½
3A   2
16E   12½   8
4   5E
7A
½ SPACE SEAM
½ SPACE SEAM
1 st GORE
SERIES
312
27B   26D
15C   27D
28C

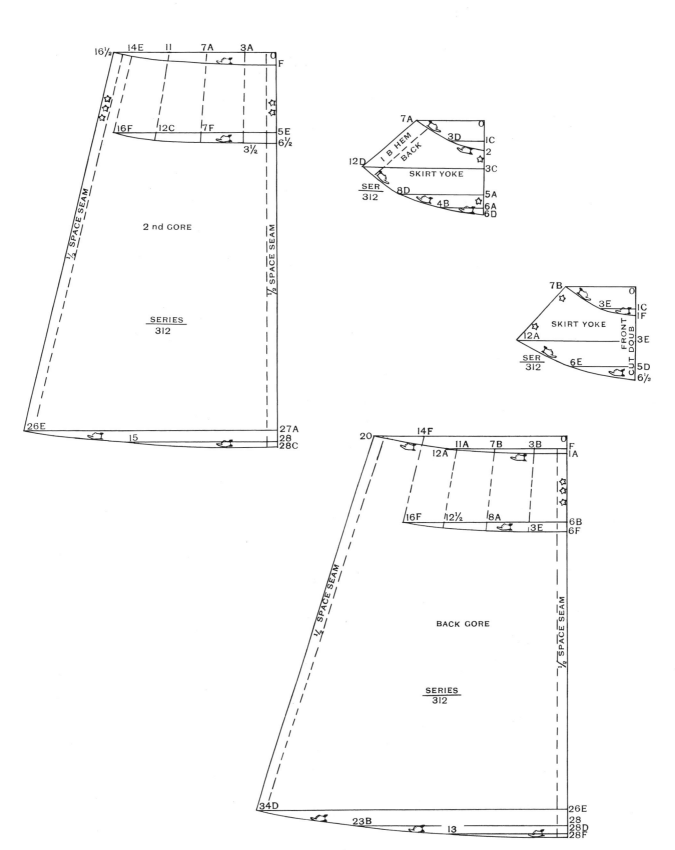

Shirtwaist and Skirt

Shirtwaist and Skirt

Five measures are taken for this dress: Bust, length of waist, around the waist, length of sleeve, and length of skirt. It is drafted in 9 pieces: Back and front of waist, sleeve puff, and an 11-gore ripple skirt drafted in 6 pieces.

To Draft. Select bust and length of waist scales for back and front of waist. For sleeve puff, use bust and length of sleeve scales. For skirt and yoke, use waist and length of skirt scales.

The difference between the waist and hip measure is 18 inches.

Before cutting back and front of waist pattern, fold dotted line to heavy line. Then make curved line for shoulder and cut pattern out on this line.

To Make. Fold dotted lines to heavy lines and stitch tucks in back of waist to waistline. Tucks in front of waist may be stitched to yoke depth or to bottom of waist. The wide space in back and front of diagram is left for lace. Sew lace to material, then cut material away. Join shoulder and underarm seams. Close seam of sleeve puff. Then gather to fit arm and armhole.

Join skirt according to stars. Stitch and press thoroughly. Finish top and bottom in the usual way.

The material used for the waist is cream nun's cloth, trimmed with guipure lace insertion. Material required for medium form, 2 1/2 yards 40 inches wide. Black panama was used for the skirt, trimmed with a 3-inch fold of taffeta and three rows of 1/2-inch taffeta ribbon. Material required for medium form, 5 yards 48 inches wide.

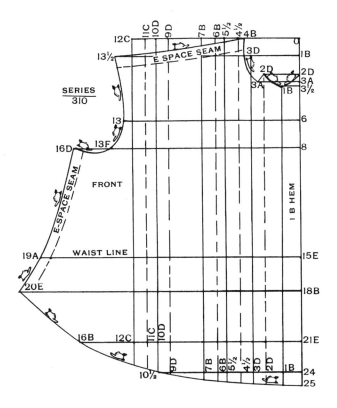

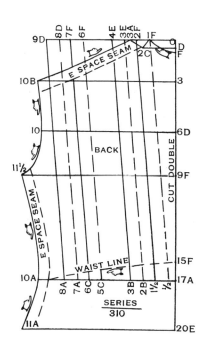

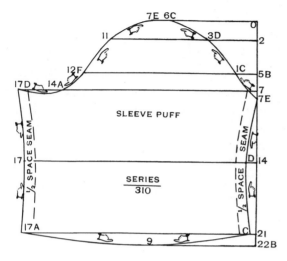

SLEEVE PUFF

SERIES
310

½ SPACE SEAM

½ SPACE SEAM

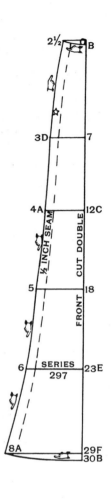

FRONT   CUT DOUBLE

½ INCH SEAM

SERIES
297

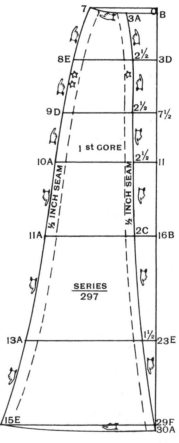

1 st GORE

½ INCH SEAM

½ INCH SEAM

SERIES
297

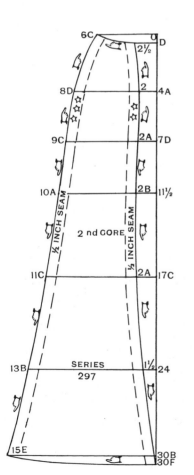

2 nd GORE

½ INCH SEAM

½ INCH SEAM

SERIES
297

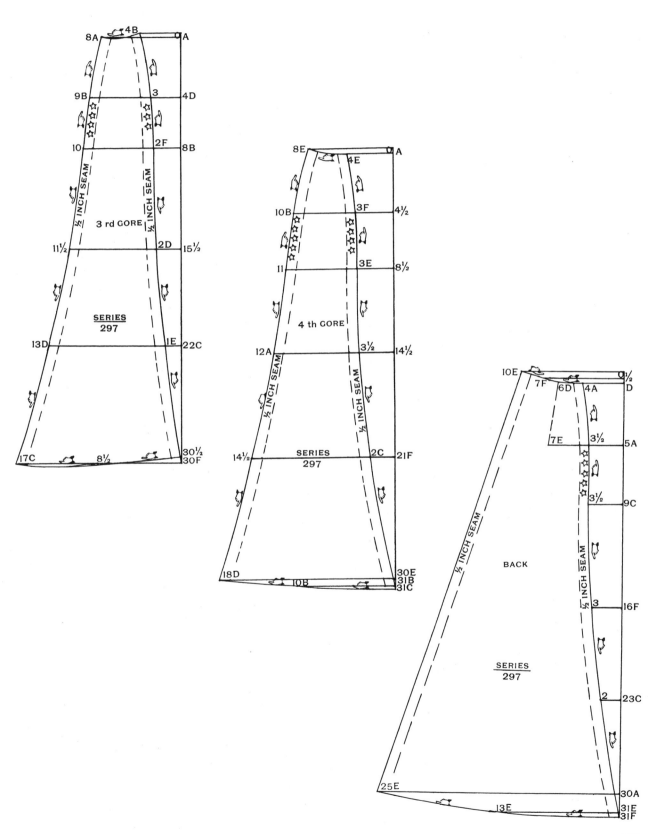

Kimono Wrapper

Four measures are taken for this garment: Bust, length of waist, full length, and sleeve. It is drafted in three pieces: Back and front of kimono and sleeve.

To Draft. Select bust and length of waist scales. Draft to waistline on back and front. Then subtract length of waist measure from full-length measure. This will give desired scale for baseline from waistline to bottom of garment. Use bust scale for all crosslines. For sleeve, use bust and length of sleeve scales.

No diagram is given for sash as it is a long straight piece 4 inches wide.

Before cutting front of pattern out, fold dotted lines to heavy lines, making three backward-turning tucks. Then draw line for shoulder and cut out on that line.

To Make. Stitch three backward-turning tucks. Then join back, shoulder, and underarm seams. Close seam of sleeve. Gather to fit armhole.

One of the many pretty kimono materials was used for this garment. Persian ribbon was used to trim fronts, sleeves, and sash. Material required for medium form, 9 yards 27 inches wide.

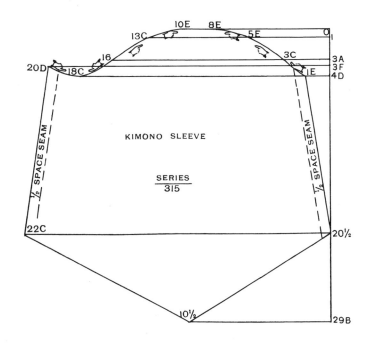

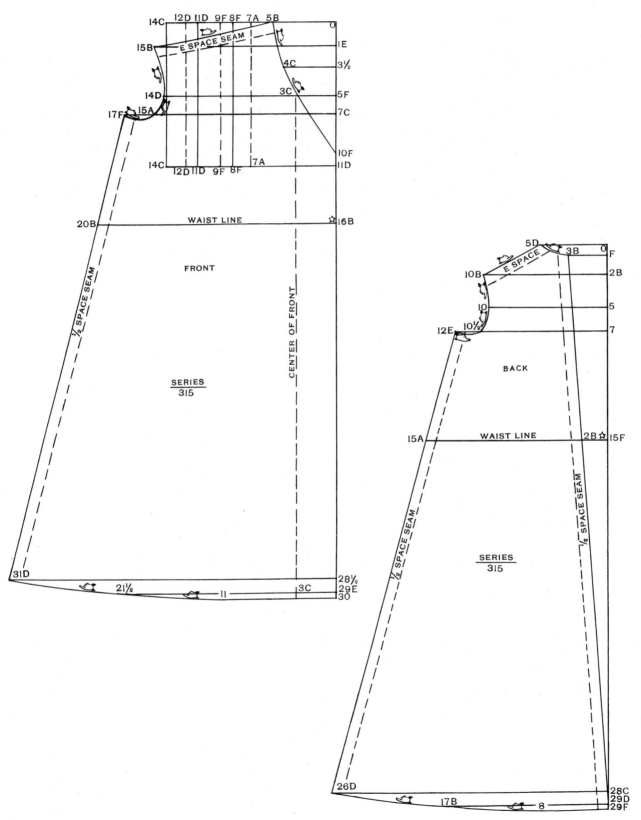

Storm and Motor Coat

Four measures are taken for this coat: Bust, length of waist, full length, and sleeve. It is drafted in seven pieces: Back and front of coat, coat sleeve (two pieces), full sleeve, collar, and cuff.

To Draft. Select bust and length of waist scales. Draft back and front of coat to waistline. Then subtract length of waist from full-length measure. This will give desired scale for baseline from waistline to bottom of coat. Use bust scale for all crosslines. For collar, use bust and length of waist scales. For full sleeve, coat sleeve, and cuff, use bust and length of sleeve scales.

Either sleeve may be used.

To Make. Join seams of coat according to seams given in diagram. To make like illustration, use full sleeve and finish at wrist with a narrow band. Join cuff to band with center even with inseam of sleeve.

The material used for this coat is rubberized satin-striped taffeta. Collar may be made of velvet or same material as coat. Amount required for medium form, 9 yards 27 inches wide.

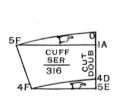

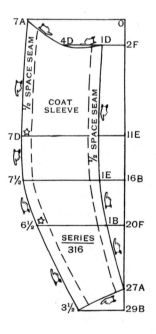

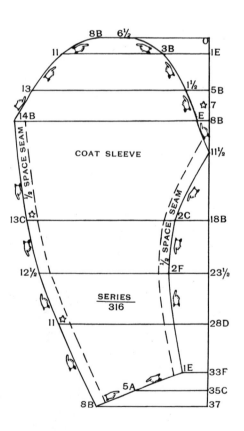

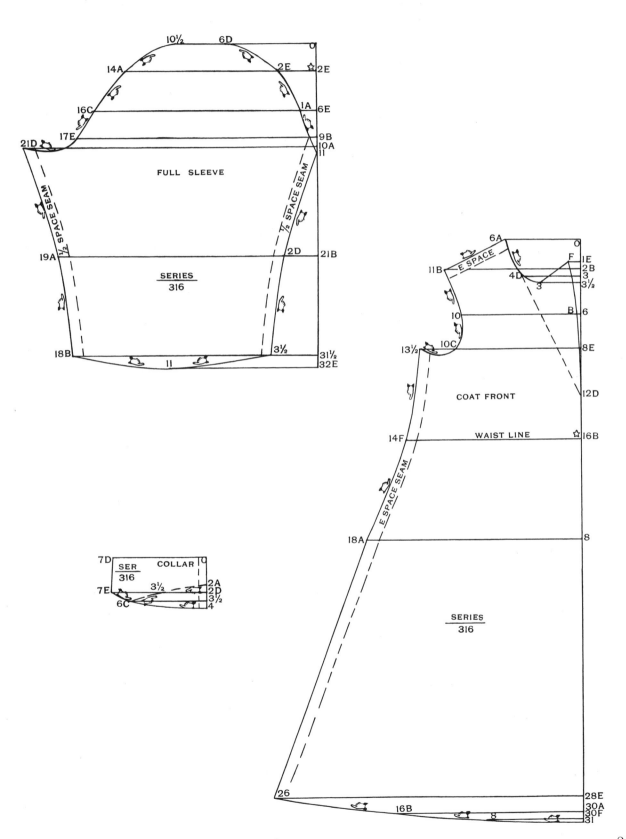

FULL SLEEVE

SERIES
316

COLLAR

SER
316

COAT FRONT

WAIST LINE

SERIES
316

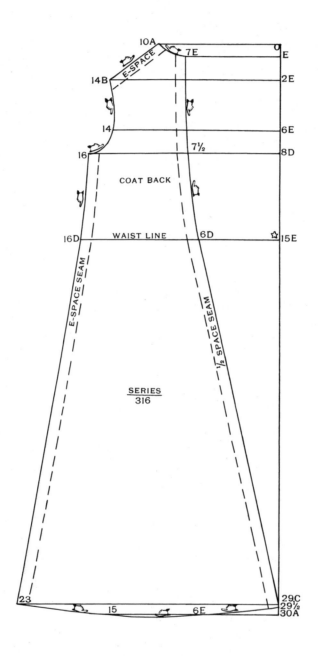

July 1908 American Modiste

Nowhere is the classic influence more apparent than in the cloaks and wraps for carriage and evening wear. They are made of soft chiffon cloths, of the beautiful heavy silks and satins, of rough pongee, and of almost every material that can be trusted to fall in ideal lines and folds.

Black taffeta coats have returned to popularity. They are trimmed in many elaborate ways with bands of colored satin, while they are decorated around the neck with a lace collar. These coats are useful, for they are not too warm, yet they provide that finish to the costume which is necessary when driving or automobiling is in order. Sometimes, too, they are made of satin and lined with a soft pongee, which makes them serviceable and dressy at the same time. The three-piece combination suits are wonderfully convenient, for if the gown is too cool for the late afternoon, one can always slip on the accompanying little coat. It is not necessary to have these coats match the gown in color, although they are usually made of the material or the trimmings of the gown.

Silks and linens show the gown of striped material, with the coat of plain color matching the stripe, or vice versa. The gowns are usually built along jumper lines and the coats are long or short, as preferred. A novelty is the short coat of lace, trimmed and strapped with material.

The vogue for lace, which is one of the leading characteristics of the fashions of today, naturally finds expression in the wearing of dainty blouses, made either entirely in lace or in lace mounted on esprit net or chiffon, and trimmed with touches of velvet. Embroidered waists are very fashionable indeed this season. The embroidery appears on the collar, cuffs, and front. Others are made of allover embroideries, some of the patterns being rings of eyelet or tiny leaf designs in the eyelet. Others show equally simple designs in blind embroidery.

A good many of the newest neckbands have quite wide frills standing out around the face, sometimes of starchy lace and sometimes of crimped puffed chiffon. Some are quite Elizabethan in their stiff preciseness, while others again incline more toward the toby frill variety. They are carried out in lawn and muslin frilled with lace, so that they fall quite softly around the throat over bands of gold or silver galloon, fastened in front with tasseled ends.

Ladies' Visiting Gown

Five measures are taken for this garment: Bust, length of waist, around the waist, length of sleeve, and length of skirt. It is drafted in 11 pieces: Back and front of waist, back and front yoke, tucked portion for waist, sleeve puff, and a 9-gore tucked skirt drafted in 5 pieces.

To Draft. Select bust and length of waist scales for back and front of waist, two yoke portions, and tucked overblouse. For sleeve puff, use bust and length of sleeve scales. For skirt, use waist and length of skirt scales.

The difference between the waist and hip measure is 18 inches.

To Make. Gather back and front of waist and sew to yoke on dotted lines. Close shoulder and underarm seams. Gather to fit waist measure.

To make tucked overblouse, fold dotted line to heavy line and stitch four wide backward-turning tucks. Join to waist with star at shoulder seam. Fold tucks over at waistline like illustration. Back of waist is the same as front, only the tucked portion is a little nearer center of back at waistline.

Join skirt according to stars by folding last dotted line on front over to first gore. Make the seam on first gore the same width as seam on front. Stitch tucks 1/4 space or B space. Fold on all dotted lines making 20 backward-turning B-space tucks. Fold last tuck to center of back. Join skirt below tucks in 1/2-space seam.

White dotted silk voile was used for this dress. Tucked portion of waist is taffeta silk, with trimmings of lace. Material required for medium form, 11 yards 27 inches wide.

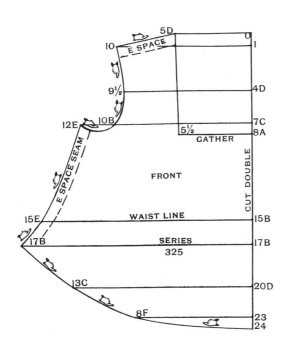

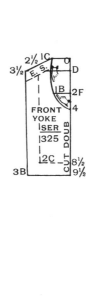

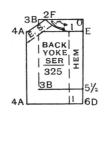

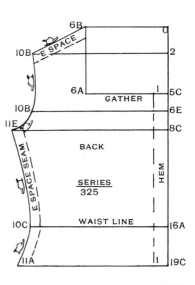

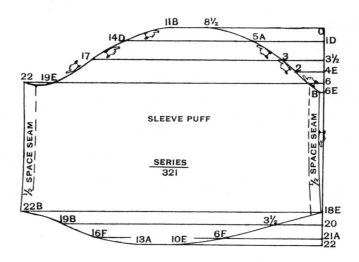

SLEEVE PUFF

SERIES
321

11B   8½
14D   5A   1D
17   3   3½
               2   4E
                        6
                        B   6E
22 19E

½ SPACE SEAM   ½ SPACE SEAM

22B   18E
  19B   3½   20
16F   13A   10E   6F   21A
                        22

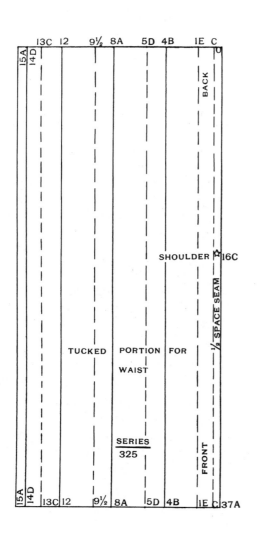

15A
14D
13C 12 9½ 8A 5D 4B 1E C 0

BACK

SHOULDER 16C

½ SPACE SEAM

TUCKED   PORTION   FOR

WAIST

SERIES   FRONT
325

15A
14D
13C 12   9½   8A   5D   4B   1E C 37A

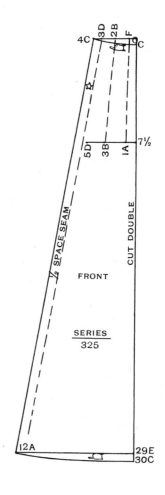

4C 3D 2B F
            C
5D 3B 1A 7½

½ SPACE SEAM

CUT DOUBLE

FRONT

SERIES
325

12A   29E
               30C

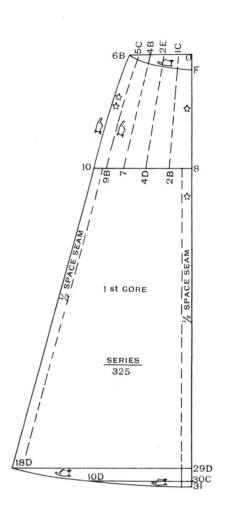

1 st GORE

SERIES
325

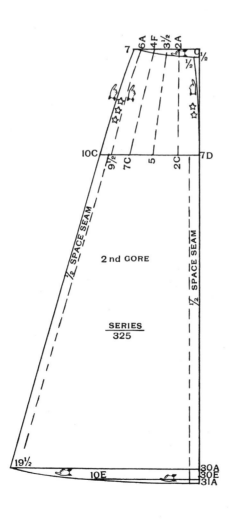

2 nd GORE

SERIES
325

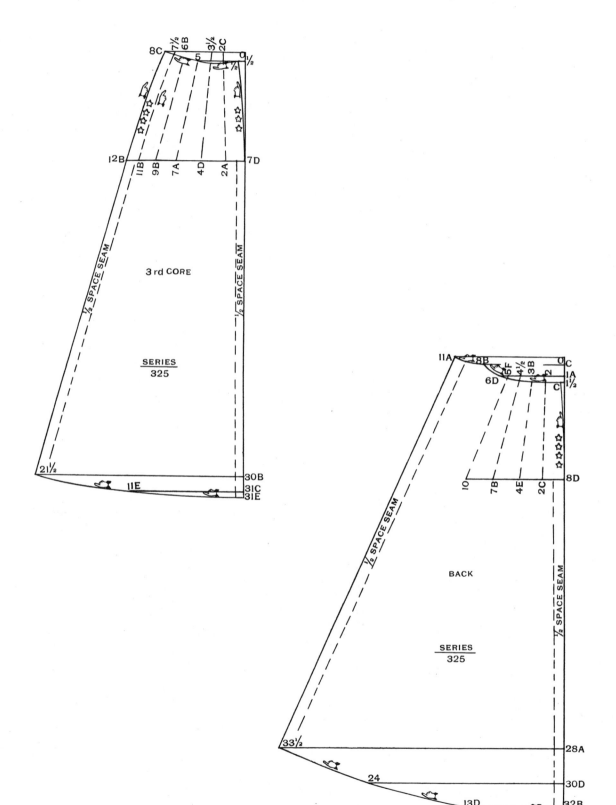

Attractive Model for Summer

Five measures are taken for this costume: Bust, length of waist, around the waist, length of sleeve, and length of skirt. It is drafted in 15 pieces: Blouse back and front, overblouse, ruffle for overblouse, collar, sleeve cap, sleeve puff, tight sleeve, and a 13-gore tucked skirt drafted in 7 pieces.

To Draft. Select bust and length of waist scales for blouse back and front, overblouse, ruffle for overblouse, collar, and sleeve cap. For tight sleeve and sleeve puff, use bust and length of sleeve scales. For skirt, use waist and length of skirt scales.

The difference between the waist and hip measure is 18 inches.

To make like illustration, use sleeve puff.

To Make. Join shoulder and underarm seams of blouse. Sew sleeve cap to blouse with star at shoulder seam. Join ruffle to overblouse (notice stars) and arrange like illustration.

Join skirt according to numbers. Fold first dotted line on first gore to dotted line on front, and second dotted line on first gore to heavy line on second gore, making a box pleat each of front gore. Stitch to any desired depth. Join all other gores with 1/2-space seam. Finish in the usual way.

The material used for this suit is white and one of the new checked taffeta silks. Panel effect and overblouse are embroidered in white silk, also the folds on skirt and sleeve. Silk required for medium form, 15 yards 21 inches wide.

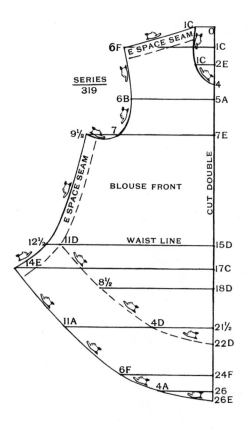

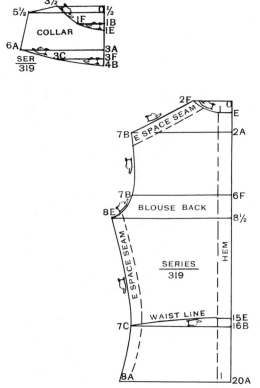

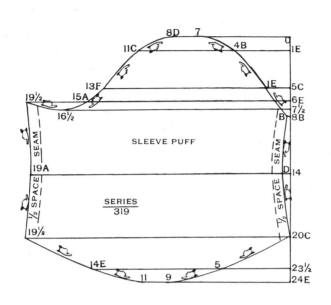

SLEEVE PUFF

SERIES
319

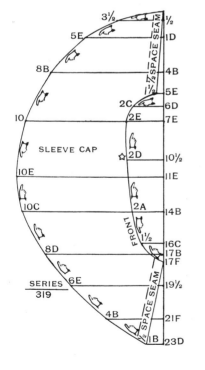

SLEEVE CAP

SERIES
319

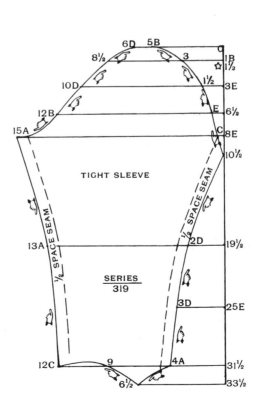

TIGHT SLEEVE

SERIES
319

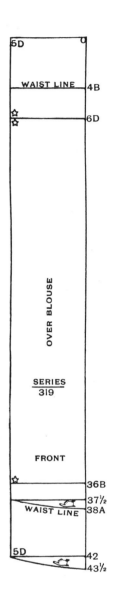

OVER BLOUSE

SERIES
319

FRONT

WAIST LINE

229

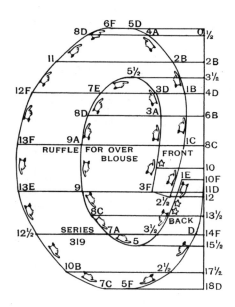

RUFFLE FOR OVER BLOUSE FRONT

SERIES 319

BACK

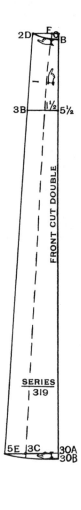

FRONT CUT DOUBLE

SERIES 319

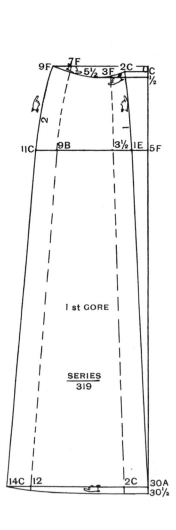

1 st GORE

SERIES 319

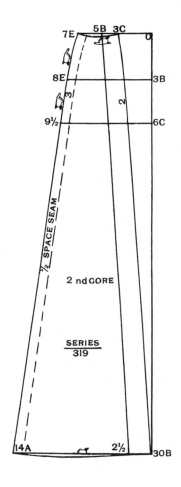

½ SPACE SEAM

2 nd GORE

SERIES 319

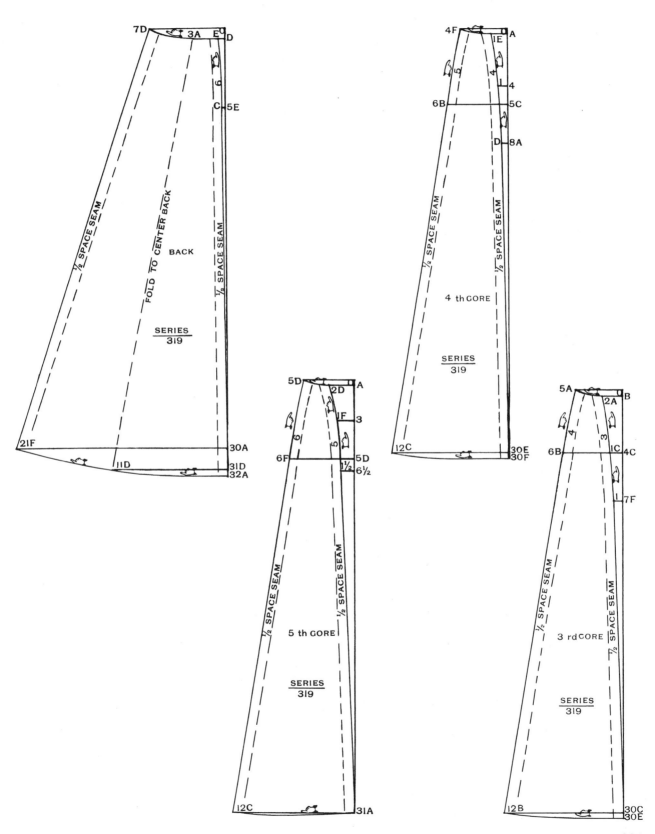

A Chic Toilette

Five measures are taken for this suit: Bust, length of waist, around the waist, length of sleeve, and length of skirt. It is drafted in ten pieces: Back and front of jacket, side front and sleeve, side back and sleeve, cuff, collar, and a seven-gore side-pleated skirt drafted in four pieces.

To Draft. Select bust and length of waist scales for jacket back, front, side front, side back, and collar. For cuff, use bust and length of sleeve scales. For skirt, use waist and length of skirt scales.

To Make. Join the different parts of jacket according to seams. Finish sleeve with cuff; place star on cuff even with underarm seam of sleeve.

Finish neck with collar. To make like illustration, slash through center of side front and bind around with braid.

Join skirt according to stars by folding dotted lines to heavy lines, making eight backward-turning pleats on each side of skirt. Stitch to any desired depth. Finish bottom in the usual way.

Golden brown mirage silk was used for this attractive suit, with trimming of silk braid 5/8 inch wide and silk soutache braid. Material required for medium form, 16 yards of silk.

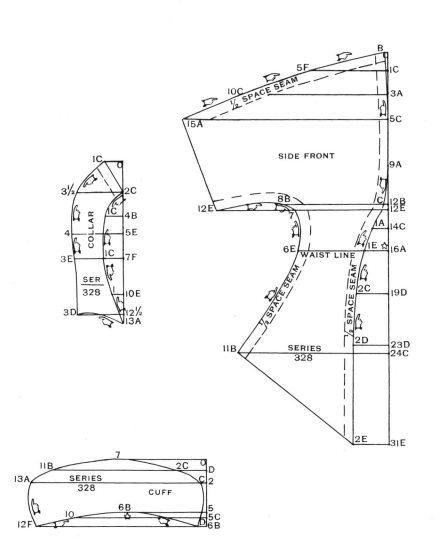

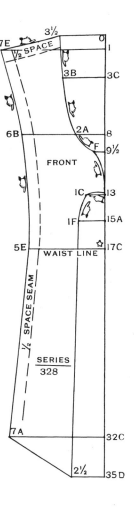

233

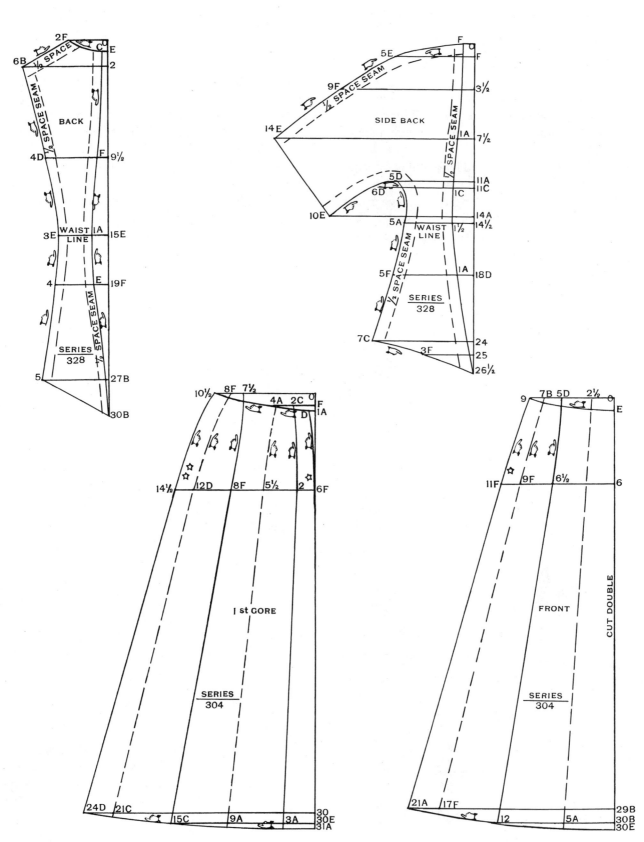

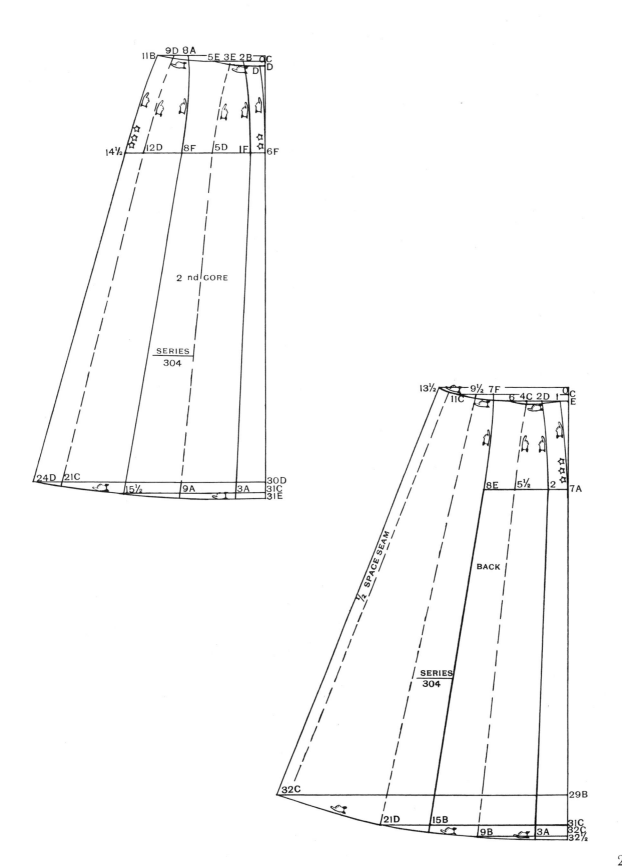

235

A Pretty Creation for Summer

Five measures are taken for this suit: Bust, length of waist, around the waist, length of sleeve, and length of skirt. It is drafted in 12 pieces: Blouse back and front, jumper back and front, sleeve puff, girdle, belt, and double skirt drafted in 5 pieces.

To Draft. Select bust and length of waist scales for blouse back and front and jumper back and front. For sleeve puff, use bust and length of sleeve scales. For belt and girdle, use waist and length of waist scales. For upper and lower flounce of skirt, use waist and length of skirt scales.

To Make. Join back and front of blouse. Gather at waistline between stars and sew to belt. Place star in belt even with underarm seam of waist.

Join shoulder and underarm seams of jumper. Gather at waistline and 1 1/2 inches above waistline. Then sew to girdle. Place bottom of jumper even with star at 8F on lower edge of girdle. Sew sleeve to blouse waist.

Join first and second sections of upper flounce before cutting goods. Then fold dotted lines to heavy lines and stitch 1/4 inch from fold, making 17 small tucks on each side of skirt. Join the three sections of lower flounce before cutting goods. Join to upper flounce with dotted lines even.

Materials required for medium form, 2 yards of plain goods for blouse waist and sleeve, and 10 yards of embroidered flouncing for skirt and jumper.

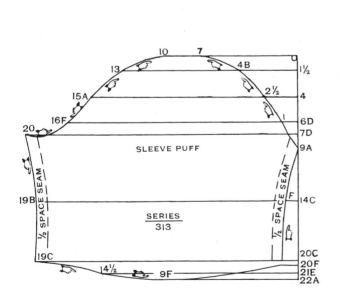

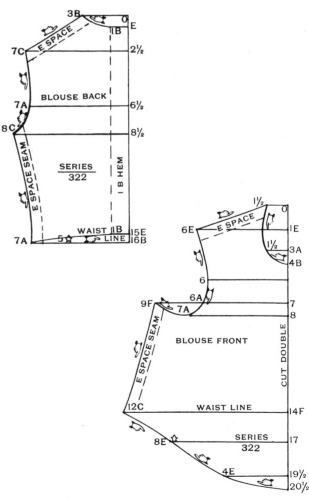

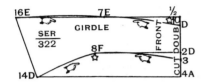

GIRDLE

SER
322

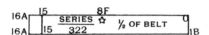

16A 15 SERIES 8F ½ OF BELT
16A 15 322

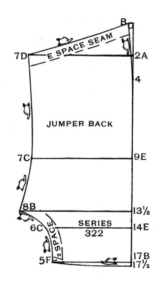

JUMPER BACK

E SPACE SEAM

SERIES
322

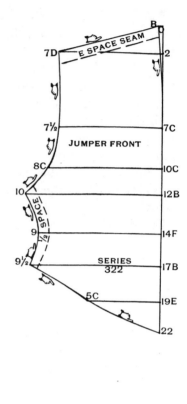

JUMPER FRONT

E SPACE SEAM

SERIES
322

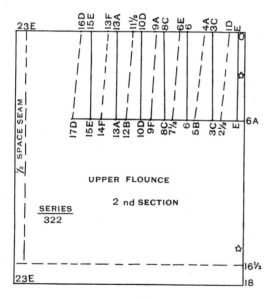

UPPER FLOUNCE

2 nd SECTION

SERIES
322

½ SPACE SEAM

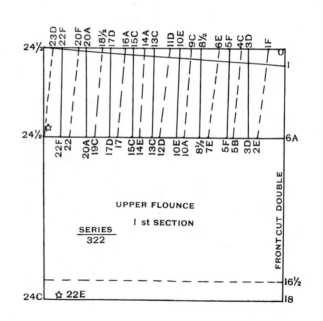

UPPER FLOUNCE

1 st SECTION

SERIES
322

FRONT CUT DOUBLE

238

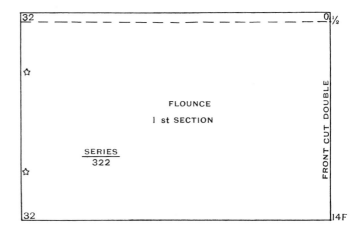

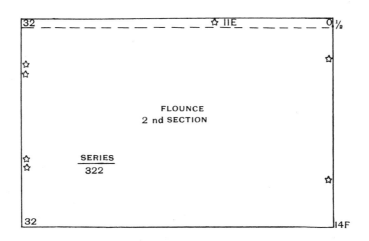

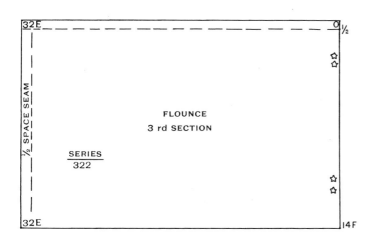

Golf and Outing Suit

Five measures are taken for this suit: Bust, length of waist, around the waist, length of sleeve, and length of skirt. It is drafted in 14 pieces: Back and front of waist, neckband, sleeve, sleeve facing, cuff, and a 15-gore ripple skirt drafted in 8 pieces.

To Draft. Select bust and length of waist scales for back and front of waist and neckband. For sleeve, sleeve facing, and cuff, use bust and length of sleeve scales. For skirt, use waist and length of skirt scales.

The difference between the waist and hip measure is 19 inches.

To Make. On waist, fold dotted lines together and stitch two backward-turning tucks. Fold pleat for right front of waist on dotted lines and stitch on heavy lines. For left front, cut on second heavy line for hem. Join shoulder and underarm seams. Cut back of sleeve open at point 8C and join sleeve facing. Finish underlap with straight piece 1/2 inch wide when finished. Close seam and join cuff.

Close seams of skirt according to numbers, with 1/2-space seams. Stitch and press.

White and colored linen was the material used for this suit. Skirt is trimmed with three folds of white linen the same as the waist. Material required for medium form, 9 yards 27 inches wide without folds.

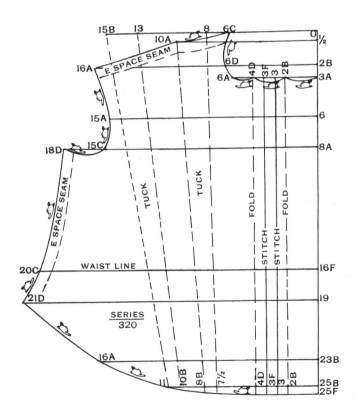

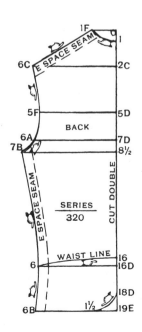

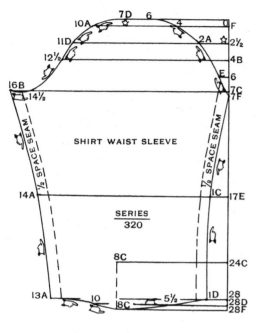

SHIRT WAIST SLEEVE

SERIES
320

SLEEVE FACING

SER 320

CUFF

SER 320 CUT DOUB

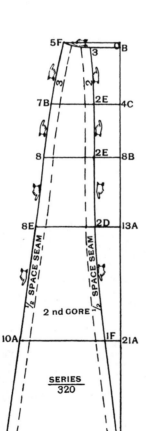

2 nd GORE

SERIES
320

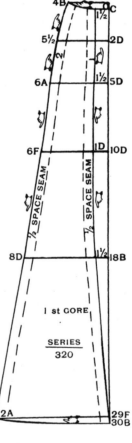

1 st GORE

SERIES
320

FRONT CUT DOUBLE

SERIES
320

Golf and Outing Suit

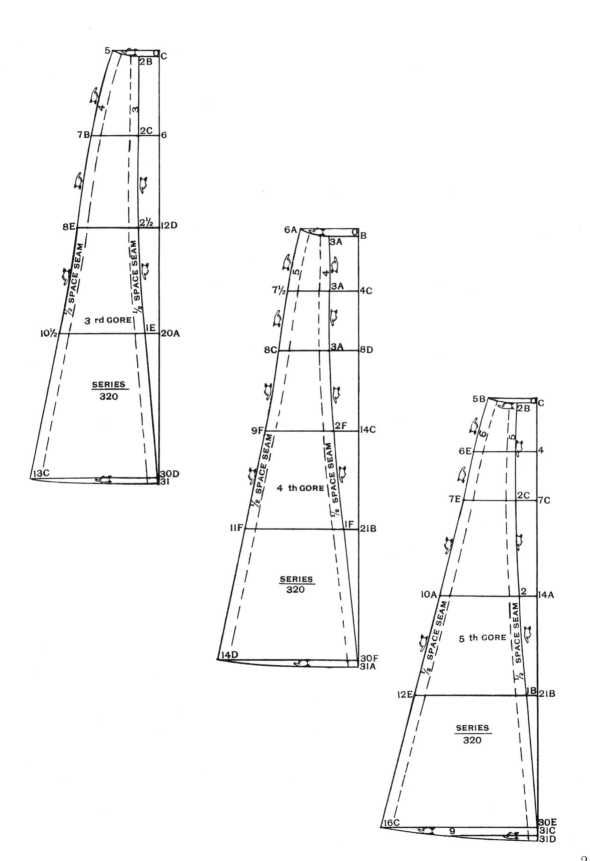

3 rd GORE

½ SPACE SEAM ½ SPACE SEAM

SERIES 320

5 · 2B · C · 7B · 2C · 6 · 8E · 2½ · 12D · 10½ · 1E · 20A · 13C · 30D · 31

4 th GORE

½ SPACE SEAM ½ SPACE SEAM

SERIES 320

6A · 0 · B · 3A · 7½ · 3A · 4C · 8C · 3A · 8D · 9F · 2F · 14C · 11F · 1F · 21B · 14D · 30F · 31A

5 th GORE

½ SPACE SEAM ½ SPACE SEAM

SERIES 320

5B · 2B · C · 6E · 4 · 7E · 2C · 7C · 10A · 2 · 14A · 12E · 1B · 21B · 16C · 30E · 31C · 31D

243

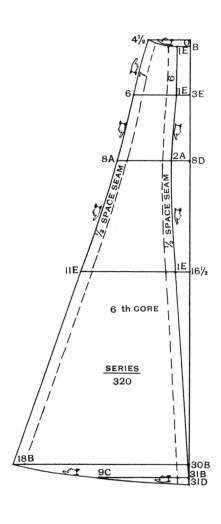
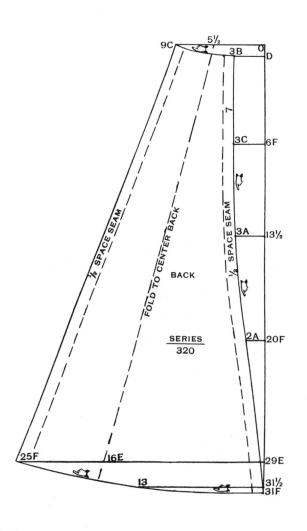

Ladies' Combination Suit

Four measures are taken for this suit: Bust, length of waist, around the waist, and length of drawers. It is drafted in five pieces: Corset cover back and front, sleeve, ruffle, and drawers.

To Draft and Make. Select bust and length of waist scales for corset cover back, front, and sleeve. For drawers and ruffle, use waist and length of drawers. Length of drawers is taken from waist-line over hip to desired length.

Join shoulder and underarm seams of corset cover. Gather to fit waist measure. Join seam of sleeve. Sew to armhole with seam in sleeve even with star on front of waist.

If straight ruffle is desired, cut off lower part of drawers on dotted line and join ruffle to same. Gather at waist or fit with four darts. Lap the backs 1 inch and join to corset cover. Finish with narrow belt and beading.

Material required for medium form, 3 1/2 yards 36 inches wide.

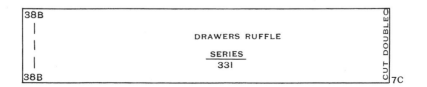

38B

DRAWERS RUFFLE

SERIES
331

CUT DOUBLE

38B   7C

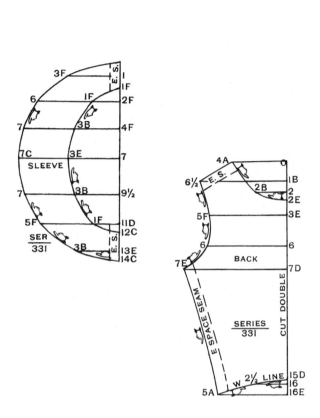

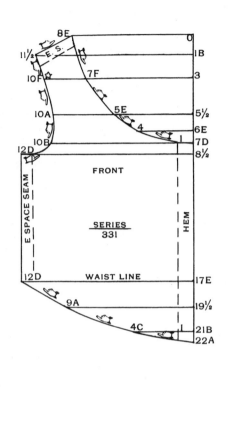

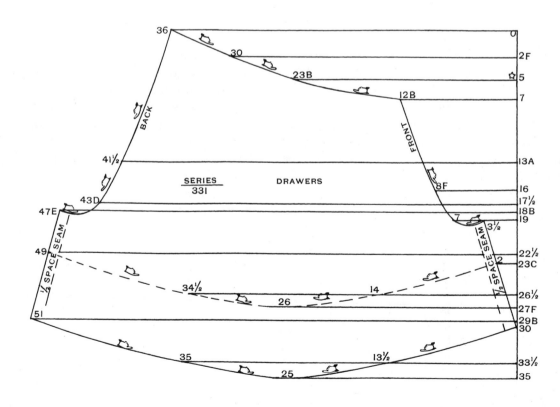

October 1908 American Modiste

The ruffled and starched white petticoats will be things of the past. The underwear must be close fitting, to accord with the skirt.

The smartest walking costumes are made with short skirts which for the most part reach 1 inch below the top of the boots. Where the skirt is designed for afternoon wear, it is made a trifle longer. The carriage and reception gowns call for a length that barely escapes the ground.

Some of the many gored and gored circular skirts have the habit back, which, however, have the flare beginning where the pleat would. This is especially noticeable with the skirts that close at the center or side front, buttoning to the lower edge. For wash skirts the large pearl buttons are removable like those of a man's waistcoat.

The skirts buttoned down the front, side, or back have been well liked in washing fabrics, and promise to be very smart in cloths for general autumn and winter wear. The buttons are not ornamental alone; they are used to close the skirt either its entire length or for a convenient distance on the hip. Not only skirts, but waists are buttoned all the way down the front or back, and sometimes both.

Then there is the tunic skirt, which style is seen in many of the smartest new gowns. The underskirt often shows much width at the edge, being pressed in fine pleats or gathered full or cut circular so as to flare prettily, while the tunic or overskirt is close and narrow. Many bands are used to suggest the tunic, the arrangement being so cleverly done as to defy anything but careful scrutiny.

The coats follow the Directoire lines in length, usually extending 3 or 4 inches below the hips and sometimes nearly reaching the bottom of the skirt. Some of the coat sleeves are so snug that the coat is put on and more especially taken off with difficulty.

The sleeves of the lingerie blouses and shirtwaists for next winter will be long, with few exceptions, and these will be for the elaborate lace blouses to be worn with afternoon costumes. One frequently sees the extremes, the long close-fitting sleeves coming over the hand. Or such short, small ones that they scarcely deserve the name of sleeves–and buttons really or apparently button them the entire length of the outside seam, or in some diagonal line from the elbow to wrist on the top, where they hold in place some fancy inset of lace, tucks, or embroidery. A note not to be overlooked is that of trimming the sleeves of garments on the outer seam with small buttons, straps, passementerie, silk braids, or bands of ribbon velvet crossing over and apparently serving as fastenings.

The newest sleeve is skintight. Plain long lace sleeves are seen in dinner and theater gowns–not any perceptible fullness even at the shoulder.

Net gowns are now a feature in the way of dressy wear for evenings and afternoons. The nets used are of many varieties, plain, dotted, large mesh, small mesh, white, cream, solid color or cream striped or figured with cashmere colors, gold, black, or combinations.

Effective Street Design

Six measures are taken for this suit: Bust, length of waist, full length, length of sleeve, around the waist, and length of skirt. It is drafted in 15 pieces: Coat back, side back, front, side front, coat collar, shawl collar, sleeve (2 pieces), cuff, and an 11-gore ripple skirt drafted in 6 pieces.

To Draft. Select bust and length of waist scales for coat and shawl collar. Draft coat back, front, side back, and side front to waistline. Then subtract length of waist from full-length measure. This will give desired scale for baseline from waistline down. Use bust scale for all crosslines. For sleeve and cuff, use bust and length of sleeve scales. For skirt, use waist and length of skirt scales.

The difference between the waist and hip measure is 18 inches.

If cutaway style of coat is desired, draw a straight line from point B to point 1A. If shawl collar is desired, cut revere off on dotted line.

To Make. Join the coat according to directions. Finish back and side back with lap or close in seam to bottom of coat. Join seam of sleeve and ease in extra fullness at the elbow. Join skirt according to stars. Finish top and bottom in the usual way.

Material required for medium form, 7 yards 50 inches wide.

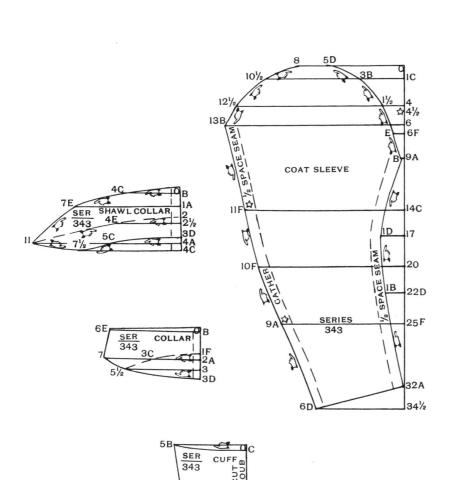

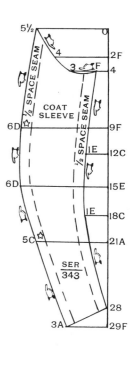

249

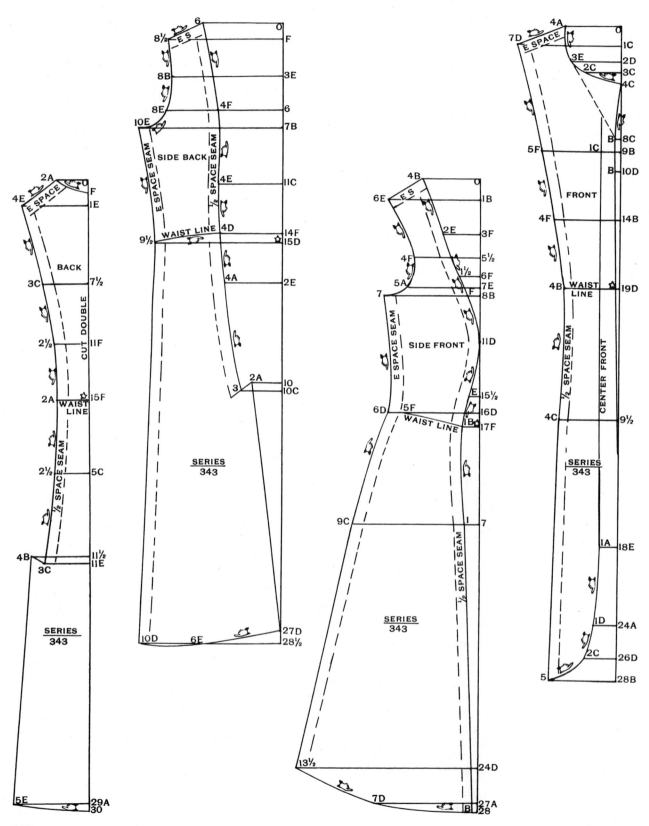

SERIES 343

250

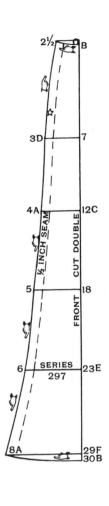

Right pattern piece (CUT DOUBLE / FRONT, SERIES 297):

2½ — B
3D — 7
4A — 12C
5 — 18 (½ INCH SEAM, CUT DOUBLE, FRONT)
6 — 23E (SERIES 297)
8A — 29F / 30B

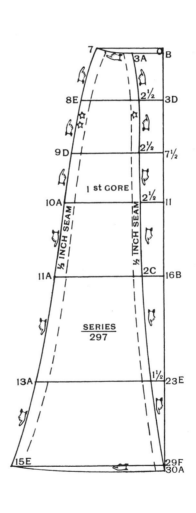

Center pattern piece (1st GORE, SERIES 297):

7 — 3A — B
8E — 2½ — 3D
9D — 2½ — 7½
10A — 2½ — 11 (1 st GORE)
11A — 2C — 16B
½ INCH SEAM   ½ INCH SEAM
13A — 1½ — 23E (SERIES 297)
15E — 29F / 30A

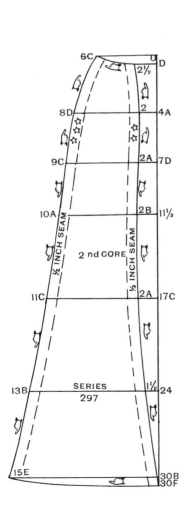

Left pattern piece (2nd GORE, SERIES 297):

6C — O — D
8D — 2 — 4A
9C — 2A — 7D
10A — 2B — 11½
11C — 2A — 17C
½ INCH SEAM   ½ INCH SEAM   2 nd GORE
13B — 1½ — 24 (SERIES 297)
15E — 30B / 30F

251

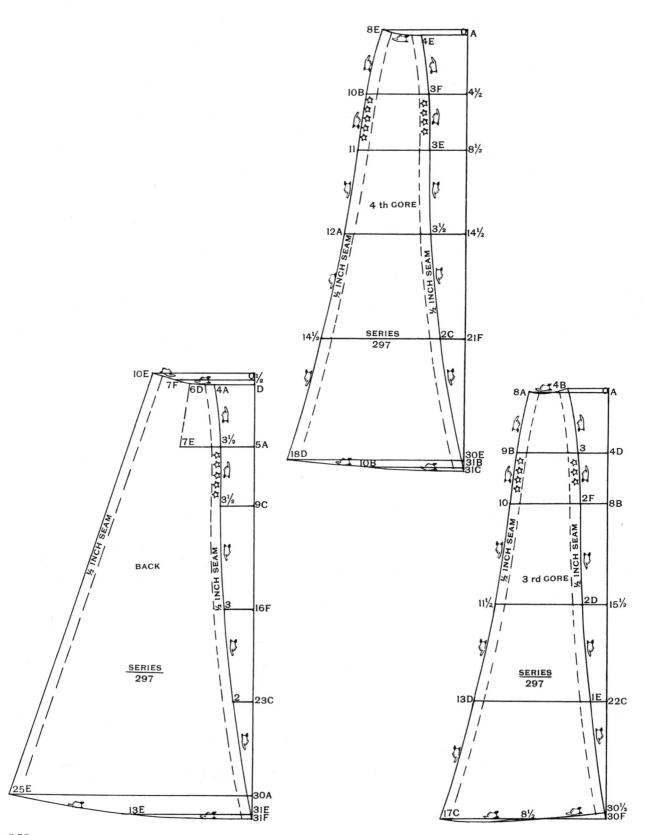

Ladies' Reception Gown

Five measures are taken for this costume: Bust, length of waist, around the waist, length of sleeve, and length of skirt. It is drafted in 15 pieces: Back and front lining, upper back and front, vest back and front, bretelle, overskirt drafted in 3 pieces, and a 9-gore flared skirt drafted in 5 pieces.

To Draft. Select bust and length of waist scales for back and front lining, upper back and front, vest back and front, and bretelle. For skirt and overskirt, use waist and length of skirt scales.

The difference between the waist and hip measure is 18 inches.

To Make. Make lining and outside separate if so desired. Face back and front to yoke depth. Join shoulder and underarm seams. Take up darts. Join upper back and front crossing and front. The

backs meet at waistline, the right front crossing slightly over to the left side. Fold dotted lines to heavy lines on bretelle and stitch three backward-turning tucks. Then join to back and front of waist. Gather to fit waist measure.

Join foundation skirt according to stars. Stitch and press. Join side gore and back of overskirt pattern before cutting goods and cut in one piece. Join front to side gore and finish back with inverted pleat. Join skirt and overskirt in one belt.

Flowered silk was the material used for this toilette, with yokes of white tucked silk and vest and sleeve of filet lace, all prettily trimmed with velvet ribbon. 17 yards of silk 22 inches wide will be required for medium form.

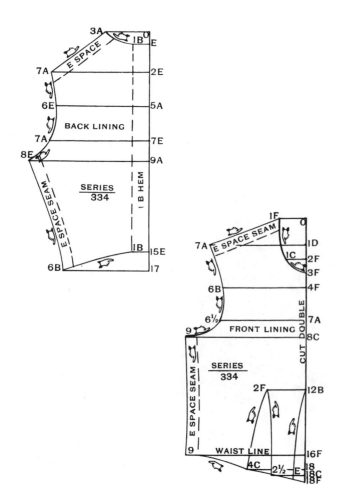

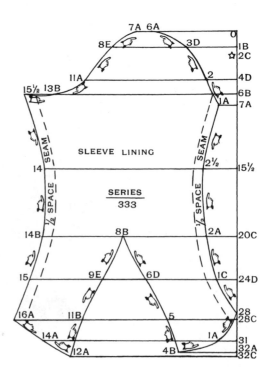

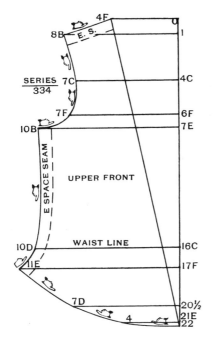

UPPER FRONT

WAIST LINE

E SPACE SEAM

SERIES 334

4F
8B E. S.
1
4C
6F
7E
SERIES 334   7C
7F
10B
10D
11E
16C
17F
7D
20½
4
21E
22

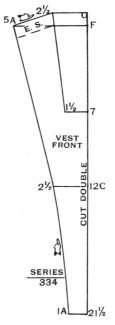

VEST FRONT

CUT DOUBLE

SERIES 334

5A   2½
E. S.
F
1½   7
2½   12C
1A   21½

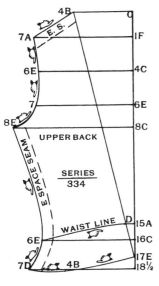

UPPER BACK

SERIES 334

E SPACE SEAM

WAIST LINE

4B
E. S.
O
7A
1F
6E
4C
7
6E
8E
8C
6E
7D   4B
D 15A
16C
17E
18½

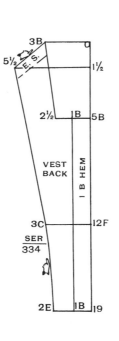

VEST BACK

1 B HEM

SER 334

3B
E. S.
O
5½
1½
2½   1B   5B
3C   12F
2E   1B   19

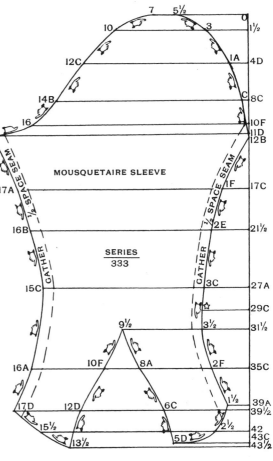

MOUSQUETAIRE SLEEVE

½ SPACE SEAM

½ SPACE SEAM

GATHER

GATHER

SERIES 333

7   5½
10   3   1½
12C   1A   4D
14B   C 8C
19   16   10F
11D
12B
17A   1F 17C
16B   2E 21½
15C   3C 27A
29C
9½   3½ 31½
16A   10F   8A   2F 35C
1½ 39A
17D   12D   6C 39½
15½   2½ 42
13½   5D 43C
43½

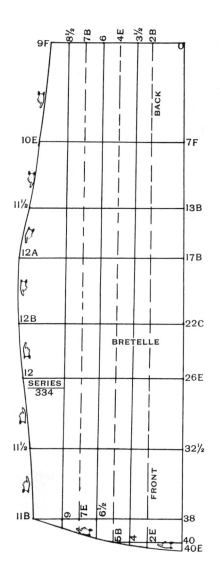

9F 8½ 7B 6 4E 3½ 2B O

BACK

10E — 7F

11½ — 13B

12A — 17B

12B — 22C

BRETELLE

12
SERIES
334 — 26E

11½ — 32½

FRONT

11B — 38
9 7E 6½ 40
5B 4 2E 40E

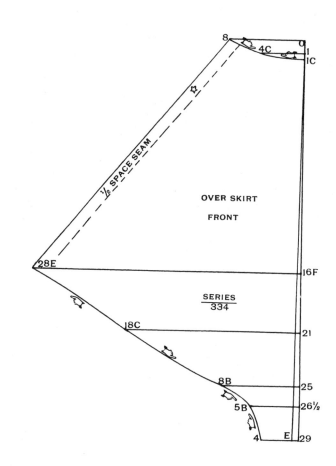

8   4C   O
IC

½ SPACE SEAM

OVER SKIRT
FRONT

28E — 16F

SERIES
334

18C — 21

8B — 25
5B — 26½
4   E   29

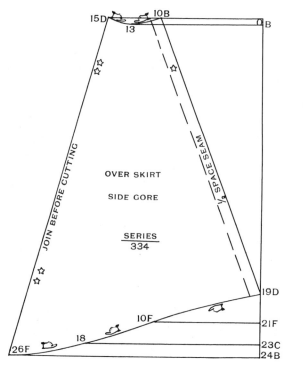

15D 10B O B
13

JOIN BEFORE CUTTING

½ SPACE SEAM

OVER SKIRT
SIDE GORE

SERIES
334

19D

10F — 21F
18 — 23C
26F — 24B

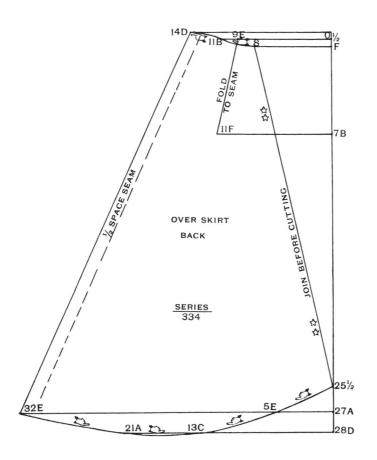

OVER SKIRT
BACK

SERIES
334

½ SPACE SEAM

FOLD TO SEAM

JOIN BEFORE CUTTING

14D 11B 9E 8 0½
F
11F 7B
32E 5E 25½
27A
21A 13C 28D

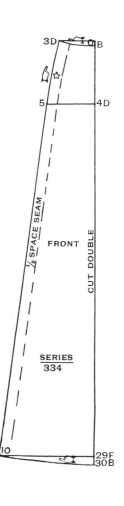

FRONT

CUT DOUBLE

½ SPACE SEAM

SERIES
334

3D B
5 4D
10 29F
30B

October 1908

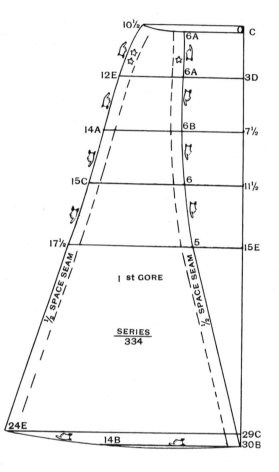

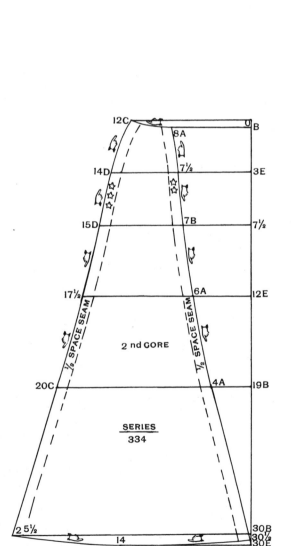

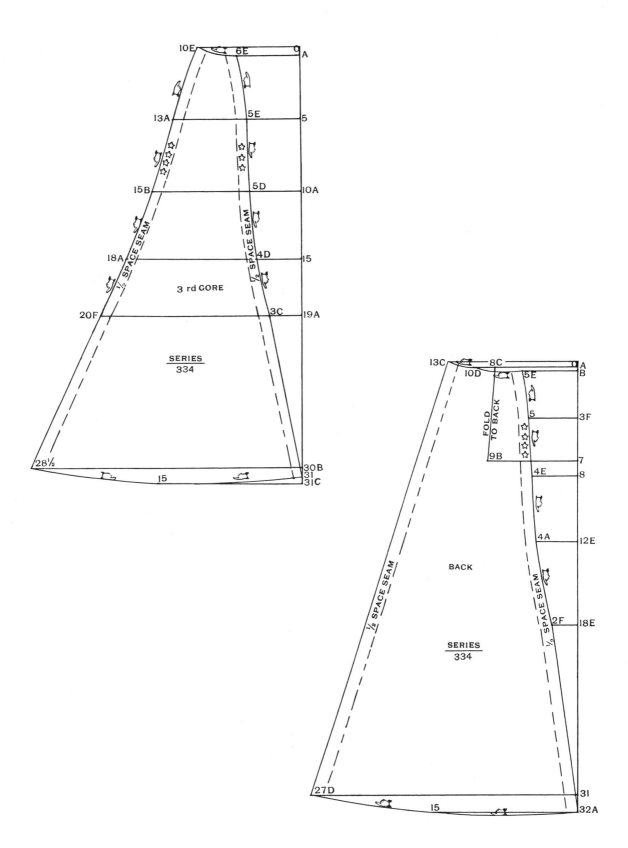

Artistic Directoire Coat

Four measures are taken for this coat: Bust, length of waist, full length, and length of sleeve. It is drafted in nine pieces: Coat back, front, side back, and side front; stock; rolling collar; new sleeve drafted in two pieces; and cuff.

To Draft. Select bust and length of waist scales for coat back, front, side back, and side front; stock; and rolling collar. Draft back, front, side back, and side front to waistline. Then subtract length of waist from full-length measure. This will give desired scale for baseline. Use bust scale for all crosslines. For sleeve and cuff, use bust and length of sleeve scales.

To Make. Join the different parts of coat. Make waistlines meet. Stitch and press thoroughly. To make skirt part like illustration, cut open on dotted line on side front. To make sleeve, either join in seam or fold upper part over to under and stitch a flat seam. Join rolling collar to stock. Then sew to coat.

Navy blue broadcloth was used to develop this coat, with trimming of velvet, satin, silk cable cord, and satin buttons. Material required for medium form, 2 1/2 yards 54 inches wide.

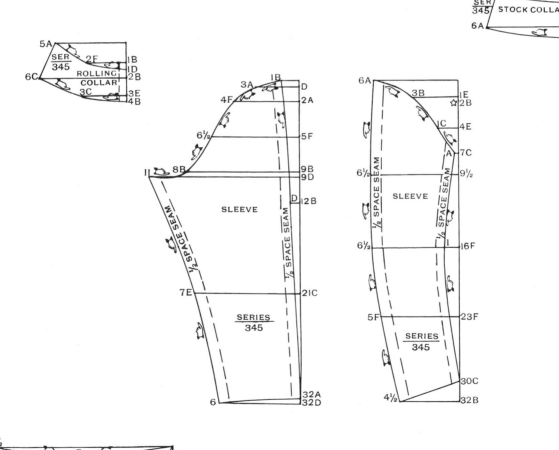

261

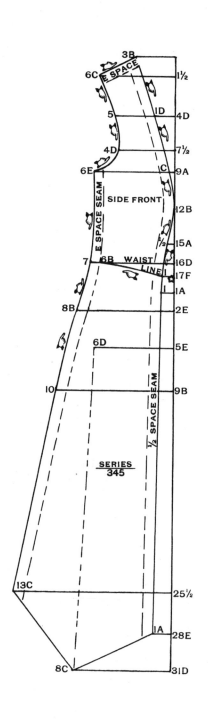

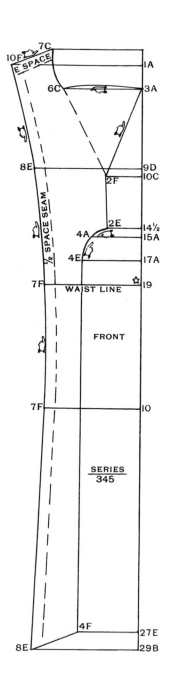

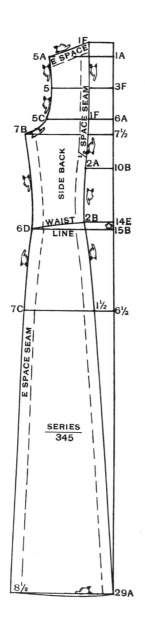

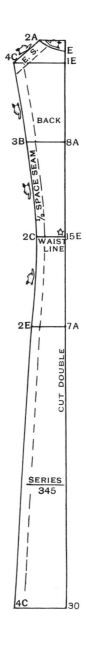

For Autumn and Winter

Five measures are taken for this costume: Bust, length of waist, around the waist, length of sleeve, and length of skirt. It is drafted in 15 pieces: Blouse back and front, jumper back and front, collar, sleeve lining, mousquetaire sleeve, and a 16-gore skirt drafted in 8 pieces.

To Draft. Select bust and length of waist scales for blouse back and front, jumper back and front, and collar. For sleeves, use bust and length of sleeve scales. For skirt, use waist and length of skirt scales.

The difference between the waist and hip measure is 19 inches.

When making pattern for jumper back and front, fold dotted lines to heavy lines, making two backward-turning tucks. Then draw curved line for shoulder and cut out on that line.

To Make. Each half of skirt and blouse is made separately. Join shoulder and underarm seams of blouse. Gather to fit waist measure. Join collar to neck. Baste mousquetaire sleeve to lining as far as elbow. Then gather inseam of sleeve from star to fit inseam of lining. Close both in one seam. Close back of sleeve to elbow with 1/2-space seams.

Join skirt according to numbers. To make like illustration, cut on line for habit back. Stitch seams and press well. Make belt 1 1/2 inches wide. Join skirt and jumper in same belt. Button skirt, back and front.

Chiffon broadcloth was used for this gown; 7 yards will be required for medium form. Waist and sleeve are of dark ecru allover embroidery; 4 yards required.

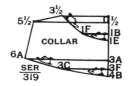

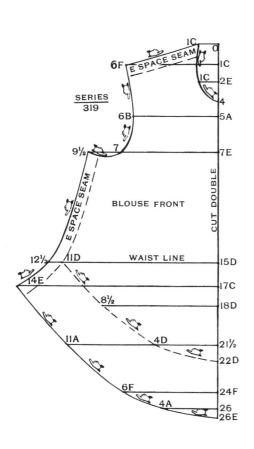

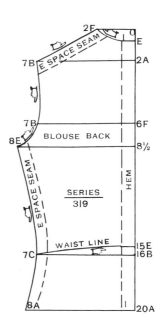

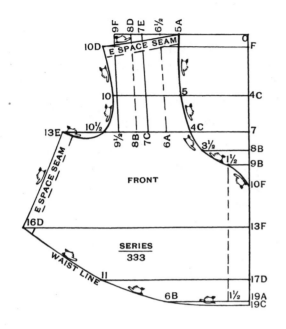

FRONT

SERIES
333

WAIST LINE

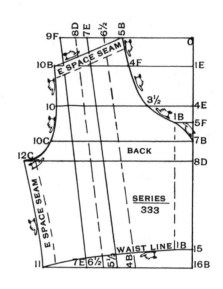

BACK

SERIES
333

WAIST LINE

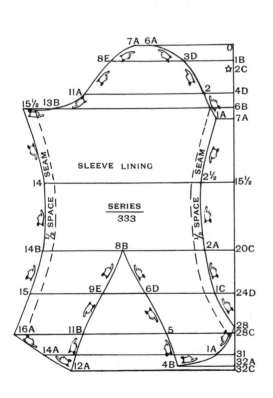

SLEEVE LINING

SERIES
333

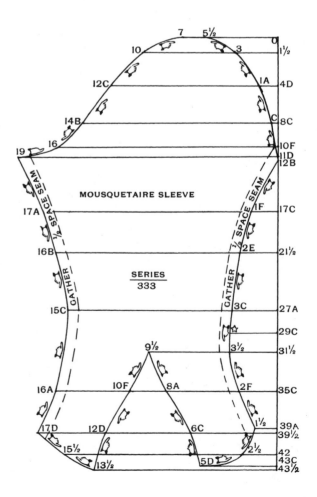

MOUSQUETAIRE SLEEVE

SERIES
333

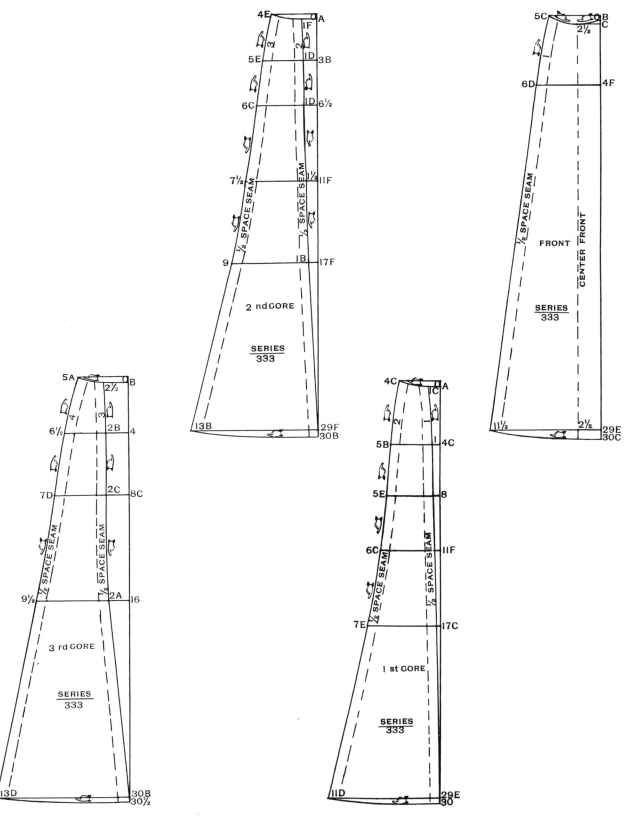

267

October 1908

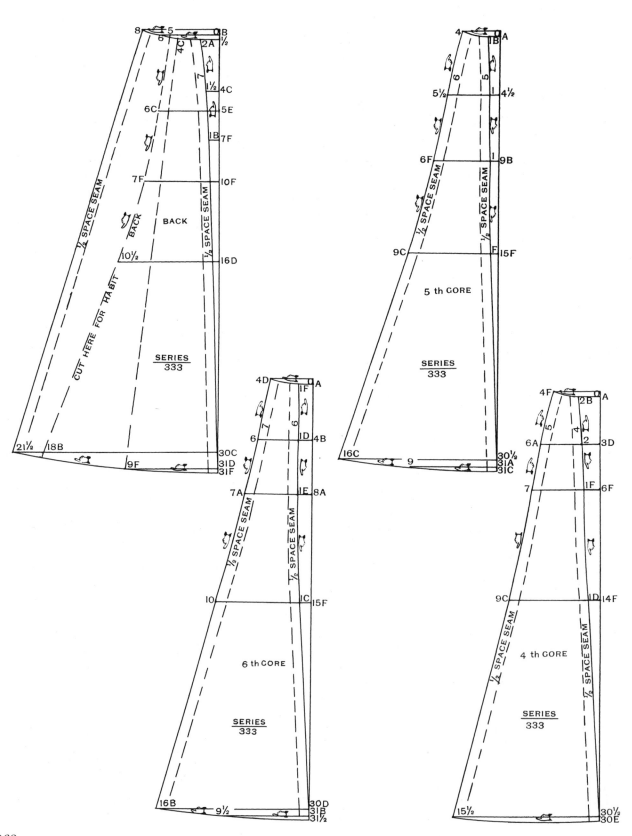

268

January 1909 American Modiste

The true Directoire styles are most becoming to young women, but in their modified form they are wearable by the majority—for "at home" gowns. The tight, clinging skirts make it almost impossible to adopt them for the street, since they cannot well be held up, and really look best when allowed to trail the floor.

Generally speaking, skirts must be sheath fitting over the hips. A noticeable feature of the very long skirts is the finishing of the lower edge. In most cases the hem or facing is about 3 inches wide at the front and deepens gradually to a depth of 8 inches or more at the back of the gown. This of course tends to make the back of the gown heavier, drawing any fullness from the front. Very little trimming appears on skirts, especially long ones. Some are absolutely plain, but perfect in cut; others show tiny frills, braiding, stitched bands, etc.

Net is perhaps the favorite material for blouses. There are many kinds—big mesh, little and medium, fish filch, octagon, silk, cotton, dotted, plain, figured, striped, and barred.

The oversleeve must not interfere with the desired effect of length and slenderness in the arm. It is almost as close fitting as the long tight undersleeve, and if draped at all the folds are of the closest and most clinging sort.

All of the new satins and silks are very soft and flexible, even the taffetas having lost their stiffness. The favored goods are very soft satin-finished cloths, voile grenadines with floral designs, cream panne, soft corded silk, both plain and striped moiré, and oriental satin.

Braidings, passementeries, laces, and appliqués are used in profusion. Galloon of many colors is employed on plain color grounds, while silks, laces, and nets are made more elaborate by appliquéing the most luxurious flowers and other motifs of chenille, silk braid, and needlework.

No costume is complete nowadays without a touch of black. In most instances it takes the form of pipings, bindings, or folds of black satin, large buttons covered with the same rich material being added wherever at all possible—for ornament, if not for use. Then, too, the wide Directoire sash of black satin plays an important part.

The spring wearings in woolens show broad diagonal, fancy coatings, ribbed cloth, also checks and stripes. In cotton goods, ring and spot designs will be worn, also pompadour and dresden patterns. Shadow-striped voiles are in preparation.

A Practical Street Suit

A Practical Street Suit

Six measures are taken for this suit: Bust, length of waist, full length, length of sleeve, around the waist, and length of skirt. It is drafted in 14 pieces: Coat back, front, side front, side back, 2 sleeve portions, 2 collar portions, cuff, and 10-gore skirt drafted in 5 pieces.

To Draft. Select bust and length of waist scales for collars, coat back, front, side back, and side front to waistline. Then subtract length of waist from full-length measure. This will give desired scale for baseline from waistline to bottom of coat. Use bust scale for all crosslines. For sleeve and cuff, use bust and length of sleeve scales. For skirt, use waist and length of skirt scales.

The difference between the waist and hip measure is 17 inches.

To Make. Join the different parts according to seams given. Close seams of sleeve. Join cuff with star point, 6F, even with inseam of sleeve. Cut collar and collar band double. Join collar to band with stars even and sew to neck of coat.

To make skirt like illustration, allow a seam out from center of front. Skirt may instead be made with lapped seam at center front and finished with buttons. Join skirt according to stars. Stitch, press, and finish top and bottom in the usual way.

Striped material was used for this suit; material required for medium form, 7 1/2 yards 44 inches wide. A fashionable striped silk was used to face revers, cuffs, and Napoleon collar; for medium form, 1 yard 22 inches wide.

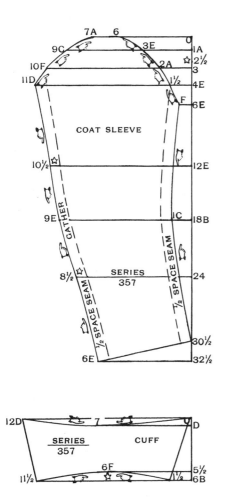

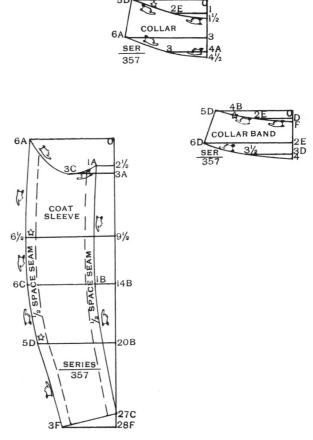

271

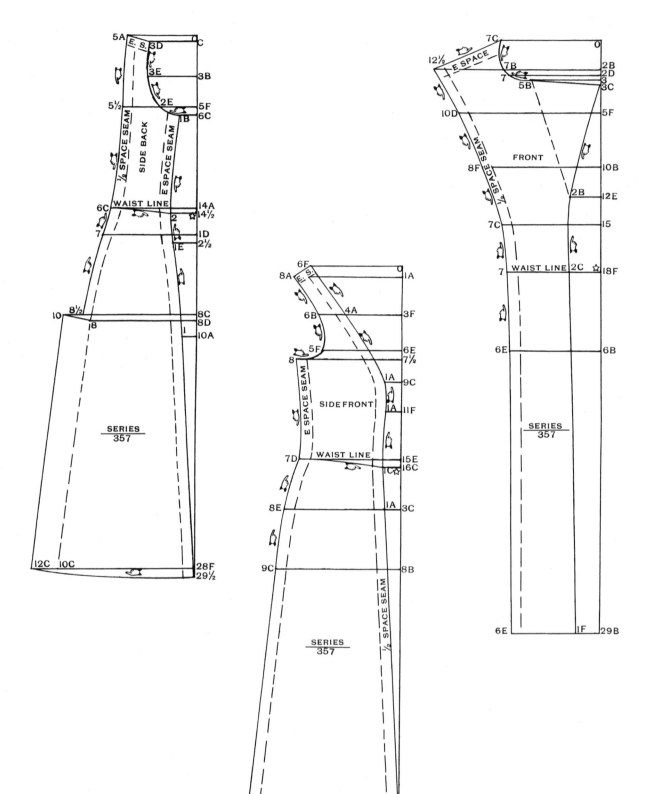

A Practical Street Suit

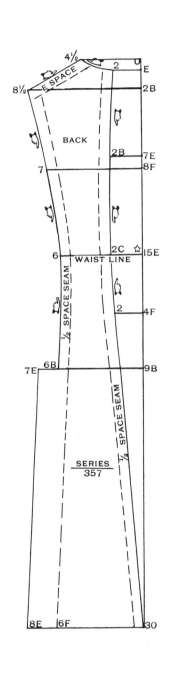

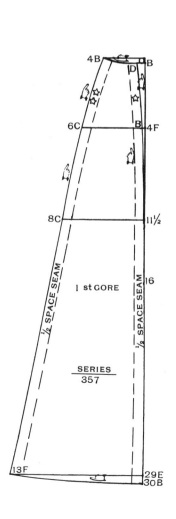

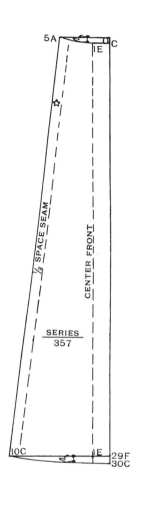

273

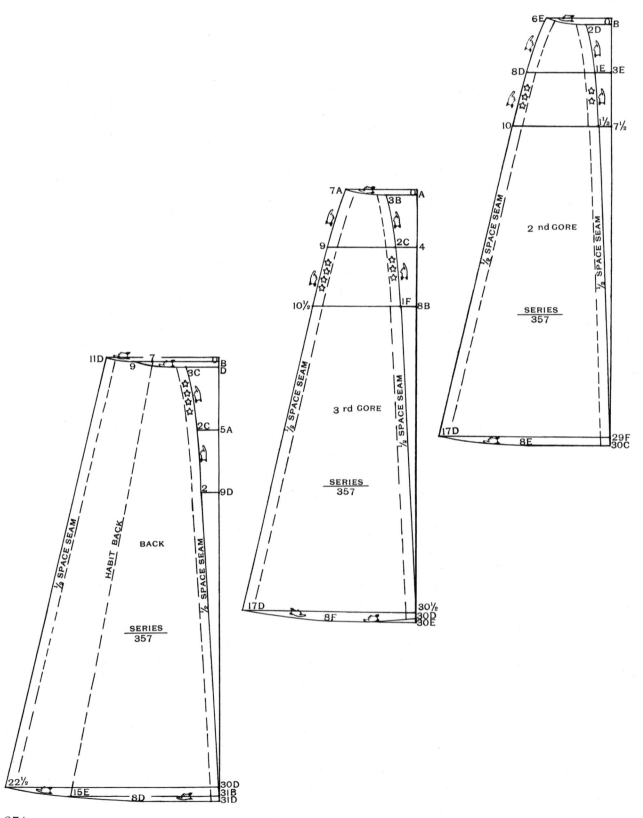

A Gown for Dressy Occasions

Five measures are taken for this dress: Bust, length of waist, around the waist, length of sleeve, and length of skirt. It is drafted in 13 pieces: Back and front lining, upper back and front, tight sleeve (2 pieces), oversleeve, belt, and a 7-gore skirt with overskirt front drafted in 5 pieces.

To Draft. Select bust and length of waist scales for back and front lining and upper back and front. For sleeve and oversleeve, use bust and length of sleeve scales. For belt, use waist and length of waist scales. For skirt and overskirt front, use waist and length of skirt scales.

To Make. Make lining and outside separate. Close lining darts, shoulder, and underarm seams. Also close seams of plain sleeve. Join to armhole of lining.

To make upper waist, join shoulder seams. Then make two backward-turning tucks by folding dotted lines to heavy lines. Stitch. Finish bottom of waist with narrow band. Close seam of oversleeve and join to upper waist.

The skirt is slightly gathered in all gores but front and overskirt section. Join the different parts of skirt according to stars. Also join seam of overskirt to right side, where front and first gore join, and allow free edge of overskirt to drape over left front and first gore seam. Gather the remaining gores and sew to belt.

Liberty satin was used for this gown, with lace bodice and sleeves. Buttons and silk soutache braid for trimmings. Material required for medium form, 12 yards 27 inches wide.

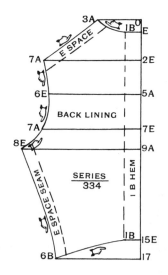

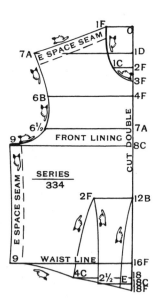

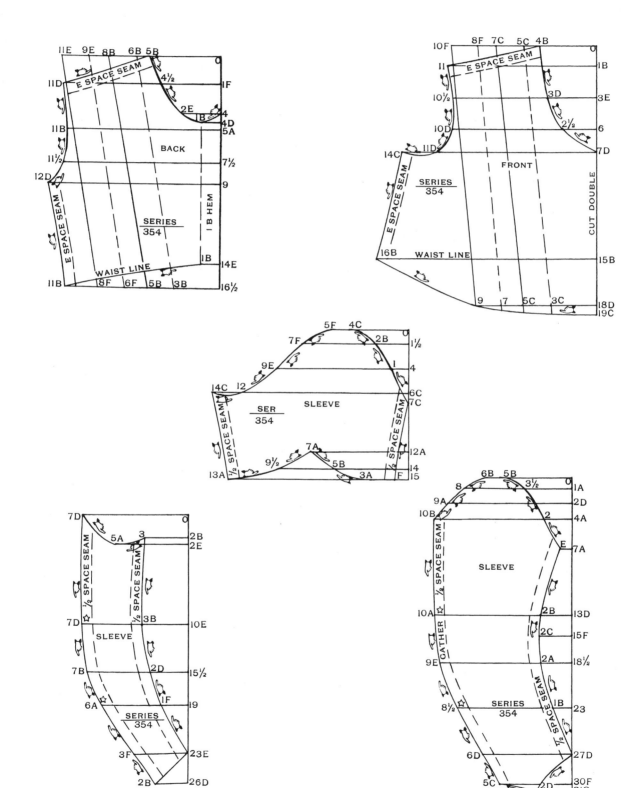

277

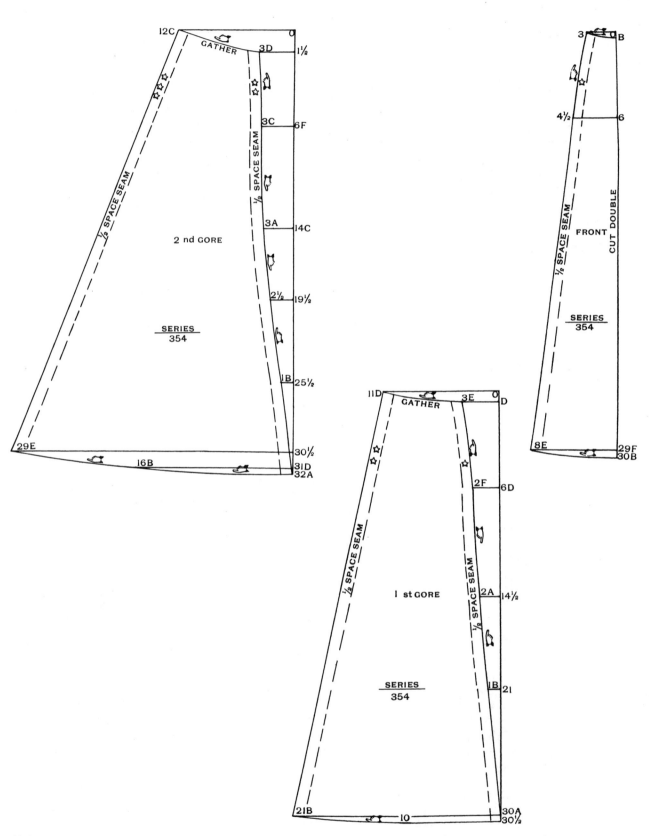

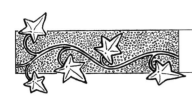 

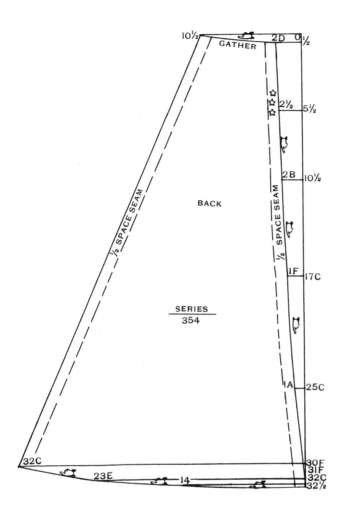

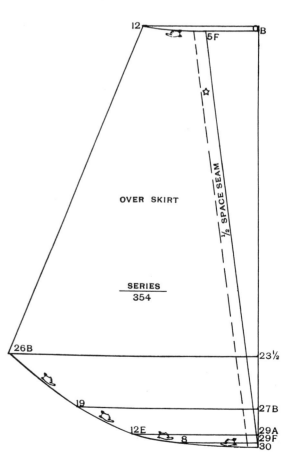

For Day or Evening Wear

Five measures are taken for this empire dress: Bust, length of waist, around the waist, length of sleeve, and length of skirt. It is drafted in 18 pieces: Lining back, front, and side back; upper back and front; back and front yoke; back and front yoke strap; belt; sleeve (2 pieces); sleeve puff; collar; and a 7-gore gathered skirt drafted in 4 pieces with natural and empire waistline.

To Draft. Select bust and length of waist scales for lining back, front, and side back; upper back and front; two yoke portions; back and front yoke strap; collar; and belt. For sleeve and sleeve puff, use bust and length of sleeve scales. For skirt, select length of waist scale. Copy points on baseline as far as star with that scale. Then select length of skirt scale and copy points on baseline from star to bottom of skirt. Use waist scale for all crosslines.

To make as illustrated, cut lining away to yoke depth.

To Make. Make lining and outside seams separate. Gather upper back and front to fit lining and yoke straps. Gather lower part of waist and top part of skirt. Join to lining on dotted lines. Notice dotted lines above waistline. Cover seams with belt and stitch to position.

Join seams of sleeve. Finish bottom in the usual way. Gather sleeve puff and join to band the same width as yoke band. Arrange on tight sleeve and gather to fit armhole.

Green silk voile was used for this garment, with sleeve of colored lace to match. Yoke band, sleeve band, and belt of oriental embroidery. Material required for medium form, 11 yards 21 inches wide.

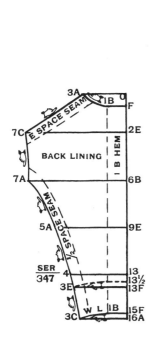

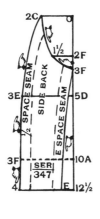

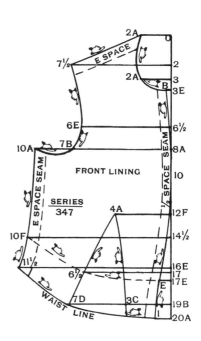

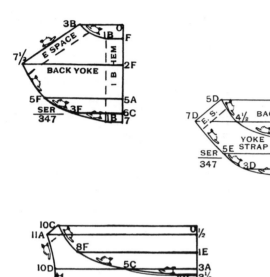
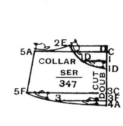
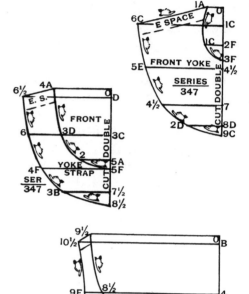
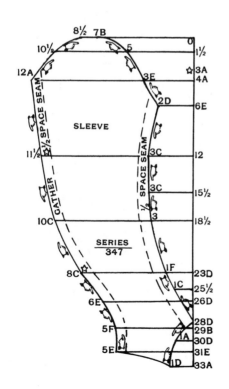
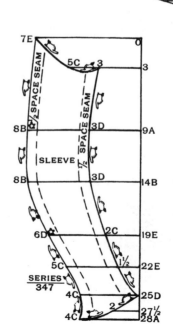

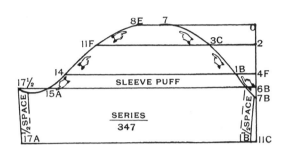
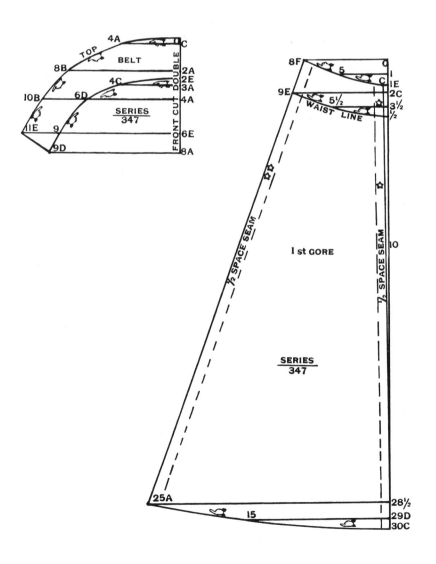
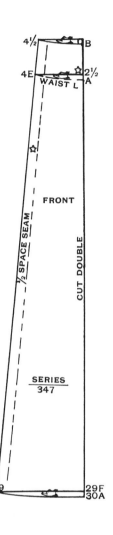

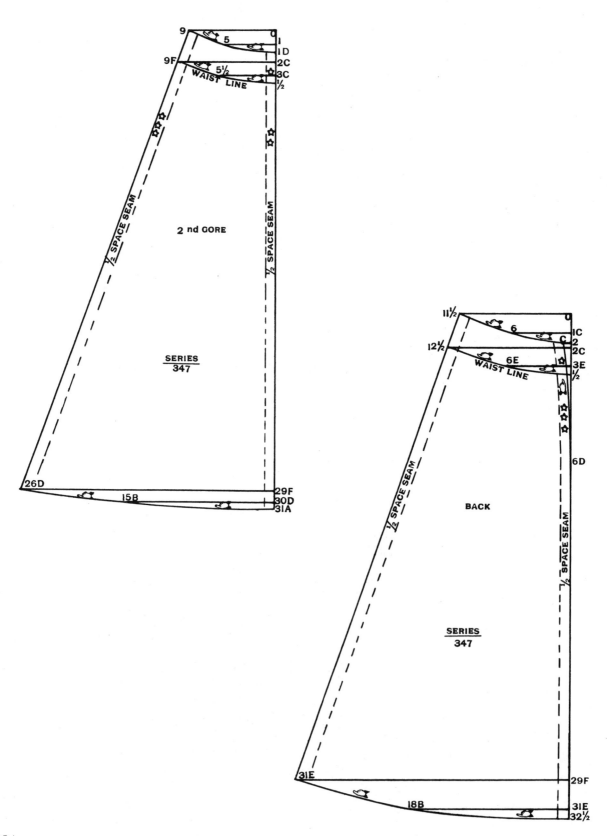

A Smart Creation for Street Wear

Six measures are taken for this suit: Bust, length of waist, full length, length of sleeve, around the waist, and length of skirt. It is drafted in 12 pieces: Coat back, front, side back, side front, collar, sleeve (2 pieces), and a 9-gore gathered skirt drafted in 5 pieces.

To Draft. Select bust and length of waist scales for collar and coat back, front, side back, and side front. Draft to waistline. Then subtract length of waist measure from full-length measure. This will give desired scale for baseline from waistline down. Use bust scale for all crosslines. For sleeve, use bust and length of sleeve scales. For skirt, use waist and length of skirt scales.

The difference between the waist and hip measure is 18 inches.

To Make. Join the different parts of coat according to seams given. The lower part of the coat, where back and side back join, may be finished open or closed as desired. Sleeve top may be gathered or finished with flat darts, stitched on the outside making three forward on two backward darts. Join sleeve seams and ease in any extra fullness at elbow.

Join seams of skirt according to stars. Finish top and bottom in the usual way.

Black velvet was used to develop this design, with trimmings of ermine. Material required for medium form, 12 yards 27 inches wide.

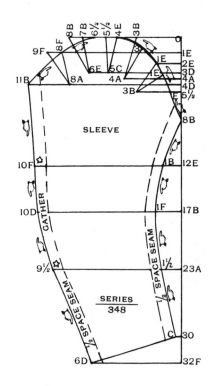

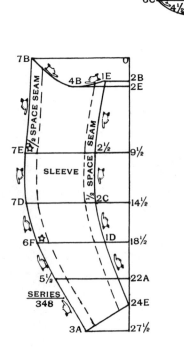

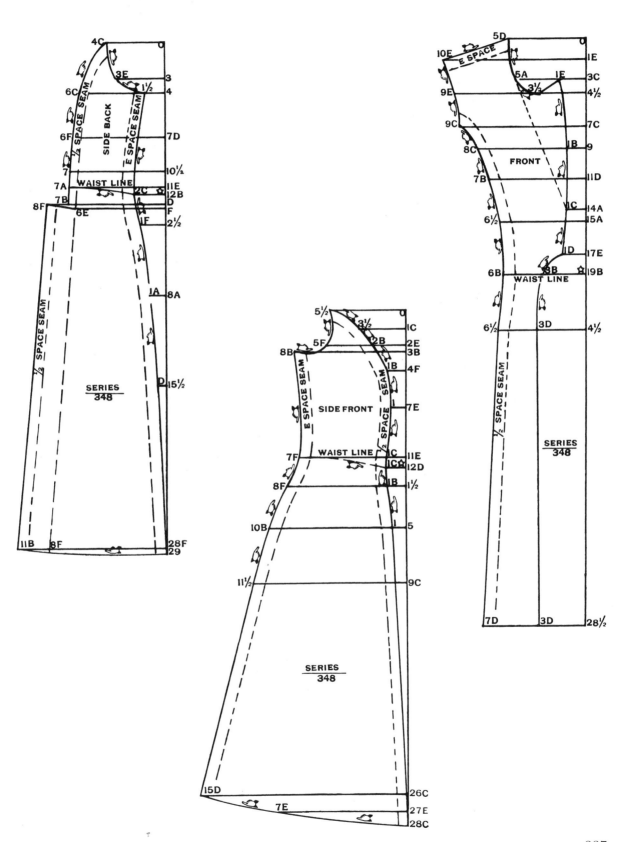

SIDE BACK

½ SPACE SEAM

E SPACE SEAM

WAIST LINE

½ SPACE SEAM

SERIES
348

SIDE FRONT

E SPACE SEAM

½ SPACE SEAM

WAIST LINE

SERIES
348

E SPACE

FRONT

WAIST LINE

½ SPACE SEAM

SERIES
348

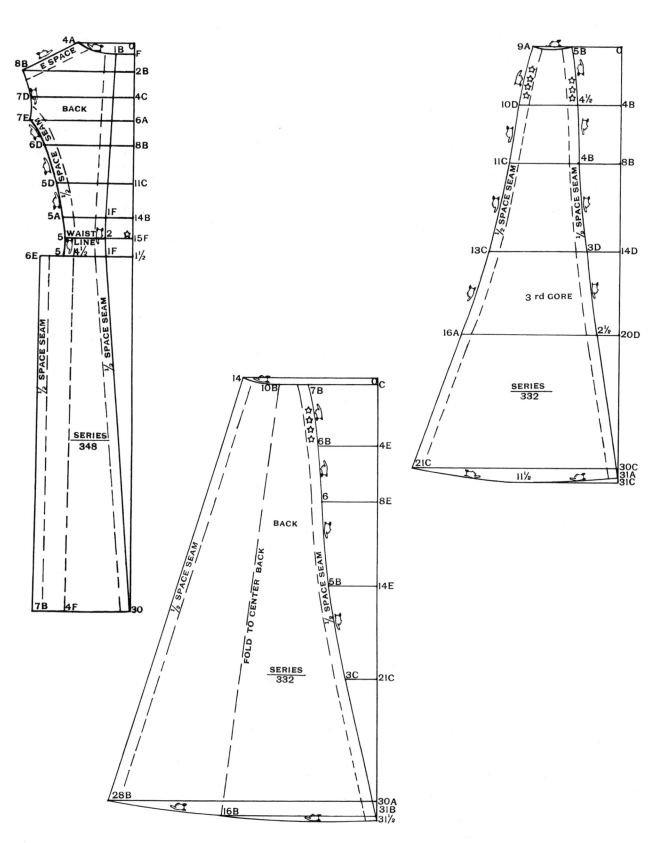

288

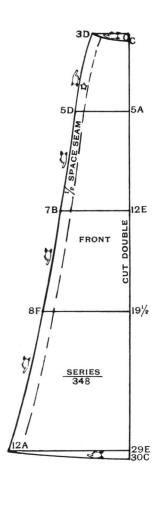

SERIES
348

FRONT

CUT DOUBLE

½ SPACE SEAM

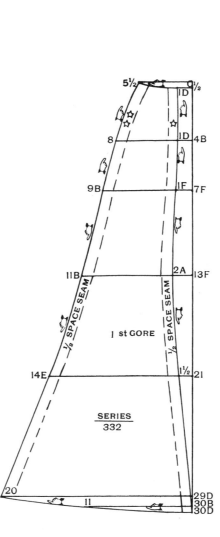

1 st GORE

½ SPACE SEAM

½ SPACE SEAM

SERIES
332

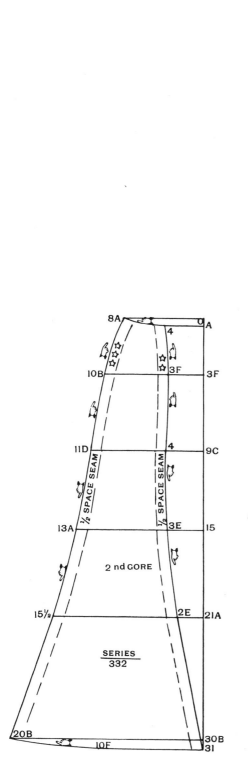

2 nd GORE

½ SPACE SEAM

½ SPACE SEAM

SERIES
332

Evening or Opera Coat

Three measures are taken for this coat: Bust, length of waist, and full length. It is drafted in three pieces: Back, front, and under part of sleeve.

To Draft. Select bust and length of waist scales for under part of sleeve and back and front to waistline. Then subtract length of waist from full-length measure. This will give desired scale for baseline from waistline to bottom of coat. Use bust scale for all crosslines.

To Make. Cut sleeve open under arm to point 11B and 10D (notice stars). Join under part of sleeve to upper part, back and front, two stars toward front and three to back portion. Join underarm seam and finish armhole of sleeve to remaining material. Close center back and shoulder seams.

Faced cloth was used for the coat, trimmed with a wide band of satin, buttons to match, and front finished with silk braid and braid ornaments. Material required, 3 yards 50 inches wide.

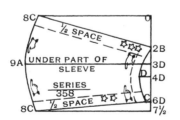

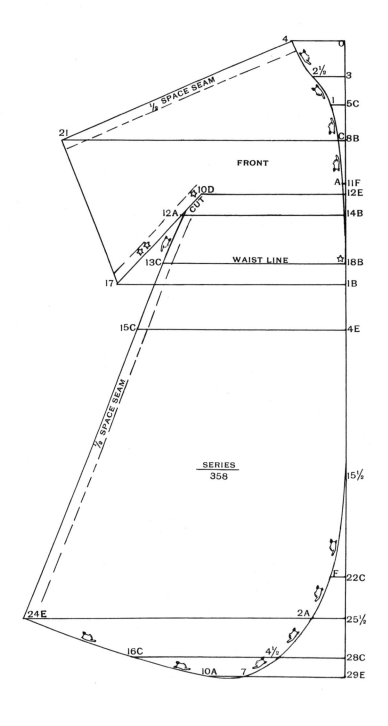

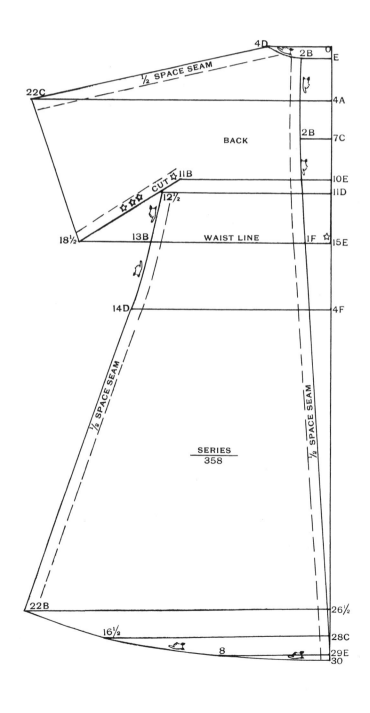

A Pretty Net Waist

Four measures are taken for this waist: Bust, length of waist, around the waist, and length of sleeve. It is drafted in 11 pieces: Back and front lining, upper back and front, back and front yoke, collar, plain sleeve (2 pieces), shirred sleeve, and cuff.

To Draft. Select bust and length of waist scales for back and front lining, upper back and front, two yoke portions, and collar. For shirred sleeve, sleeve lining, and cuff, use bust and length of sleeve scales.

To make sleeve like illustration, cut lower part of sleeve lining off at point 2B (notice star).

To Make. Make lining and outside separate. Gather upper back and front and join to yoke. Join shoulder and underarm seams. Gather to fit waist measure.

Gather lower part of shirred sleeve to cuff. Close back seam of sleeve lining. Gather seam of shirred sleeve to fit inseam of lining. Close upper sleeve and sleeve lining in one seam. Gather to fit armhole.

Filet net was used for this waist, with lace yoke and insertion for trimming. Material required for medium form, 3 yards 27 inches wide.

294

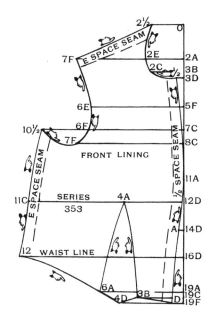

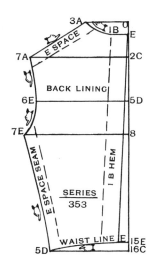

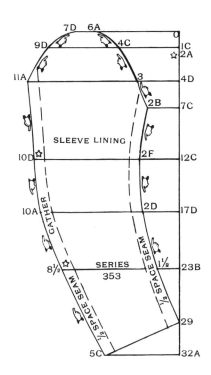

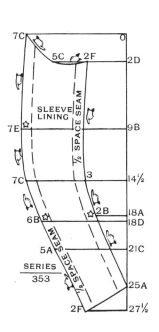

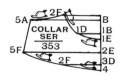

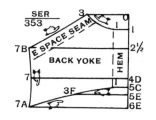

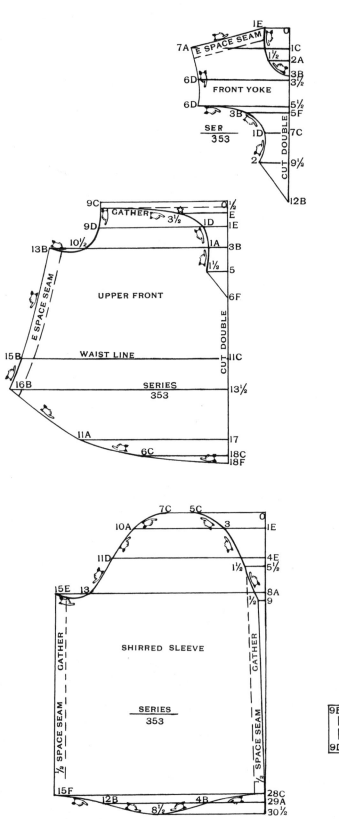

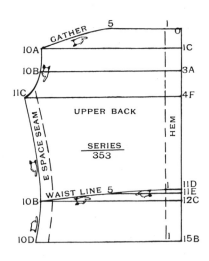

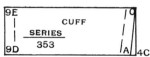

296

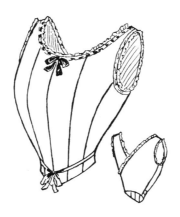

Fitted Corset Cover

Three measures are taken for this garment: Bust, length of waist, and around the waist. It is drafted in four pieces: Back, front, side front, and underarm.

To Draft and Make. Select bust and length of waist scales for all parts of corset cover. Join ac-

cording to stars. Leave seam open between stars where back and underarm join, so as to pass small end of back through and tie in front, like illustration. Join shoulder seam. Finish neck and armhole as desired.

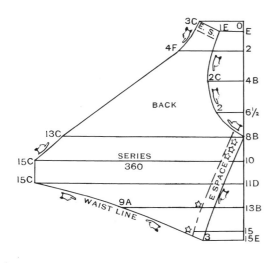

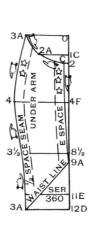

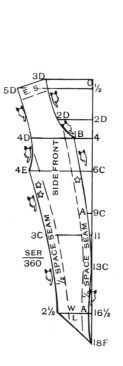

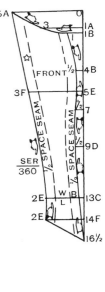

April 1909 American Modiste

For the average woman who takes delight in making her own clothes, the style now worn is a welcome change from the stiff tailored coats formerly in vogue. The absence of excessive padding and multiplicity of seams has simplified the construction considerably, and places the garment well within the range of the amateur dressmaker.

The skirt can be long or short as desired—short, most decidedly, when worn on the street, and long for dressy occasions. Skirts, although wider, still fit the hips closely; the fullness beginning higher than formerly. The trimmings for useful wear are stitchings and strappings, but for dressy skirts much soutache in elaborate designs is seen. It is often set in points, or pyramidal figures punctuated with crochet buttons.

There seems to be a tendency to the restoration of the regular waistline in many dresses. The new cloth and wash dresses show this characteristic. The extreme plainness of some of the new models necessitates the lavish use of embroideries and braidings. All lines introduced by the trimming are long and straight.

Net and lace blouses of every description are worn over soft silk slips. Waists of wash nets and other fabrics are more or less enriched with real lace—such as irish, cluny, torchon, and venice make. Sleeves tucked regularly or in groups are the popular favorites.

Buttons to trim all garments are yet much in favor, as are soutache braid trimmings of all varieties. Some designs have the effect of braid sewn in a design on net. These give the garment the appearance of having been actually hand trimmed. The new colors are rather brilliant—such as bright rose, cerise, olive green, sea-wave blue, duck's-breast blue-green, brick-dust red, old rose pink, white, soft browns, and black.

April 1909

A Dressy Street Suit

Five measures are taken for this suit: Bust, length of waist, around the waist, length of sleeve, and length of skirt. It is drafted in 11 pieces: Coat back, front, side back, side front, collar, sleeve (2 pieces), cuff, and a 5-gore side-pleated skirt drafted in 3 pieces.

To Draft. Select bust and length of waist scales for coat back, front, side back, side front, and collar. For sleeve and cuff, use bust and length of sleeve scales. For skirt, use waist and length of skirt scales.

The difference between the waist and hip measure is 16 inches.

To Make. Join the different parts of coat according to seams. Line front and side front with a good linen canvas, also collar and cuffs. Join sleeve

seams, easing in extra fullness at elbow. Finish sleeve with cuff. Place center of cuff 1/2 inch in front of inseam of sleeve. Gather to fit armhole.

Fold dotted line on front of skirt to heavy line on side gore, also dotted line on side gore to heavy line on center of side gore. Fold second dotted line to same heavy line, and dotted line on back to heavy line on side gore, making two forward- and two backward-turning pleats on side gore. This skirt has a habit back. Stitch pleats to any desired depth. Press them thoroughly to bottom of skirt.

The material used for this garment is one of spring's novelties in a beautiful shade of gray, with trimmings of a darker shade of satin. Material required for medium form, 5 1/2 yards 50 inches wide.

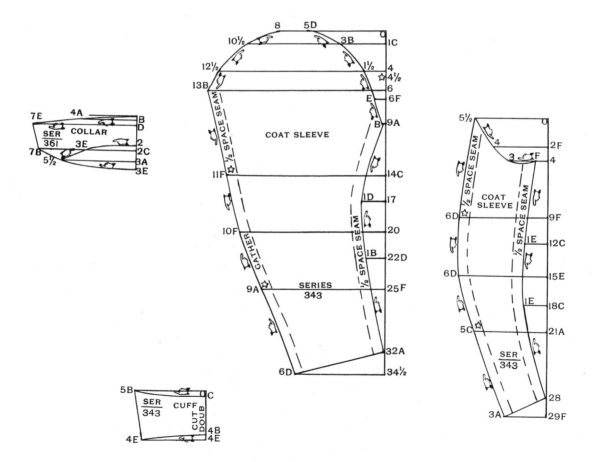

300

A Dressy Street Suit

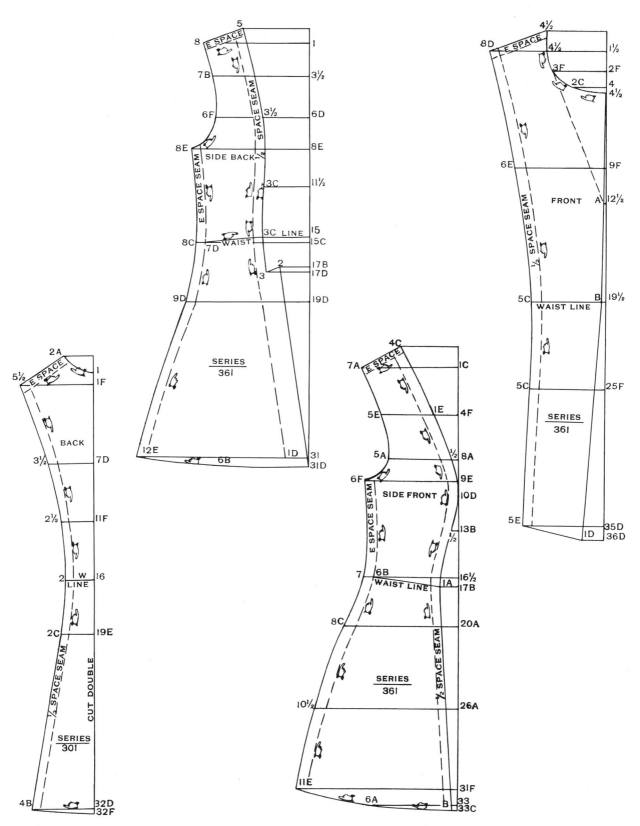

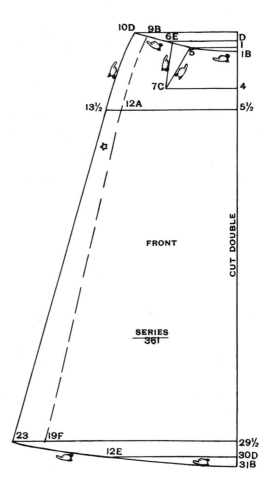

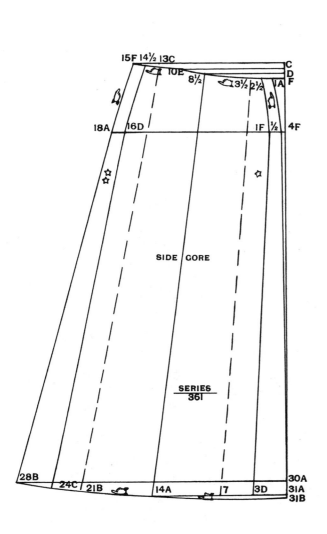

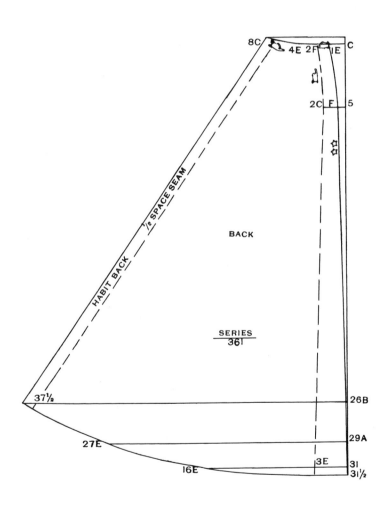

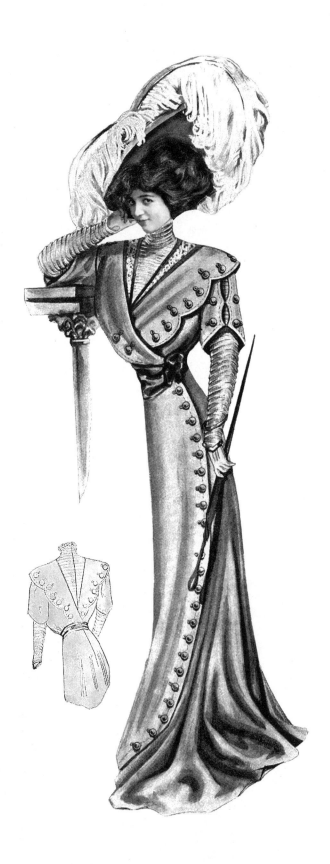

Stylish Street Gown

Five measures are taken for this gown: Bust, length of waist, around the waist, length of sleeve, and length of skirt. It is drafted in 14 pieces: Back and front lining, upper back and front, back and front yoke, sleeve (2 pieces), oversleeve or sleeve cap, bretelle, and a 5-gore gathered skirt drafted in 4 pieces.

To Draft. Select bust and length of waist scales for lining back and front, upper back and front, two yoke portions, and bretelle. For sleeve and sleeve cap, use bust and length of sleeve scales. For skirt, use waist and length of skirt scales.

The difference between the waist and hip measure is 17 inches.

To Make. Make waist and lining separate. Place back and front yoke on back and front lining and stitch to position. Take up darts. Close shoulder and underarm seams. Join shoulder and un-derarm seams of upper back and front. Make bretelle double and sew to waist. Gather upper waist at waistline to fit lining. Finish with narrow belt.

Join seam of sleeve with 1/2-space seam. Ease in extra fullness at elbow. Gather top of sleeve and sew to armhole of lining. Join oversleeve to upper waist with points 1 inch in front of shoulder seam.

Cut one skirt right front, one left front, and one back, as back is made with box pleat. Illustration shows inverted pleat, but small cut is to show back of waist only. Join skirt according to stars. Fold first dotted line on right front to heavy line on left front 1B and 1C. Stitch 1 space from folded edge. Join side gores to right front and left front. Fold dotted line on back to heavy line on side gore. Stitch to any desired depth. Finish placket on left side of back.

Lightweight chiffon broadcloth was the material used for this gown, with tucked net for yoke and sleeve.

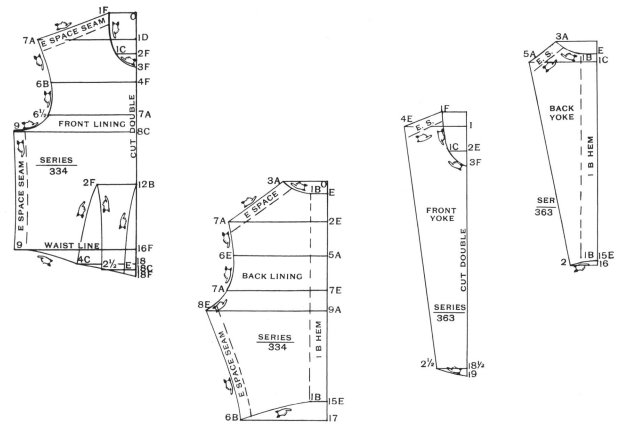

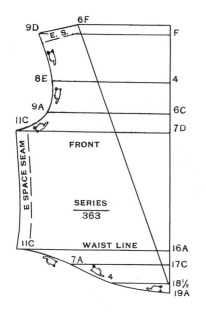

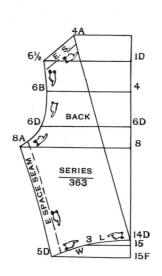

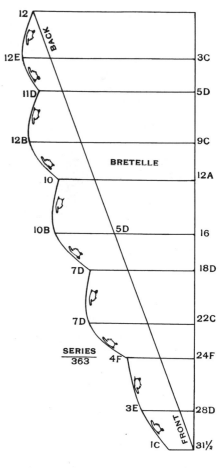

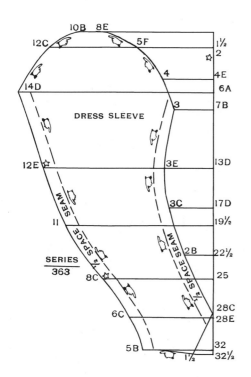

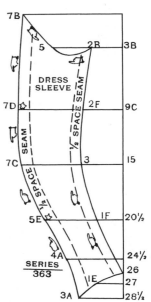

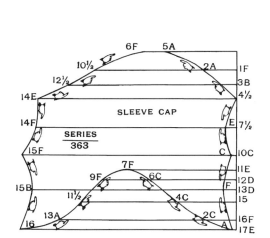

SLEEVE CAP

SERIES
363

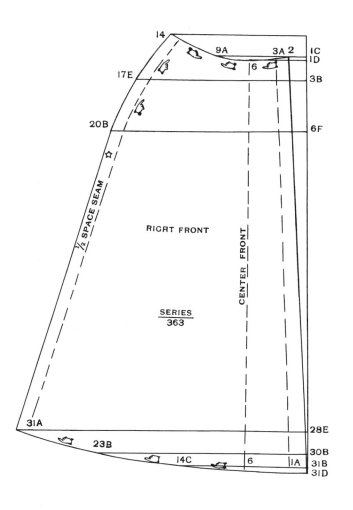

RIGHT FRONT

CENTER FRONT

½ SPACE SEAM

SERIES
363

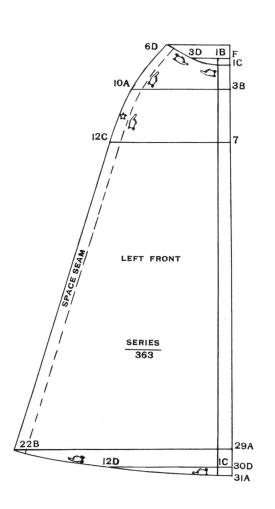

SPACE SEAM

LEFT FRONT

SERIES
363

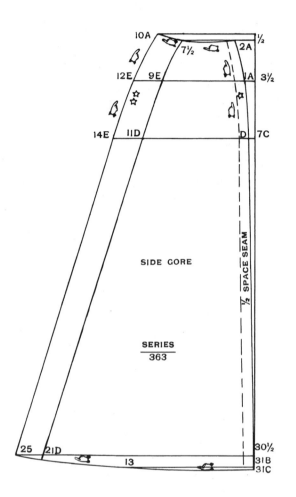

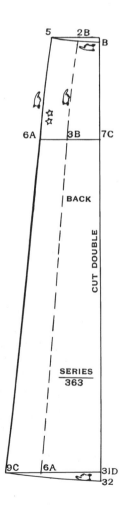

Stylish Evening Gown

Five measures are taken for this gown: Bust, length of waist, around the waist, length of sleeve, and length of skirt. It is drafted in eight pieces: Back, side back, front, side front, stock and large collar, sleeve lining, and mousquetaire sleeve.

To Draft. Select bust and length of waist scales for collars, back, side back, front, and side front to waistline (notice star). Then select length of skirt measure scale. Copy all points on baseline from waistline to bottom of princess. Use bust scale for all crosslines. For sleeve and sleeve lining, use bust and length of sleeve scales.

Use any tight waist lining or guimpe with this princess.

To make like illustration, cut front off at waistline. Or leave as diagram is given and finish with princess front.

To Make. Take up dart on side front. Join the different parts according to seams given. Arrange large collar around yoke of dress with stars on collar even with stars on back and front of princess. To make sleeve, close back of lining to elbow with 1/2-space seam. Fold on dotted lines of mousquetaire sleeve and gather two 1/4-inch tucks. Gather inseam of sleeve to fit lining and join in one seam. Gather to fit armhole.

The material used for this garment was black Directoire satin, with black crepe de chine for sleeve, trimming of same material, soutache braid, and jet buttons. Material required for medium form, 8 yards 27 inches wide.

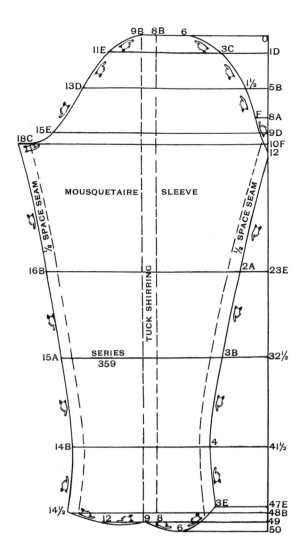

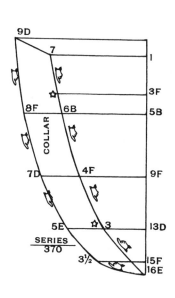

COLLAR

SERIES
370

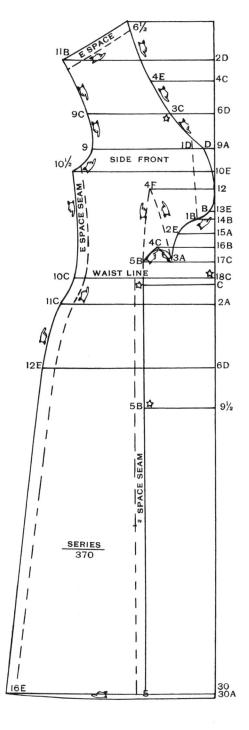

SIDE FRONT

E SPACE SEAM

WAIST LINE

½ SPACE SEAM

SERIES
370

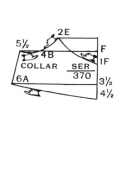

COLLAR   SER
370

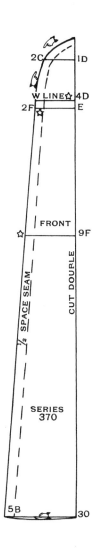

W LINE

FRONT

CUT DOUBLE

½ SPACE SEAM

SERIES
370

311

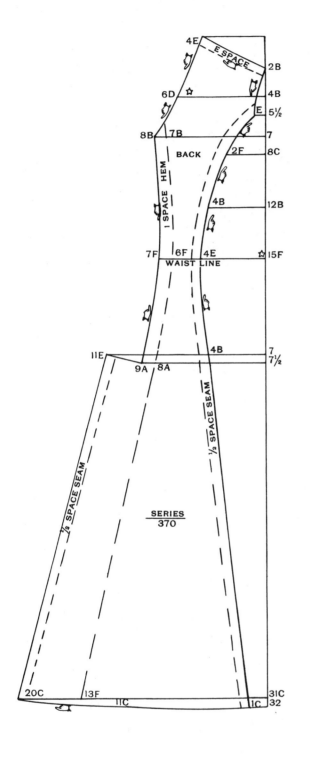

BACK

SERIES
370

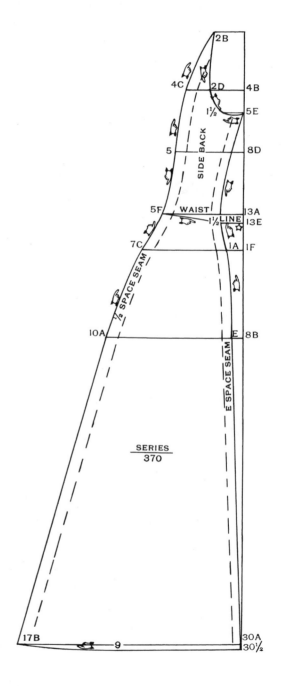

SIDE BACK

SERIES
370

Smart Design for Easter

Five measures are taken for this garment: Bust, length of waist, around the waist, length of sleeve, and length of skirt. It is drafted in 15 pieces: Back and front lining, upper back and front, back and front yoke, collar, sleeve, and a 13-gore plain skirt drafted in 7 pieces.

To Draft. Select bust and length of waist scales for back and front lining, upper back and front, two yoke portions, and collar. For sleeve, use bust and length of sleeve scales. For skirt, use waist and length of skirt scales.

The difference between the waist and hip measure is 17 inches.

To Make. To make waist without lining, fold dotted line to heavy line on back and front. Stitch to position. Join shoulder and underarm seams. Make yoke separate from waist if desired. Join back of sleeve to elbow with 1/2-space seam, also inseam of sleeve. Gather to fit armhole.

Join skirt according to numbers. Fold dotted line on first gore to heavy line on front. Stitch to position. The skirt is made with habit back. Finish top and bottom in the usual way.

One of the beautiful satin foulards was used for this design, with plain satin to trim. Buttons to match plain satin. Yoke of crepe de chine and lace. Material required for medium form, 12 yards 22 inches wide.

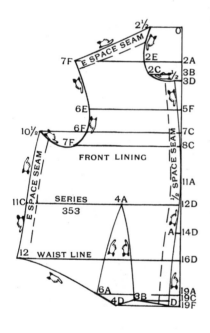
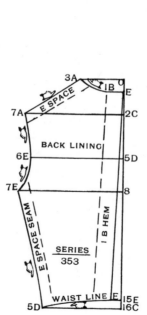
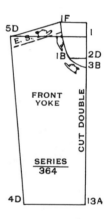
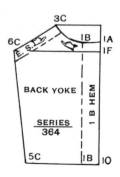

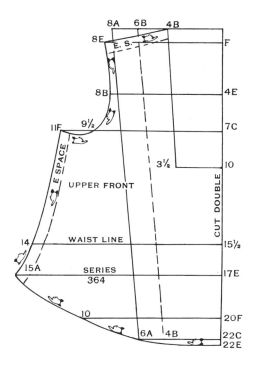

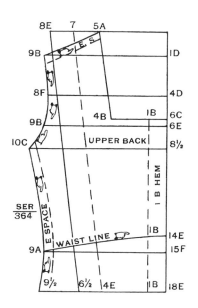

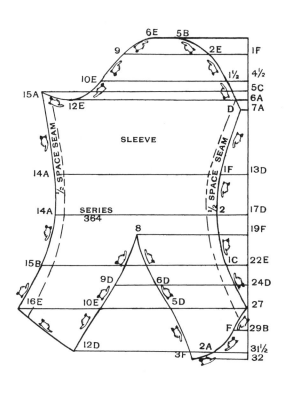

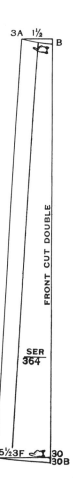

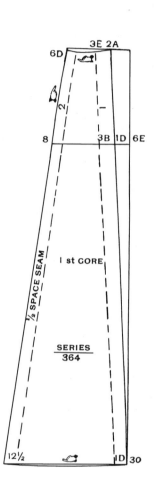

3E 2A
6D
2
8   3B 1D 6E

½ SPACE SEAM

1 st GORE

SERIES
364

12½   1D 30

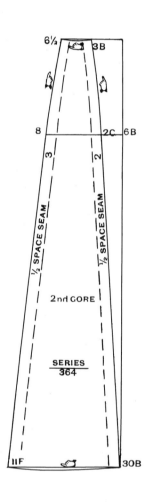

6½   3B

½ SPACE SEAM   ½ SPACE SEAM
8   2C 6B
3   2

2nd GORE

SERIES
364

11F   30B

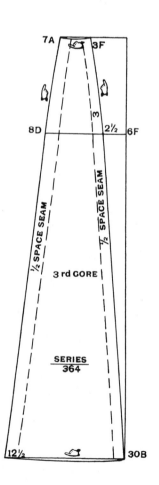

7A   3F

3
8D   2½ 6F

½ SPACE SEAM   ½ SPACE SEAM

3 rd GORE

SERIES
364

12½   30B

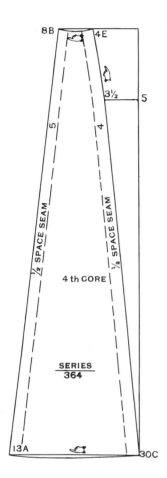

8B — 4E
3½ — 5
5 — 4
½ SPACE SEAM — ½ SPACE SEAM
4 th GORE
SERIES
364
13A — 30C

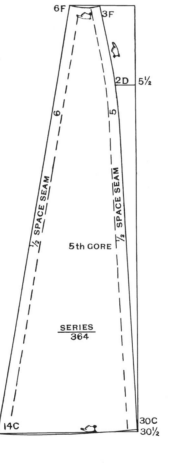

6F — 3F
2D — 5½
6 — 5
½ SPACE SEAM — ½ SPACE SEAM
5 th GORE
SERIES
364
14C — 30C
30½

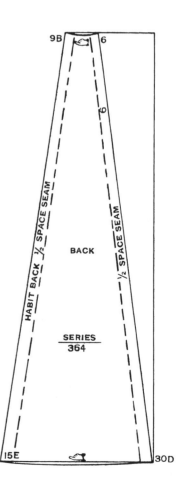

9B — 6
6
HABIT BACK ½ SPACE SEAM — ½ SPACE SEAM
BACK
SERIES
364
15E — 30D

317

April 1909

Dressy Afternoon Waist

Three measures are taken for this waist: Bust, length of waist, and length of sleeve. It is drafted in six pieces: Waist back and front, vest back and front, and sleeve (two styles).

To Draft. Select bust and length of waist scales for waist back and front and vest back and front. For sleeves, use bust and length of sleeve scales.

Illustration shows a small shirtwaist sleeve gathered at wrist. If this style is desired, use shirtwaist sleeve pattern. To make the other sleeve, use plain sleeve pattern.

To Make. Join back and front of waist to back and front vest. Stitch to position. Join shoulder and underarm seams. Gather to fit waist measure.

To make shirtwaist sleeve, join sleeve seam. Cut open on dotted line and finish with lap and facing. Gather to fit cuff and armhole. To make plain sleeve, join seams and gather to fit armhole.

The material used for this waist was cherry-colored satin, with deep yoke and sleeve trimmings of irish crochet lace, with tiny quillings of black satin ribbon.

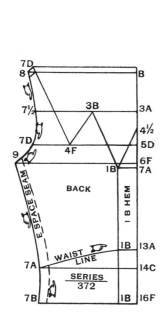

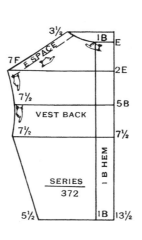

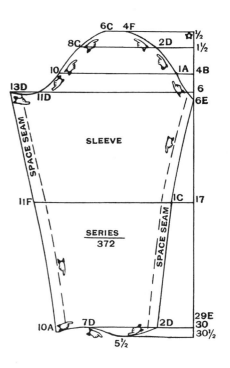

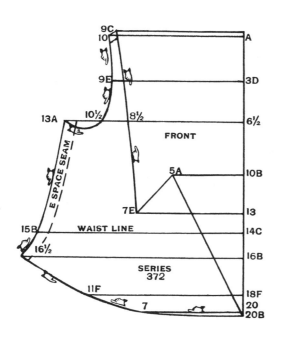

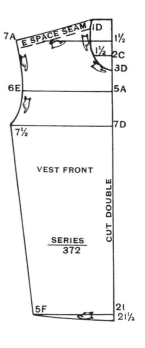

VEST BACK

SERIES
372

I B HEM

BACK

I B HEM

WAIST LINE

SERIES
372

SLEEVE

SPACE SEAM

SPACE SEAM

SERIES
372

FRONT

E SPACE SEAM

WAIST LINE

SERIES
372

VEST FRONT

SERIES
372

CUT DOUBLE

E SPACE SEAM

July 1909 American Modiste

The newest materials are much embroidered, as well as having insertions of lace set in, and tiny tucks galore.

Fullness is introduced by delicate shirrings, pleats, tucks on the side and at the back, while the first breadth is left to hang plain and straight. Skirts of the heavier materials have the fullness cunningly fitted in over the hips. All walking skirts must clear the ground. Skirts for traveling and shopping are all walking length. Genuine princess gowns should always have trains. All evening frocks except those for dancing are being made with trains.

The separate blouse is not lost sight of, as it is useful to wear under the sleeveless jumper or pinafore style, also with the high-waisted or ordinary shaped skirts.

The coat has become a recognized feature of summer fashions. White serge or panama, tropical suiting, pongee, linen, poplin, or cotton rep would be very smart if the coat is made up as part of a suit, the skirt being of the same material. But if intended for wearing with any dress, ottoman silk, soft satin, or a lightweight cloth might more appropriately be chosen, while black would be the most practical color.

Detachable collars of linen are very popular. Most are embroidered by hand, though many are inserted with lace. Collars of baby irish lace are very stylish and are suitable for wear with all materials. Collars and buttons made from black satin are considered very smart on linen coats of both white and colors.

Lace will be more than ever worn, not only as a trimming, but also in the form of complete gowns and coats. Real crochet laces, both french and irish, will enjoy a considerable vogue for these garments, especially when they are intended for day wear. The finer kinds of brussels and alençon point laces, very delicately tinted to match the materials in whose company they will be seen, will be used to make complete bodices. Lace coats are popular, from the real irish lace models to the lace and braid makes, which are very effective in all white, or black.

Guimpes will lose nothing in favor for summer wear. Many of the separate blouses, even, are worn over guimpes usually in self-tone. All women appreciate this style, especially if the guimpe is of white material. Or often the yoke-facing only will be white, and the sleeves will be of light material dyed the color of the dress with which it is worn. The effect may be rendered more severe by making the sleeves of the dress goods. The net guimpes usually have linings of fine brussels net. This lining is also much used with allover lace, and it gives an unusually pretty effect beneath chiffon. Figured net with chiffon makes a very pretty guimpe. Washable guimpes are generally made of allover embroidery or dotted and figured swiss, mull, and batiste. Much fancy tucking is used for this purpose. A white guimpe may be embroidered in a color corresponding to the dress. Cotton marquisette is largely used and generally toned to the dress.

Shantung is lovely in its natural color and much used this season for coats and skirts, and long coats for motoring, also the princess dress.

The pretty spot, ring, or tiny flowered foulard is most serviceable. Dark tones are being much utilized this season. The lovely wisteria and catawba shades are wonderfully beautiful in this material, but such standbys as dark blue are also much worn.

Bordered materials are in vogue, some being quite wide and others narrow in design. For practical use the narrow ones are to be preferred, as they can be cut off and used as bandings in any way the gown demands.

Unique Style for Summer

Five measures are taken for this dress: Bust, length of waist, around the waist, length of sleeve, and length of skirt. It is drafted in 12 pieces: Waist back and front, back and front yoke, lace yoke back and front, belt, sleeve, and a 7-gore tucked skirt drafted in 4 pieces.

To Draft. Select bust and length of waist scales for waist back and front and four yokes. For sleeve, use bust and length of sleeve scales. For belt, use waist and length of waist scales. For skirt, use waist and length of skirt scales.

The difference between the waist and hip measure is 16 inches.

To Make. Tuck goods for back and front of waist, yoke portions, and sleeves before cutting. Make yoke and waist separate. Join shoulder and underarm seams of lace yoke. Stitch to waist.

Join skirt according to stars. Fold dotted lines to heavy lines, making nine tucks on each side of skirt. Stitch tucks 1/4 inch from folded edge to yoke depth. Join waist and skirt into belt. Join sleeve seam and gather top to fit armhole. Sleeve may be sewn to waist or yoke as preferred.

Foulard silk was the material used to develop this garment, trimmed with lace insertion and a frill of lace around bottom of skirt. Yokes of tucked ninon. Material required for medium form, 10 yards 27 inches wide.

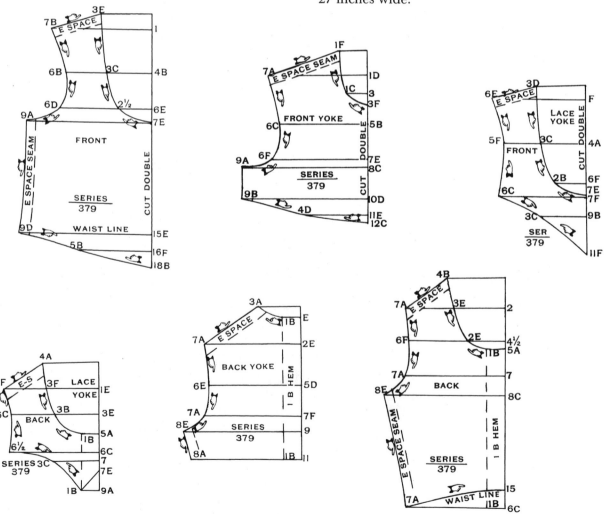

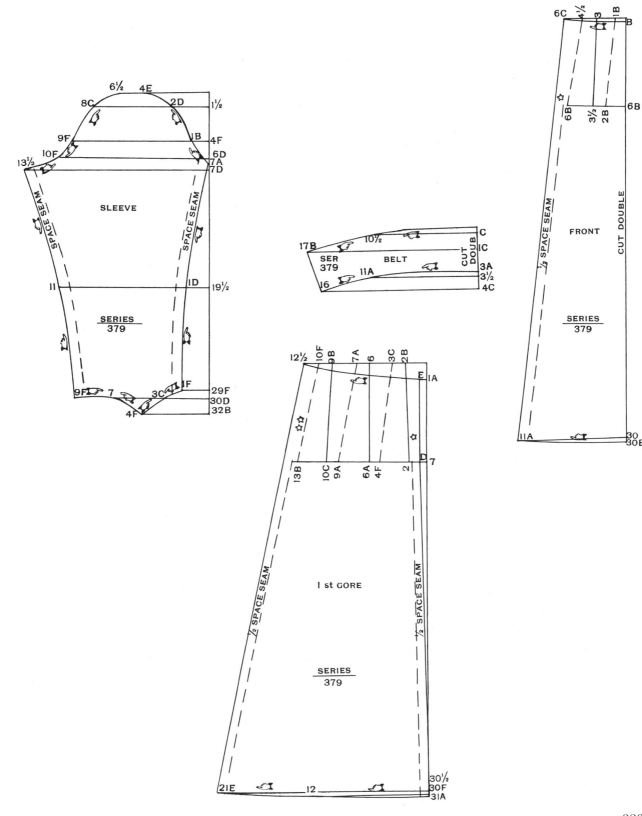

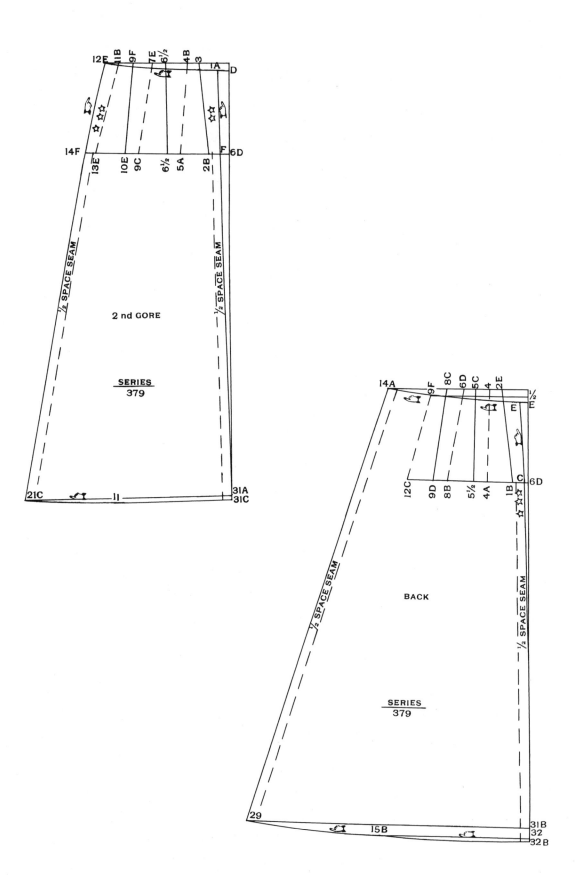

Silk and Net Waist

Four measures are taken for this waist: Bust, length of waist, around the waist, and length of sleeve. It is drafted in six pieces: Waist back and front, back and front yoke, sleeve, and oversleeve.

To Draft. Select bust and length of waist scales for waist back and front and back and front yokes. For sleeve and oversleeve, use bust and length of sleeve scales.

To Make. Make two E-space tucks in back and front of waist. Join shoulder and underarm seams. Gather to fit waist measure. Make yoke and

waist separate. Close back seam of sleeve to elbow, also inseam of sleeve and oversleeve. Sew to armhole.

A pretty shade of blue lansdowne was used for this waist. Scallops of waist and oversleeve are embroidered in white. Yoke and cuff are made of tucked net, finished with bands of silk. Two and one-half yards of silk will be required for medium form.

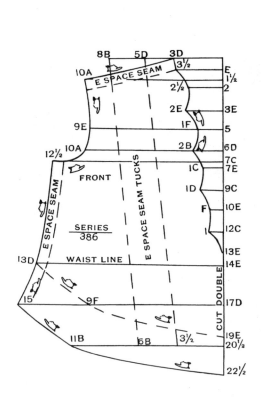

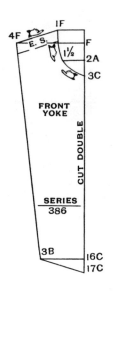

FRONT YOKE

CUT DOUBLE

SERIES 386

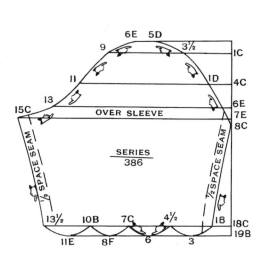

OVER SLEEVE

SERIES 386

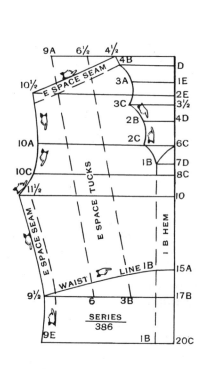

FRONT

SERIES 386

WAIST LINE

E SPACE SEAM TUCKS

CUT DOUBLE

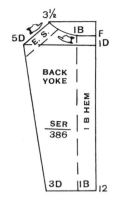

BACK YOKE

SER 386

I B HEM

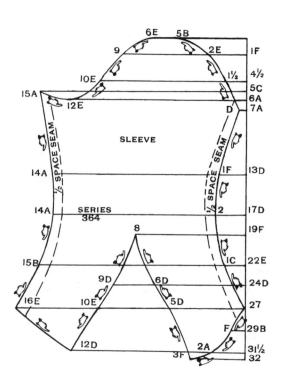

SLEEVE

SERIES 364

Outing Suit

Six measures are taken for this suit: Bust, length of waist, full length, length of sleeve, around the waist, and length of skirt. It is drafted in 13 pieces: Coat back, front, side back, side front, collar, sleeve (2 pieces), cuff, and an 8-gore skirt drafted in 5 pieces.

To Draft. Select bust and length of waist scales for collar and coat back, front, side back, and side front. Draft to waistline. Then subtract length of waist from full length. This will give correct scale for baseline from waistline to bottom of coat. Use bust scale for all crosslines. For sleeve and cuff, use bust and length of sleeve scales. For skirt, use waist and length of skirt scales.

The difference between the waist and hip measure is 18 inches.

To Make. Join the different parts of coat according to seams given. Finish seams running to shoulder with insertion. Join seam of sleeves, and ease in extra fullness at elbow between stars. If cuff is used, place star 4D even with inseam of sleeve. Gather to fit armhole.

Join skirt according to stars by folding dotted lines to heavy lines. Turn under side edges of front, second gore, and back 1 space. Lap three gores over to heavy lines on first and third gores. Stitch as shown in illustration. Finish top and bottom in the usual way.

This is one of the new half-fitted coats, and is especially good for linens. Material required for medium form, 10 1/2 yards 27 inches wide.

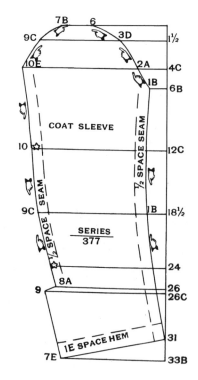

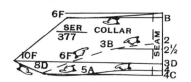

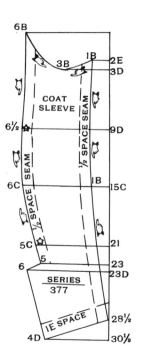

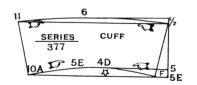

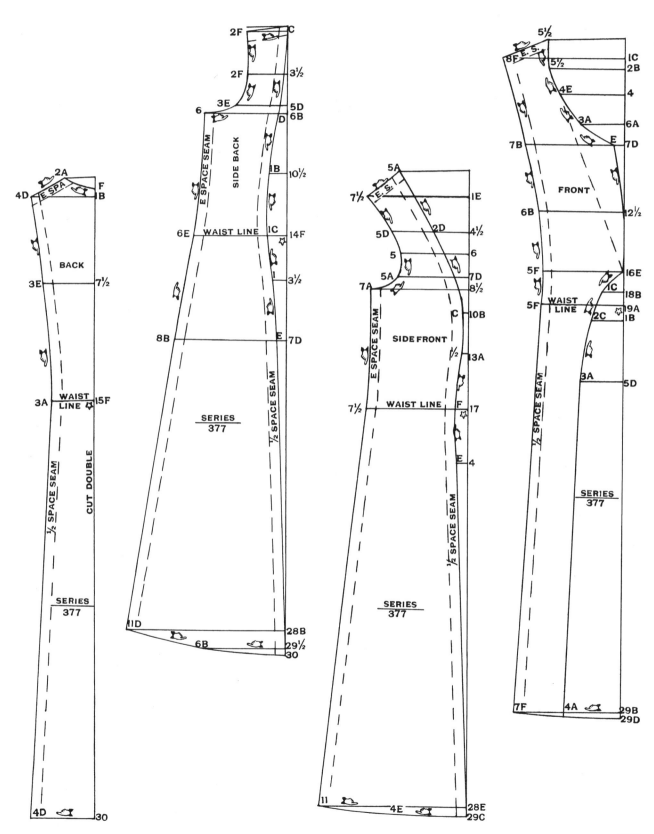

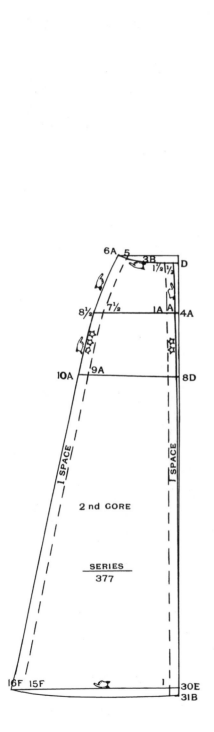

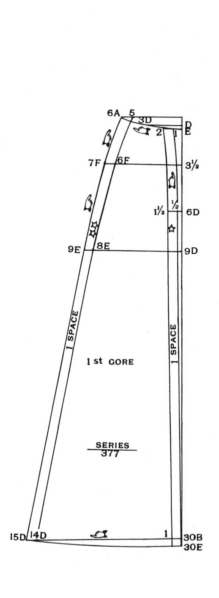

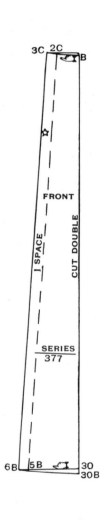

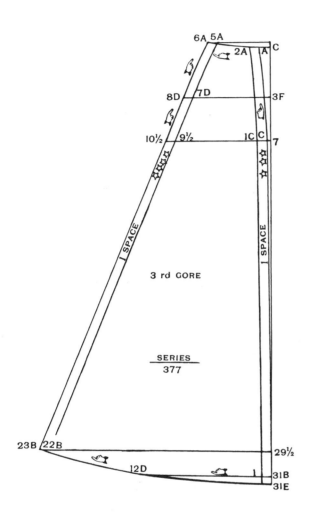

6A 5A
2A A C

8D 7D 3F

10½ 9½ 1C C 7

1 SPACE

1 SPACE

3 rd GORE

SERIES
377

23B 22B 29½
12D 1 31B
31E

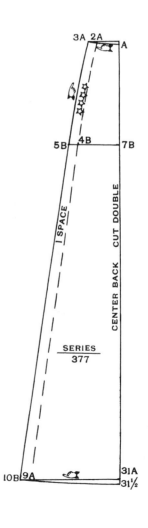

3A 2A A

5B 4B 7B

1 SPACE

CENTER BACK CUT DOUBLE

SERIES
377

10B 9A 31A
31½

331

Ladies' Bathing Suit

Five measures are taken for waist and skirt: Bust, length of waist, around the waist, length of sleeve, and length of skirt. For knickerbockers two measures are taken: Waist and length. The length is taken from waistline over hips to desired length. Diagram allows for finish.

This suit with knickerbockers consists of 15 pieces: Waist back and front, underwaist for knickerbockers (back, front, and side back), belt, collar, sleeve, knickerbockers (2 pieces), and a 9-gore pleated skirt drafted in 5 pieces including panel front.

To Draft. Select bust and length of waist scales for waist back and front; underwaist back, front, and side back; collar; and panel front to waistline. For sleeve, use bust and length of sleeve scales. For belt, use waist and length of waist scales. For skirt, use waist and length of skirt scales. For knickerbockers, use waist and length scales.

The difference between the waist and hip measure of skirt is 16 inches.

To Make. Join shoulder seam of waist. Fold goods on dotted line and stitch a 1 B-space tuck. Join underarm seams. Join first, second, third, and back gores of skirt according to stars by folding dotted lines to heavy lines, thus making a pleat over each seam. Sew skirt to waist and cover seam with belt. Before sewing belt to side front of waist, fold 3B over to 6B (notice stars). This gives a continuation of deep pleat over shoulder.

Now join panel front to waist and skirt by folding dotted line to heavy line on waist and skirt. Stitch right side as illustrated and finish left side for closing. Close shoulder seam and finish with collar.

For knickerbockers, join the three sections of underwaist according to seams given. Join the two sections of knickerbockers before cutting goods. One and one-half space is allowed for hem. Close seams as given. Join to underwaist.

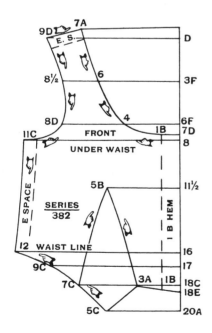

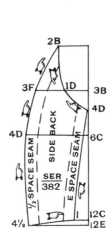

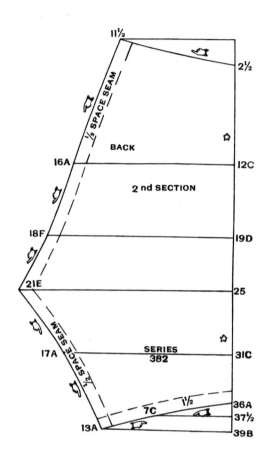

BACK

2 nd SECTION

SERIES
382

½ SPACE SEAM

½ SPACE SEAM

11½
2½
16A
12C
18F
19D
21E
25
17A
31C
7C
1½
36A
37½
13A
39B

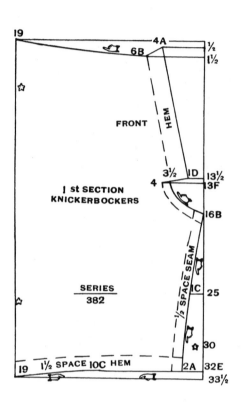

FRONT

1 st SECTION
KNICKERBOCKERS

SERIES
382

HEM

½ SPACE SEAM

19
4A
6B
½
1½
3½
1D
13½
4
3F
16B
1C
25
30
19
1½ SPACE 10C HEM
2A
32E
33½

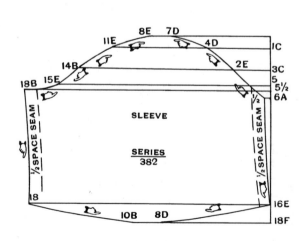

SLEEVE

SERIES
382

½ SPACE SEAM

½ SPACE SEAM

8E
7D
11E
4D
1C
14B
2E
3C
18B
15E
5
5½
6A
18
16E
10B
8D
18F

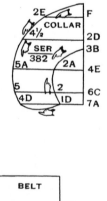

COLLAR

SER
382

2E
F
4½
2D
3B
5A
2A
4E
5
2
6C
4D
1D
7A

15	SERIES	BELT
15	382	2B

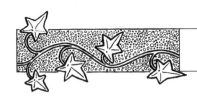

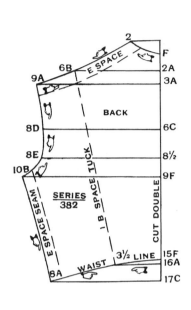

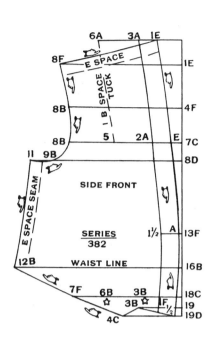

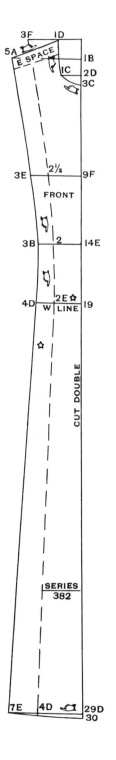

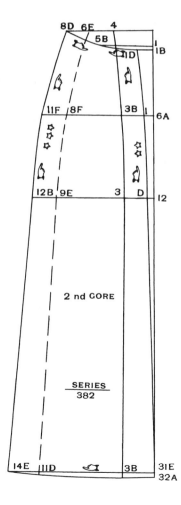

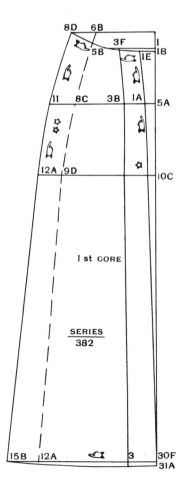

335

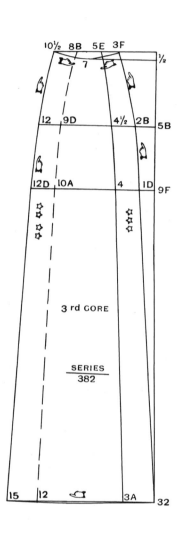

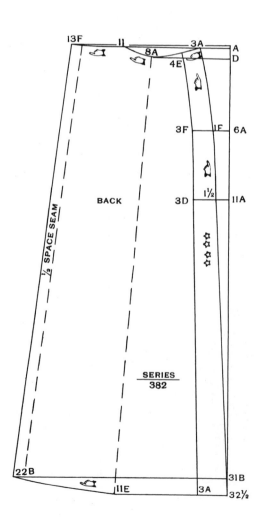

Ladies' Reception Gown

Five measures are taken for this gown: Bust, length of waist, around the waist, length of sleeve, and length of skirt. It is drafted in 12 pieces: Back and front waist, back and front bretelles, collar, dress sleeve (2 pieces), oversleeve, and a 5-gore skirt drafted in 4 pieces.

To Draft. Select bust and length of waist scales for waist back and front, bretelles back and front, and collar. For sleeve and oversleeve, use bust and length of sleeve scales. For skirt, use waist and length of skirt scales.

This gown has the raised waistline. Take the measures the same as for natural waistline. Allowance is made in diagrams for raised waistline on skirt.

To Make. Use back and front lining for body part of waist. Take up darts or gather to fit waist measure. Join shoulder seams of bretelles and arrange on waist like illustration. Tuck material for dress sleeve before cutting. Join dress sleeve and oversleeve to armhole.

Join first and second section of back gore before cutting goods. Skirt may be made with habit back or inverted pleat. Join according to stars and seams. Sew to waist. Finish with belt or sash.

The material used for this gown was old rose Liberty satin, trimmed with a heavy wide insertion. Yoke and sleeve of tucked net. Nine yards 27 inches wide will be required for medium form.

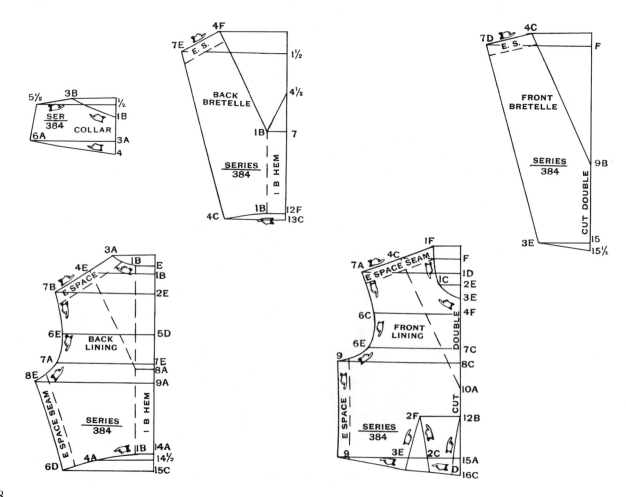

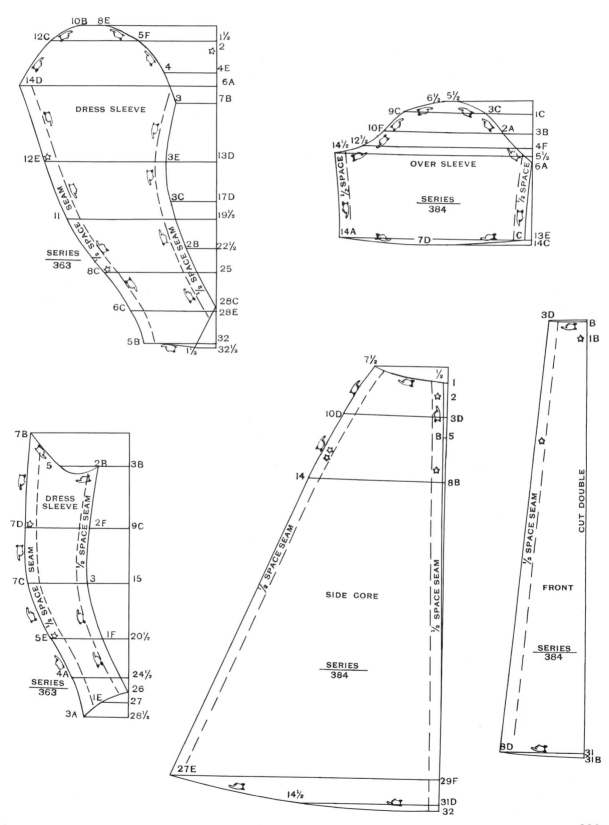

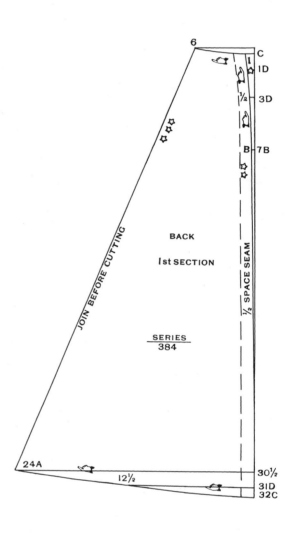

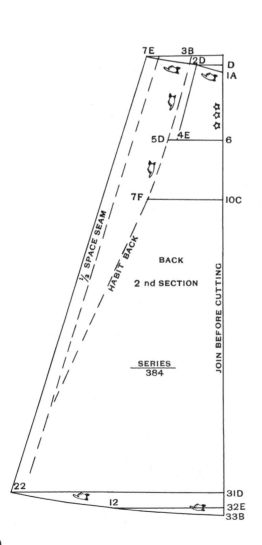

Ladies' Empire Raincoat

Ladies' Empire Raincoat

Four measures are taken for this coat: Bust, length of waist, full length, and length of sleeve. It is drafted in ten pieces: Coat back, side front, front, collar, sleeve (two pieces), cuff, belt, back coat skirt, and side gore.

To Draft. Select bust and length of waist scales for collar, belt, and coat back, side front, and front to star 19D. Draft to waistline. Then subtract length of waist measure from full-length measure. This will give desired scale for baseline from star 19D to bottom of coat. Use bust scale for all crosslines. Use same scales for back and side gores. For sleeve and cuff, use bust and length of sleeve scales.

To Make. Join back and side gores of coat skirt. Also join back and side front of body part at underarm seam. Sew skirt to upper part. Join front with lapped seam like illustration. Close shoulder seams. Cover seam with belt. Stitch under fronts or finish as illustrated. There is no seam in body part of coat at center back (though small illustration shows one). If you desire a seam add 1/2 space. Close seams of sleeve and ease in extra fullness at elbow. Finish with cuff.

This design is equally attractive in broadcloth, pongee, and heavy silk (as in the popular rubberized silk). Material required for medium form, 4 yards 42 inches wide.

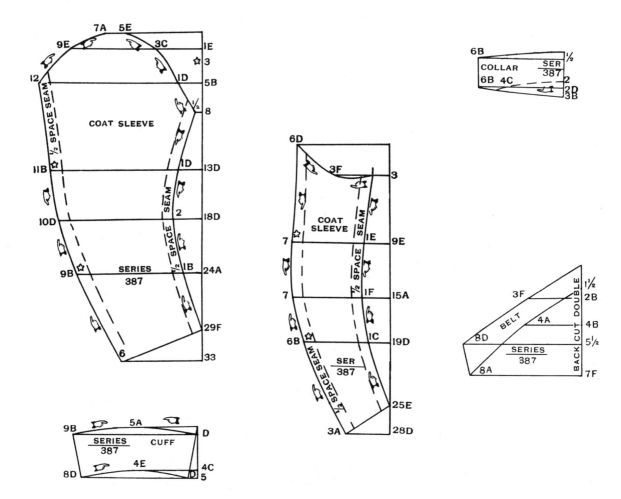

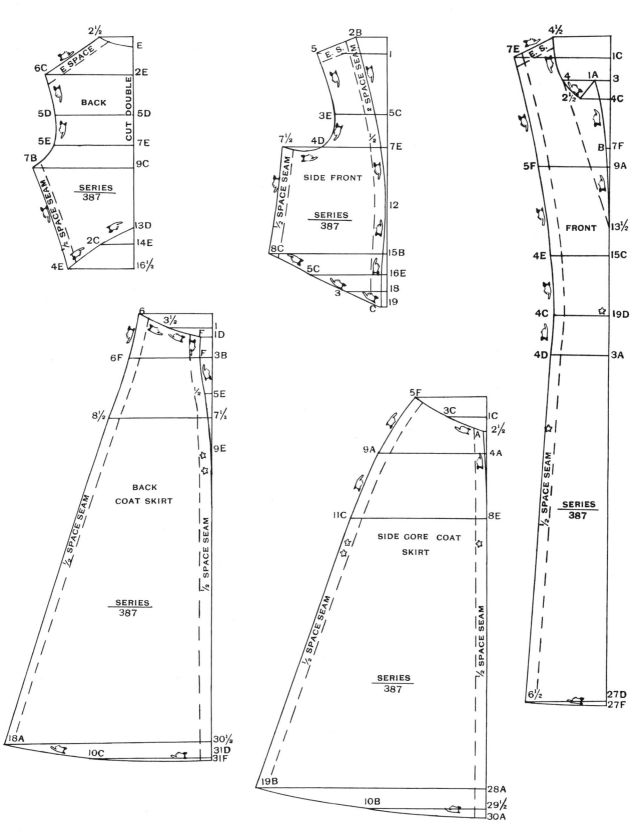

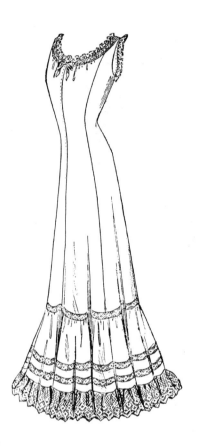

Princess Slip

Four measures are taken for this garment: Bust, length of waist, around the waist, and length of skirt. It is drafted in four pieces: Back, front, side front, and side back.

To Draft and Make. Select bust and length of waist scales. Draft each piece to waistline (notice stars). Then select length of skirt scale. Copy points on baseline from waistline to bottom of skirt. Use bust scale for all crosslines.

Join the four pieces according to seams given. Gather the upper edge of front and side front, or finish with draw ribbon. No diagram is given for flounce as it is one straight piece.

To make with flounce, 6 yards 36 inches wide will be required for medium form.

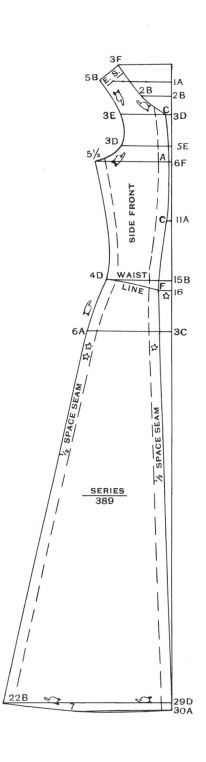

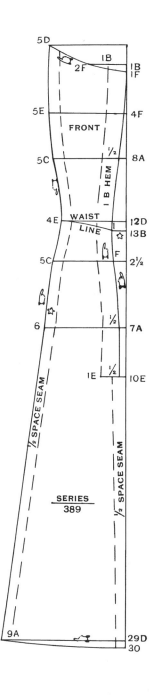

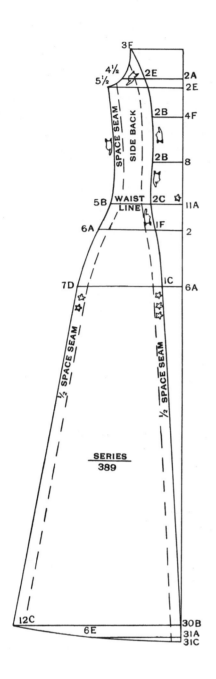

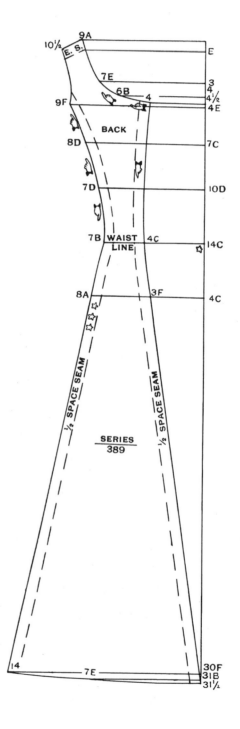

October 1909 American Modiste

Perhaps the materials which are most popular are the stripes which make the figure look more slender and the diagonals in all widths. Many persons ordering an autumn suit intending it to do duty throughout winter, prefer a medium-weight material, sufficiently interlined, to that heavier quality which looks too rough-and-ready for the early fall days.

The waistlines of the newest frocks have descended to the normal length, and often even beyond.

While lingerie waists are still popular, many tailored models in linen, madras, and shirtings are worn. Although white waists are particularly desirable, some pretty models are being shown with white grounds and colored markings in stripes and checks. Many net waists are displayed in the stores in both white and colors. For morning wear nothing is in better taste than the mannish well-tailored waist.

Among the high-class novelty materials are rough weaves and corded effects. Plan and fancy cheviots and homespun fabrics will be very smart this season for suits. They are shown in both plain and two-tone effects. Diagonals hold a prominent position and are shown in various wales. Materials with a satin finish will enjoy the same, if not greater, popularity.

October 1909

Ladies' Reception Gown

Five measures are taken for this gown: Bust, length of waist, around the waist, length of sleeve, and length of skirt. It is drafted in 12 pieces: Back and front lining, upper back and front, bretelle, sleeve (2 pieces), oversleeve, and a 7-gore empire skirt drafted in 4 pieces.

To Draft. Select bust and length of waist scales for back and front lining, upper back and front, and bretelle. For sleeve and oversleeve, use bust and length of sleeve scales. For skirt, use waist and length of skirt scales.

The difference between the waist and hip measure is 16 inches.

Waist may be made with or without tight lining. The skirt diagram may be used for plain skirt or empire. For plain skirt, cut off on dotted waistline.

To Make. Trace yoke from upper back and front on dotted lines. Cut 1 1/2 inches larger to allow for finish. Close shoulder and underarm seams. Gather to fit waist measure. Fold bretelle on dotted lines and stitch tuck 1 space deep. Face the outside edge; make the facing 1 space wide when finished. This will give the effect of three 1-space tucks as shown in illustration. Sew to waist along yoke line. Pleat or gather lower edge of bretelle into a 3-inch band and sew to waist. Cut out oversleeve between points 4F and 6E. Finish with straps of velvet and buttons. Join skirt according to stars and seams.

The material used for this costume is a changeable chiffon taffeta, with velvet and lace for trimming.

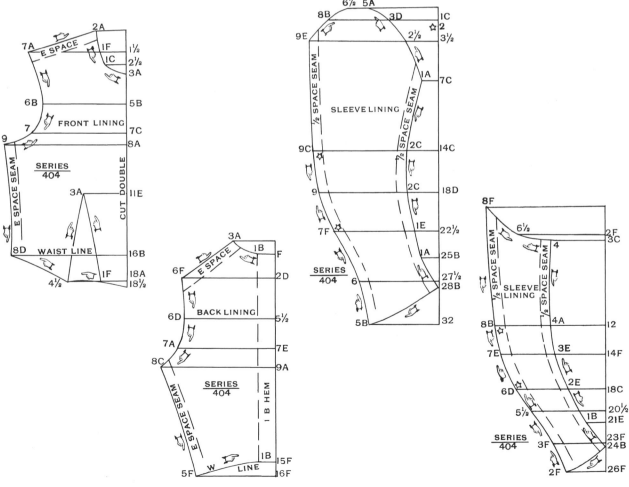

349

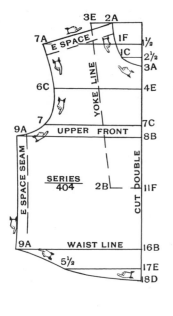

3E 2A
7A E SPACE 1F ½
1C 2½
3A
6C 4E
YOKE LINE
7
UPPER FRONT 7C
9A 8B
CUT DOUBLE
E SPACE SEAM
SERIES
404 2B 11F
9A WAIST LINE 16B
5½ 17E
8D

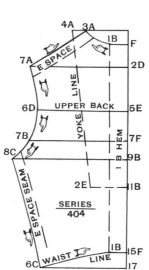

4A 3A
1B F
7A E SPACE
2D
6D UPPER BACK 5E
YOKE LINE
7B 7F
8C 9B
1 B HEM
E SPACE SEAM
2E 1B
SERIES
404
1B
6C WAIST LINE 15F
17

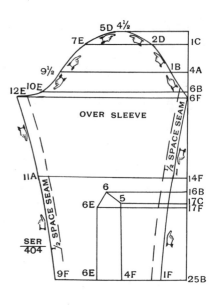

5D 4½
7E 2D 1C
9½ 1B 4A
12E 10E 6B
OVER SLEEVE 6F
½ SPACE SEAM
11A 14F
6 16B
6E 5 17C
½ SPACE SEAM 17F
SER
404
9F 6E 4F 1F 25B

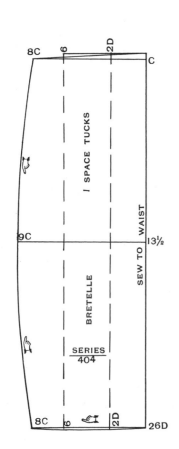

8C 6 2D
C
I SPACE TUCKS
SEW TO WAIST
9C 13½
BRETELLE
SERIES
404
8C 6 2D
26D

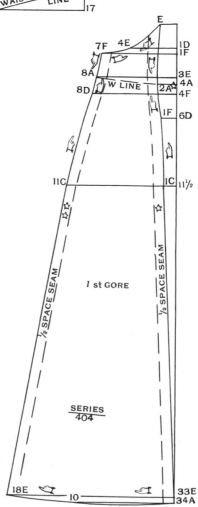

E
7F 4E 1D
1F
8A 3E
4A
8D W LINE 2A
4F
1F 6D
11C 1C 11½
☆ ☆
½ SPACE SEAM
1st GORE
½ SPACE SEAM
SERIES
404
18E 10 33E
34A

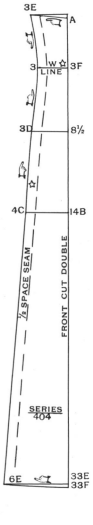

3E
A
3 W LINE 3F
3D 8½
4C 14B
½ SPACE SEAM
FRONT CUT DOUBLE
SERIES
404
6E 33E
33F

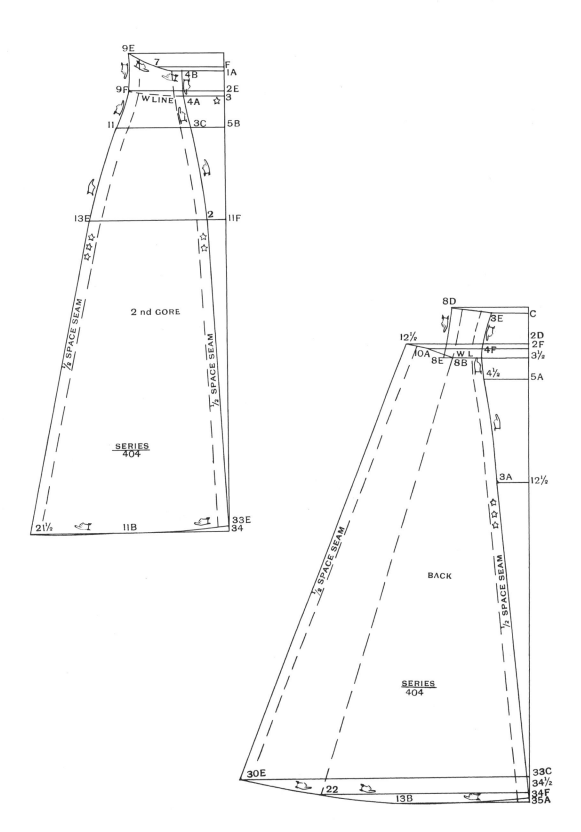

9E
7
F
1A
4B
9F
2E
3
W LINE
4A
11
3C
5B
13E
2
11F

2nd GORE

½ SPACE SEAM
½ SPACE SEAM

SERIES
404

21½
11B
33E
34

8D
3E
C
12½
2D
2F
10A
W L
4F
8E 8B
3½
4½
5A

3A
12½

½ SPACE SEAM
½ SPACE SEAM

BACK

SERIES
404

30E
33C
34½
22
34F
13B
35A

351

A Stylish Street Suit

Six measures are taken for this suit: Bust, length of waist, full length, length of sleeve, around the waist, and length of skirt. It is drafted in 13 pieces: Coat back, front, side back, side front, underarm gore, collar, sleeve (2 pieces), and a 9-gore pleated skirt drafted in 5 pieces.

To Draft. Select bust and length of waist scales for collar and coat back, front, side back, side front, and underarm gore. Draft to waistline. Then subtract length of waist from full length. This will give desired scale for baseline. Use bust scale for all crosslines. For sleeve, use bust and length of sleeve scales. For skirt, use waist and length of skirt scales.

To Make. This coat has one of the new shaped underarm gores. The front seam follows the same lines as the side front. The side back runs into the armhole instead of the shoulder as side front shows.

Join the different parts of coat according to seams and stars. Finish neck with coat collar. Join seams of sleeve, and ease in extra fullness at elbow between stars.

Join skirt according to stars by folding dotted lines to heavy lines. Fold first dotted line on first gore to heavy line on front. Fold second dotted line to heavy line on second gore. Follow these directions throughout the skirt, making seven backward-turning pleats on each side of skirt, and a box pleat where the front and first gore join. Stitch a 1/2-space tuck where the front and first gore join from waist to bottom of skirt. Other pleats are stitched to any desired depth and width.

The material used for this suit is one of the new French diagonal two-toned effects, with velvet collar and jet buttons for trimmings. Material required for medium form, 7 yards 52 inches wide.

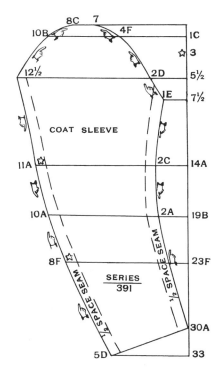

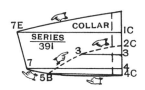

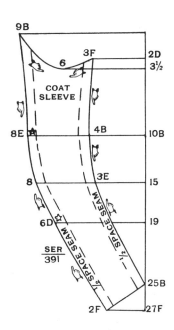

353

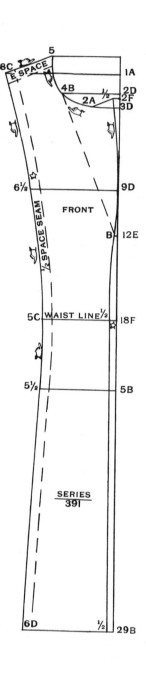

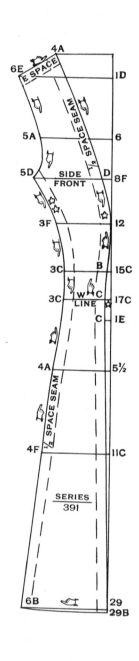

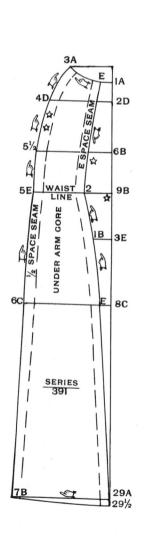

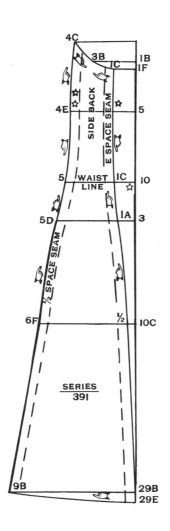

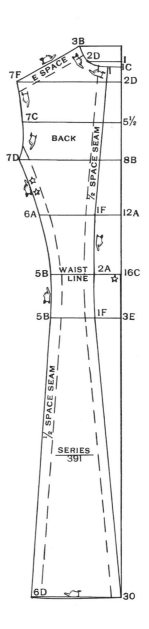

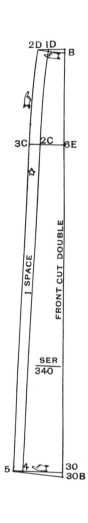

2D 1D   B

3C   2C   6E

I SPACE

FRONT CUT DOUBLE

SER
340

5   4   30
30B

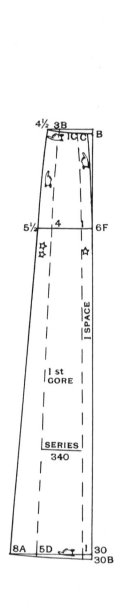

4½ 3B   B
1C C

5½   4   6F

I SPACE

1 st
GORE

SERIES
340

8A   5D   1 30
30B

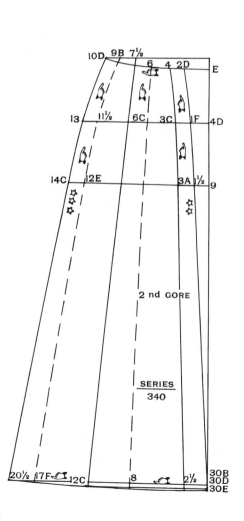

10D 9B 7½
6   4 2D   E

13   11½   6C   3C   1F   4D

14C   12E   3A 1½   9

2 nd GORE

SERIES
340

20½ 17F   12C   8   2½   30B
30D
30E

356

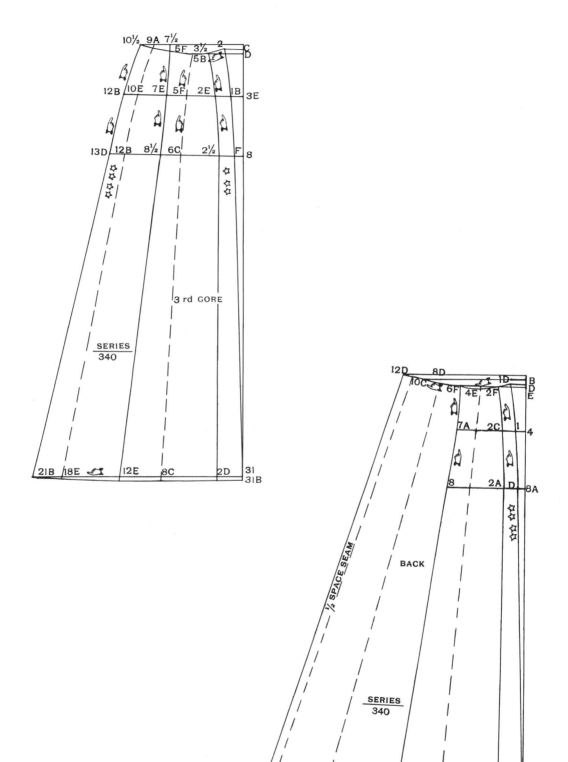

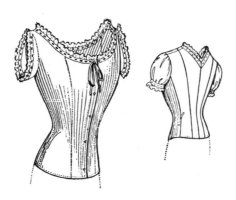

French Corset Cover

Four measures are taken for this waist: Bust, length of waist, around the waist, and length of sleeve. It is drafted in seven pieces: Back, front, side back, side front, underarm gore, small shield, and sleeve puff.

To Draft and Make. Select bust and length of waist scales for all parts of waist except sleeve puff. For sleeve puff, use bust and length of sleeve scales.

To make low neck like illustration, cut out on dotted lines.

This is a good waist for a stout form.

Join the different parts according to seams given. Cut sleeve shield double. Join to armhole with small point at shoulder seam. If small puff is preferred, sew in same as any sleeve puff.

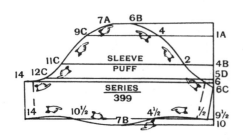

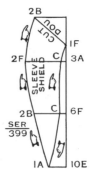

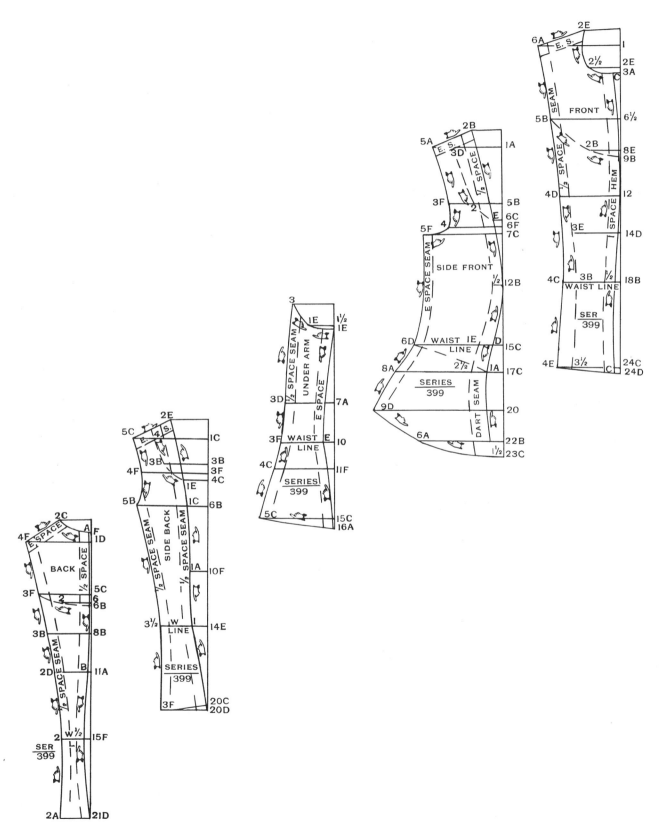

Ladies' Petticoat

Two measures are taken for this skirt: Waist and length. It is drafted in five pieces: Front; first, second, and back gore; and one-fourth of gathered flounce.

The skirt is a seven-gore with habit back, fitting perfectly through the hips. It may be cut away under flounce or left full length as desired.

To Draft and Make. Finish with placket at center back seam. Cut four pieces like flounce and gather to fit skirt. Finish top of skirt with facing or belt.

Heatherbloom required for medium form, 5 yards 36 inches wide with flounce.

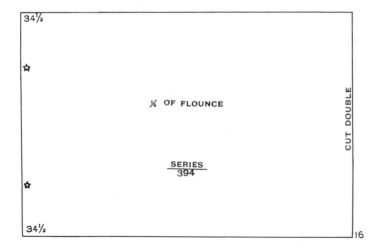

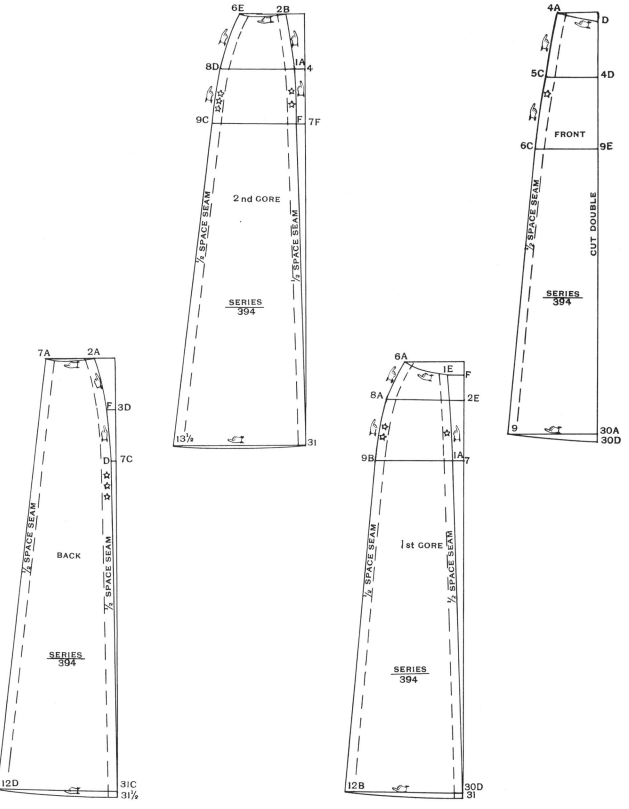

Edited Selections From

The Complete Dressmaker With Simple Directions For Home Millinery

Edited by Clara E. Laughlin

Dressmaking Instructions By Mary I. McIntyre

Originally Published in 1907 By
D. Appleton and Company in New York

From Chapter II
Underwear

How to Make Drawers

Exact measures must be taken in order that the right pattern as to size may be gotten. Decide upon the way you want to make the drawers, whether closed or open, trimmed or plain. Take the measures around the waist, from waist to the bend of the knee, and around the fullest part of the hips.

Open Drawers. Cut the legs of drawers and join them either by machine or with running stitches by hand, having the seam on right side. Turn the legs inside out and hide the raw edges in another seam and sew (by machine or running stitches); this is called a french seam or fell. Face from the top or waist of each leg at the back around to waist at front with a bias band or facing about 1 inch wide.

The legs of the drawers now may be joined to the yoke. This yoke takes the place of a band and is cut double, one for facing. The yoke is turned up on the wrong side about 1/2 inch and basted. It is, of course, the size of the waist desired. The drawers are gathered slightly so that more of the fullness is at the back. The top of the legs of the drawers are lapped about 1/2 inch and basted onto the yoke, with the turned-in edge of yoke and gathers on the right side. The other part of the yoke is turned up 1/2 inch and basted on so that it hides the gathering and raw edges of the yoke and drawer legs. Stitch close to the edge so that one stitching will hold the yoke pieces and drawer legs together.

A drawstring may be placed in a casing made at top of yoke. About 6 or 8 inches from back on each side and 3/4 inch from top make one row of stitching. The space between the top and this stitching will serve as a casing. Fasten the tapes well at the inner end and leave enough to tie at back.

Closed Drawers. Be sure that you have the proper length from the waist to the seat; otherwise the drawers will be very uncomfortable. French seam each leg and hem or trim as you desire. Then make the plackets.

Now you are ready to join the legs. Join the legs at the "crotch" by putting the seam on the right side, and be very particular that the seams meet. Sew with running stitches. Then turn the drawers and sew again with running stitches, thus hiding the first sewing; this makes the french seam.

Gather the front waist part into half the waist measure. The fullness should be placed more to the center, leaving about 2 inches from the placket plain. Gather the top of back of drawers into the other half of waist measure, more of the fullness being placed at the center, leaving about 3 inches almost without gathers at each end of the band.

To put on the band, notch the center of the strip intended for the band. Put this notch to center of drawers. Baste on the gathers. Then turn in the edge about 1/2 inch and baste over gathers. Stitch close to the edge. Turn in the ends of band and overcast very fine. The band is now ready for the buttonholes and buttons.

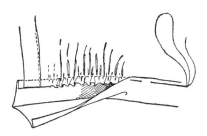

Figure 20. Putting on the band

The Trimmings Used on Drawers, and How to Make Them. To measure a tuck, cut measure on a piece of cardboard twice the width plus

space desired. Fold the tuck carefully by measure. Crease tuck down flat before measuring for next tuck. Baste and stitch or run by hand.

There are two ways of putting in insertion, with a single row of stitching or a double row. If a single row of stitching is wanted as a finish, turn the material back to within 1/16 inch of the needlework. Baste flat on the goods (if tucked, leave the width of a tuck between the last tuck and edge of insertion). Then baste the upper edge, after having folded down the edge, and stitch close to edge.

After stitching, first remove bastings. Then run the scissors carefully between the material and the insertion and cut through the center. Trim away the surplus material. Turn the other edge over like a narrow hem, then hem down. This gives a neat finish and protects the stitching when laundered.

If two rows of stitching are desired, fold the edge to within 1/8 inch of the needlework and proceed as before, making two rows of stitching 1/8 inch apart. Never finish the edges differently on the same garment.

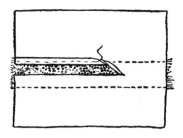

Figure 21. Insertion

To sew edging on the bottom of drawers, make one 1/4-inch tuck with 1/8 space at the bottom. Then turn back the 1/8 inch on the wrong side even with the edge of the tuck and crease center. Gather and stroke the edging. Place the wrong sides together, fastening the centers and at each end. Then baste carefully, being particular that the rows of gathering and the crease come together, and stitch. Now flatten the seam with thumb and finger. Turn tuck down over the seam, as it is best to turn the tuck back while basting on the edging. Baste down and stitch close to the edge.

Petticoats

The gores must be even at the top, any difference in length coming at the bottom. French seam the gores together, and trim off the bottom evenly. Turn up the hem and put in the tucks (in the same way as for drawers). Fit the skirt with darts at top and gather the back gores into waist measure. Make placket by binding with straight strip of material. The placket should be about 12 inches deep. Sew the band on in the same manner as the drawers band.

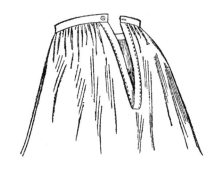

Figure 24. Bound placket

Nightgowns

The body seams are felled or french seamed.

The Yoke. The nightgown may be made with or without a yoke. A very pretty gown is made with a few clusters of tucks in the front and the back plain. It is cut low enough for the head to pass through and so does away with openings. This sort of nightgown usually has a short sleeve. Nightgowns with yokes are measured from the bottom of the yoke to the floor. The yoke is basted to the body of the gown, which has been gathered, wrong sides together, and stitched. Then the seam thus made is turned up on the right side and the front yoke turned in against it, basted close to the edge, and stitched. A yoke may also be joined to the body of the gown with a finishing braid placed over the seam.

The Opening of a Nightgown. Make an opening about 20 inches deep. Baste a facing on the button side about 3/4 inch wide, allowing 1/4 inch seam. Put the right side of facing to the right

side of goods and stitch. Turn both the edges of this seam back on the gown. Turn in the edge of the facing, baste, and stitch close to the edge. For the buttonhole side, make a hem about 1 inch wide. Turn this hem to the wrong side, baste, and stitch close to the edge. Lap the hem over the faced side so that it covers the stitching on the button side. Fasten with a double row of stitching at the bottom of opening.

To Make an Under Waist

Place your pattern on the straight of material and cut around pattern, being careful to crease or trace the waistline and amount allowed at seams. Baste the underarm seams and shoulders together (make all alterations on these seams).

Gather at the waistline to the size of waist. The gathers are usually confined to about 6 inches across the front and about 4 or 5 inches at the back waistline. Run a thread at the top or neck of under waist so that it may be drawn up to fit. Make the armhole comfortable by clipping in the depth wanted; turn under and crease down. Cut out the armhole after the waist is taken off.

The front of waist may be finished in the same way as the nightgown opening. Or the hem on the buttonhole side may be turned on the right side and stitched at each side, making a bow pleat.

Trimming. There are many ways of trimming an under waist. If lace is used, the neatest way is to overhand the insertion, beading, and lace together. Turn a narrow hem on waist and overhand the insertion to the waist. If a band is wanted at the top of waist, put on a bias facing, hemming down a second time. Embroidery beading can be put on with french fell, the stitching coming below the cord of the beading. For featherstitching, fold edge of beading, lay on wrong side of waist, stitch on wrong side, and cover with bias band on right side. If trimmed with a ruffle, lay it on and cover all with a bias band on the right side.

If trimming around the armhole, much depends on material of which waist is made. It may be finished with french hem or facing. If no trimming is used, it is better to face the armhole with a bias band. If trimmed with an embroidery ruffle, the ruffle and facing are basted in with the armhole, right sides together. Then turned on the wrong side of waist and hemmed, care being taken to stretch the bias so that it will not tighten the armhole.

Placing Belt. Measure belt, if of the material, the length, twice the width plus the seams, allowing for lap in front. Fold the edges to the center; place the center of belt to center of waist. Arrange the gathers in right place, making it smooth under the arm. Baste along the top and bottom of edges and stitch. If drawn up around waist, place straight beading at waistline and stitch top and bottom.

From Chapter VII
Skirts

The Lining Skirt

To the foundation or lining skirt much attention should be given. Experience has taught me that the best results come from the use of a five- or seven-gored pattern for this purpose.

How to Cut a Five-Gored Skirt. The measures must be accurately taken. These are:

Waist–tight.

Front–from waistline at center to the floor.

Side–from waistline to floor over fullest part of hip.

Back–from center at waistline to floor.

Around hip at fullest part–taken easily.

If the pattern is too long, fold it across through the middle in a tuck to the required length. If the reverse is the case, slit the pattern across, about in the middle, and insert a piece wide enough to make the length desired. The reason for putting in or taking out a piece in the middle, is that the shape is not interfered with at the bottom.

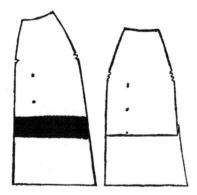

Figure 29. Making skirt pattern longer or shorter

The best cotton material for skirt lining I have found to be percaline, which sells from 12 1/2 cents per yard to 35 cents per yard. This last is very fine and silky. A very substantial and satisfactory quality can be had for 25 cents per yard.

To cut a five-gored skirt place the lining on the cutting table. If there is no fold in material make one by putting both selvages together and creasing the length of skirt on the fold thus made. Now place the front gore, which is always a straight line, on the fold. Pin the pattern on securely along the edges and once or twice through the gore so that it will not move. Allow as much below the pattern as is needed for a hem. About 2 inches makes a sufficiently deep hem. Or if a ruffle is to be placed on the bottom of the skirt, subtract the depth of ruffle less 1 inch from the length of skirt. This inch will give you space on which to sew the ruffle. This amount must be taken from all the gores. Cut out the gore, allowing about 3/4 inch for seams.

To cut the side gores place the straight side of the pattern to the selvage of the lining, with the broadest part at the cut end. Cut the larger gore first and invert the second gores and cut them from the same width. Short skirts should flare less in proportion to the size of hips than long skirts. The front breadth of skirts for large figures should be gored less than for medium-sized figures and should be broader at the hip line. This allows for the extra width, which is needed more for the front than at the hip, and prevents the skirt from drawing up in front.

To Baste the Skirt. Place the bias edge or side of front gore to the straight side of second gore and baste with uneven basting from the top to the bottom. Hold them so that the bias side will not be stretched. Repeat the same process with the second and third gores. Join the back seam. Be sure to have the top of gores even, letting any unevenness come at the bottom.

To Fit the Skirt. Put the skirt on the person wrong side out and pin the back seam together at the hip line. Be sure that the center fold of the skirt in front is pinned securely at the top to the under-clothing, so that the skirt will not be drawn more to one side than it is on the other. Make all fittings on the seams of the skirt. Keep the grain or woof thread even around the hips, and alter or fit from the hips to the waist. Trace exactly where the back seams come together, as the inverted pleat will be turned and folded back to meet at the same line.

Take the skirt off and baste the alterations. Stitch by machine and pink out the edges, then press the seams open.

The skirt lining is now ready for the last fitting. Try the skirt on again. Place a belt tape around the waistline and pin the skirt to it, arranging the inverted pleat at the back. Decide about the length of the skirt and find out how many inches from the floor it will measure. Take a ruler or yardstick. Place the end on the floor or a table and move it around the skirt, marking the number of inches from the floor as decided upon. This will give an even line when turned up. The longer the skirt is the more fullness there is at the bottom. Consequently when the hem is turned up you will find it necessary to fit the fullness into little pleats. Distribute these pleats so that they will be as nearly perpendicular as possible. Measure with a gauge the depth of hem plus 1/2 inch to turn in, and baste the hem down. Stitch close to the edge.

Finish the back seam with a placket (as for a petticoat). Turn over the belting and stitch close to the edge on right side.

The Pleated Skirt

Of the many styles in skirts the pleated skirt is undoubtedly the most popular.

The pattern from which the lining skirt was made may be used for a guide in making a pleated skirt. Once the hip line is fitted properly the measure may be divided into as many parts as there are to be pleats in the skirt. For instance, if sixteen, divide the hip measure into sixteen parts. Cut each of the sections or parts twice as wide at the bottom as they are at the top. The center front of the skirt will be placed on the fold of material. The pleats run from the center toward the back, forming a box pleat for the center front, taking the first two of the sixteen sections or gores. Mark the center of the other fourteen parts and trace with long basting stitches. Join all the parts together with 3/4-inch seams. Do not press the seams open.

Now lay the pleats evenly at the hip line, fitting them into the waist measure. Place belt on waistline and pin pleats onto it. Baste the pleats close to the edges or in as far as is desired. For slight figures the pleat may be stitched in as far as 1 inch, as it tends to make one look larger.

Join the back seam, press open, and turn skirt up as lining was turned, with the ruler or measure from the floor. Bind the seams inside and make the placket. Great care should be taken when putting the hooks and eyes on a placket. The underside of the placket for this skirt should have a fly stitched on, so that there is no chance for the skirt to spread apart and show the lining or petticoat.

Another Style of Pleated Skirt

A gored skirt with a pleat at each seam may be made very easily in this way. After the skirt pattern has been secured with the proper hip measure the skirt may be cut in the regular way, allowing as much on each gore as would make a pleat the depth desired plus a 1-inch seam. Baste the skirt together at the original gore marks, leaving the amount of goods for tuck and seam on the inside. Place the skirt on the person to be fitted. Make the alterations by pinning the seam over or letting it out where it is necessary. Be sure the material for pleat and seam is folded to the side, back, or front, to which you wish the pleat to face.

Remove the skirt from the person. Baste a line down the skirt as far in from the gore line obtained in the fitting, and to the depth you desire. Join the seam on the wrong side to the bottom of the skirt. Place the belt on the skirt, and finish placket and bottom of skirt in the usual way. Remove the bastings and press the skirt. Any number of pleats in the skirt may be obtained in this way.

A Slot-Seam Skirt

A slot seam has the appearance of two inverted pleats. To make a slot-seamed skirt, the gores should be cut with an allowance of material for a pleat, and the edges of the gores turned to the inside of the skirt. Another piece of material, the length of the skirt gores on both sides, is placed under the edges of the gores to form a rest or foundation for the edges to be stitched to. The under piece is cut narrow at the top and sufficiently wide at the bottom to hold the pleat and to allow for a flare when the person is walking.

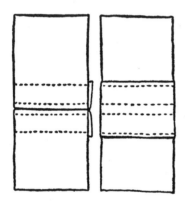

Figure 30. Slot seam, right and wrong sides

A Circular Skirt

From its name one might get the idea that such a skirt is cut in a perfect circle. This is not the case, as a perfect circle would throw a great amount of fullness at the bottom of the skirt. When a skirt is cut perfectly circular, the flutes or ripples fall regularly and there is the same amount of fullness at the front as there is at any other point. We can easily see how very lacking in grace such a skirt would be. To obviate this seams may be made at the center of the front and back. Open the fold of material and lay it flat on the cutting table. Place the front line of the pattern on a line which will extend 6 inches in from the true bias. Try to place the crease or fold of the material as near as possible over the fullest part of the hip. This will prevent much of the stretching

which happens to every bias skirt. The back seam will also fall a little off the true bias. This is also an advantage, as it prevents the back seam from dropping as much as a true bias would do.

When a circular skirt is cut and stitched it should be placed on a temporary belt tape and hung in the closet for three or four days (a week if possible) to allow the bias to sag. When striped, checked, or plaid materials are cut in this style, the stripes should be placed in such a manner that the most prominent line will form a long V. It takes quite a little planning to get similar lines or checks on both sides; but they must be worked out until the result is obtained.

Sometimes the circular skirt is made of very wide material. In that case it is often cut without a seam in the front. The straight line of the pattern is placed on the fold of the material. If the material is not wide enough piece it by joining selvage to selvage. Skirts which are known as "sunburst skirts" are made from the circular patterns seamed up front and back and pleated by a machine made purposely for them.

Cutting a Bias

The material used for a facing or binding on curved edges, folds, cords, and various other fancy trimmings, is cut on a true bias. Bias material is often preferred in facing a straight edge because it makes a smoother lining than a straight strip of cloth. Ruffles are almost always cut on the bias.

Tailor's Tacking

Fold the tucks or pleats along the tacking and baste them the desired width. In altering box-pleated skirts, the size of the box pleat itself must not be changed. But the alteration must be at the seam under the box pleat if greater width at the hip is necessary. If less width is desired lap each side of the pleat over until the right size is obtained. Do not finish the seams of a skirt as a french seam. Either bind, overcast, or pink them. A french seam is more suitable for underwear or shirtwaists.

From Chapter VIII
Making a Waist

Cutting the Lining

The first essential is a good waist pattern. Be sure your pattern is your proper size; this may be determined by the bust measure. Place cotton lining material on the cross of the goods; that is, with the selvage toward you, flat on the table. Never raise it with your hand from that position until the whole pattern is pinned to it. Place the bottom of lining at the end of the goods. Arrange all the portions economically, but in such a manner that the waistlines run evenly with the thread of material. Do not strain the pattern out of the position which this thread will determine. Pin each piece of the pattern securely, tracing at the edge of the pattern.

On the front of the waist about 2 inches is allowed for the hooks and eyes. This extra material forms a piece to turn back as a finish for the sewing on of the hooks and eyes. Allow about 1 inch extra on the underarm seams, as the alterations in fitting may have to be made there. It is also a good plan to allow 1-inch seams at the shoulders. Three-quarters of an inch is a good margin for seams on the other portions. It is much better to trim off the seams a little after the waist is fitted than to be forced to piece them or to make new ones. Allow a good seam at the neck and around the armhole. Even if these are tight they may be cut away after the proper size of armhole is determined.

In joining the portions, be sure that the waistlines are even. Pin these along the traced lines and baste from the waistline up and down with small, even basting. Do not stretch or strain any of the portions in order to make them meet, as any discrepancy should be either at the neck or armhole, and if a seam has been allowed there the lining has been protected. However, there should be no serious discrepancy.

Fitting the Lining

Put the lining on the person with the seams on the outside, pinning it firmly at the chest and waistline, then along the traced lines of the fronts, holding them together. Now look at the back of the waist. If it is too long the shoulders will need taking up. If the waist wrinkles across the back a dart across the waist at the shoulder blades makes the back fit smoothly.

Try to avoid taking in the back seam, as it often pulls the other forms out of place and away from the armhole, making the armhole too large at the back. The rounding form would then have to be taken in also. The back having cross dart does away with these alterations, except in some cases where the figure is very hollow at the back armseye. Then it is necessary to take in the round form.

Pinch in the portions at the waistline and wherever it is necessary. If the front armseye or armhole is too large pull the fullness forward, so that the grain of the front of the waist under the arm at the armhole is straight. Then smooth down from the shoulder seam over the shoulder bone until the waist feels comfortable; lay it in little pleats or tucks. If the front seam appears too long, smooth down from the neck any extra fullness and pinch it into a little dart at the hollow of the bust; be careful not to draw the waist down too much.

Ask the person being fitted if the waist is comfortable. This will help you very much, as one cannot always judge from the appearance whether it is comfortable or not. Mark the waistline, armhole, and neck with a row of pins, also make a mark with crossed pins where the front seam of the sleeve should be placed. Always fit both sides of the lining.

Remove the waist carefully after the pins have been securely fastened, as the loss of a pin from the fitted waist sometimes causes a deal of trouble. Mark both sides of the waist front with pins, before the impression made by the pins used in fitting is lost. Trace all the alterations with colored cotton. Reverse all the seams, making sure that the waist is even at the waistline, and the portions as even as possible. As figures are not always the same on both sides, it naturally follows that the waist will not be exactly the same on each side.

Finishing the Lining

After the waist is carefully stitched, remove the bastings. Notch the seams at the waistline, also 1 1/2 inches above and below the waistline, so that the waist may not be tightened, but left free to curve at the proper places. Crease the seams open with your finger and place them over some round surface. Go over the seam with the iron flat on it, so that it will lie flat to the waist. The seams may be either overcast, bound, or pinked. This is a matter of choice, but I have always found that a waist with overcast or pinked seams gives more freedom.

(For the boning of the waist, see Featherbone.)

When the featherbone is stretched in and the waist turned back it is ready for the hooks and eyes. The hooks are set in on a waist about 1/8 inch, and the eyes far enough outside the line to allow the hook to slip in easily. Fasten hooks and eyes strongly; sometimes it is well to sew them on with a buttonhole stitch.

Featherbone

Since the fashion demands a tight-fitting lining, the necessity of a well-boned waist is once more evident. We have tried many kinds of stays, but there is yet to be found anything that will secure a more firm and well-shaped waist than the Warren featherbone. Featherbone has this advantage over whalebone or any of the substitutes: it may be sewn thoroughly and easily either by hand or machine. It is put up in boxes in a nice silk or cotton casing ready for use. It is stitched fast to the seams all the way, and so becomes part of the waist and does not pull out, and the waist always retains its shape. The

bones in a waist must be sprung. To do this with featherbone is simply to stretch the goods so that there is more length of bone than seam length. This curves the waist toward the figure. Use sewing silk, a very long stitch, and a medium-sized needle. The seams must be carefully pressed and finished.

There are various kinds of featherbone, each one intended to meet a long-felt want, such as the collar bone which holds the collar upright.

Featherbone crinolette is placed in the hem of skirts or any place on a gown which needs holding out without apparent stiffening. If the effect of a small waist be desired, the shoulders and upper sleeves must be broader. Caps made somewhat like a small dress shield bound on the edge with featherbone tape are one way of obtaining a broad effect. A framework around the top of the arm, of two round stripes and two vertical stripes of wide featherbone tapes, will make a good foundation on which to tack a draped sleeve. It is light and will not crush into wads, as other materials, such as crinoline or tarlatan, have a tendency to do.

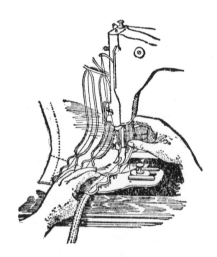

Figure 32. Darts

Darts. Place the waist wrong side up on the machine. Begin by boning the first dart. Lay the flatly pressed-open seam on top of the bone and boning attachment so that the bone is right in the center of the seam. Put the needle down about 1 inch below the top of dart, close to the seam stitching, crowd the goods (using the forefinger of each hand) up to the needle, lower the presser foot, and cut, being sure the fullness starts right with the first stitch or from the needle. This is an important point, as it prevents the bone from showing at the top, or causing a little pleat above the top of the dart. Continue crowding to within 1 inch of the waistline, following the machine stitching very closely, but never in the same stitching. Then hold the seam very firm to the bottom of a short waist. Bone both darts alike.

Finishing Bones at Top. You have allowed on each seam 1 inch of bone to extend beyond the needle. First tie the thread so that the stitching cannot rip. Rip the center row of stitching out of the extended bone. Slip the casing off and cut the bone off 1/2 inch, rounding the corners. Then turn the casing loosely over end of bone and fasten to bone and not to seam of waist, thus leaving 1/2 inch of bone loose at top of each seam.

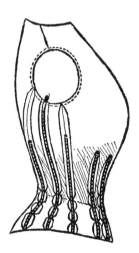

Figure 33. Finishing bones at top

To Bone a Collar. Four to six bones are used, as best suits the wearer. Two bones are tacked in about 3/4 inch from center front, two more at a point just back of the ear when adjusted, and one at each end, the bones back of the ear being cut slightly longer than the front bones. Ribbon-covered collar bone may be used without additional covering.

The Sleeves

Cut the sleeves with generous seams. It is very difficult to take the exact measures of an arm, as the muscles vary greatly. Some are much larger in the lower muscle, and some have larger upper muscles, so it is well to cut a sleeve with the back seam allowance at least 1 inch.

To baste the sleeve, place the upper sleeve piece flat on the table with the back seam nearest you. Take the undersleeve piece and place the traced seam on the seam of the upper sleeve. They should fit exactly. If they do not, find the bend or break of the arm of both pieces and place them together. Pin along the traced line. Now smooth both of the pieces until they are perfectly flat, and pin together at top and bottom. Fold the back edge of the upper sleeve over to the under piece, beginning at the top and placing the edges together. Pin the traced lines so that the edges will stand up from the table to within 1 inch of the elbow mark. Now begin to pin the lower pieces together the same as the top, to within 1 inch of the elbow mark. This will leave some fullness in the upper piece. Gather this fullness into the space which is free on the undersleeve, distribute the gathers evenly, and pin together. Baste with small, even basting.

Pull the sleeve up on the arm so that it fits well into the armhole. Pin the front seam to the cross pins on the waist. At the place where the back-sleeve seam meets the waist, turn in the top of the sleeve in little puckers and pin it to the waist around the armhole line; this line is determined by fashion.

How to Sew Hooks and Eyes on a Waist

Mark with a tracing of colored thread the front line of the waist marked by the pins in the fitting. Be sure that the waist is even. Do this by pinning the back seam of waist together, open the shoulder seams, and place one side of the waist flat on the

other. Unless there is a marked defect in the figure of the person, which you would have noticed in the fitting, the front tracings should meet. The next step is to place a stay of cambric, taffeta, or crinoline about 1 1/2 inches wide over the tracing on the inner side, so that half of the staying piece is on either side of the tracing mark. On the right or hook side turn the lining back on the wrong side of the waist, so that the fold is 1/8 inch farther out than the tracing line. Baste a line about 3/8 inch in on the waist, through the stay and piece, which has been turned over and stitched by machine from the neck to the bottom of the waist. On the left or eye side of the waist repeat the same operation, unless the fold is made from the traced line exactly.

The hooks should be placed about 1 1/8 inches apart. They should be held straight on the waist, with the end or bill exactly at the traced front, or back, line, as the same rule applies to waists opened in the back. Hooks must be sewn firmly with four stitches through each little ring, and three or four strong stitches on the bill; it is well to finish with buttonhole stitches. Coarse cotton, No. 40, or buttonhole twist, should be used to sew on hooks and eyes. The eyes must be placed on the edge of the waist front so that they extend sufficiently for the hooks to slip into them. They must be sewn with three or four strong stitches in each ring, and two or three stitches over each side of the eye. Hooks and eyes may be sewn through to the outside of waist, if that part can be hidden by the trimming; in any case they must be sewn through the staying piece.

Before the hooks and eyes are sewn on, a piece of uncovered featherbone should be slipped into the casing made by the stitching on the waist fronts, about 5 inches above and to the end of the waist below the waistline. The hooks and eyes should be sewn through this bone. The piece of lining turned back from the front tracing forming the stay or foundation through which the hooks and eyes were sewn, may be turned back over the hooks and eyes and form the facing or finish. This facing should be hemmed at the outer edge. If this piece of material is not wide enough to cover the hooks and eyes, a bias piece may be turned in and hemmed on both sides to the lining to cover the stitches used in sewing the hooks and eyes. This bias facing must extend the length of the waist.

The Collar

To fit a collar, cut a piece of crinoline on the bias about the height of the person's neck plus 1 inch. Turn both the edges over about 1/2 inch on the outer side. Shape the lower edge by stretching it with the fingers to a slight curve. Place the band on the neck of the waist and pin it there so that it fits comfortably. If this band be too high, turn the upper edge over to the proper height. If it stands out from the neck at the center front, take a little dart in it so that it fits snugly to the throat. Mark the back where the band meets with pins.

Draping the Waist

The waist is now ready to drape; that is, to apply the outside material to the waist lining. The most approved way to do this is to place the lining on a bust form.

The design of the waist should be definitely planned. If the material is a short pattern and requires much planning to obtain the design decided upon, it is well to cut a rough pattern of paper on the bust form. If you are not limited in material, the planning may be done by pinning it to the lining at once.

A Plain Draped Waist

Measure the lengths desired. For the front of a 36-inch waist one length of double-width material 24 inches in length; for the back, half a width 20 inches long, will be sufficient. Fold the length for the back so that the selvage and cut edge meet, to get the center. Trace the center with a colored cotton thread. Place the center tracing on the center seam of the waist lining, allowing the material 1 inch higher than the lining at the neck, so that it will not fall short at the point of shoulder at the neckline. Pin the material securely with pins about 3 inches apart down the center line, drawing it with the fingers to the waistline.

Pin the material across the back at the armhole line in such a way that the grain or woof threads run straight across, and are not drawn or strained out of their proper position. Pin all around the shoulders and armhole, smoothing all the superfluous fullness away toward the neck and armhole. Now smooth the material down along the underarm seam, and pin. Place the pins, if possible, in a horizontal position. This suggestion applies to the pinning on of any drapery. You will find that if you draw down the material on the grain to waistline you will have some fullness between the center and the underarm seam. This fullness is usually laid in little pleats or gathers. Pin all the material securely at the waistline.

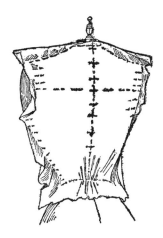

Figure 34. Draped waist back

The front of a plain waist is usually finished at the center front with a box pleat covering the opening, or a vest set in. If a vest is placed in a dress, it is done before the waist fronts are draped. Cut the double width through the fold, making one piece for each side. If a box pleat is to be the finish for the front opening, fold back the selvage edge on the wrong side. Fold the right side into a tuck which will hide the selvage edge, and stitch. Then stitch the other side the same distance from the edge, forming the box pleat. This, of course, will be placed at the hook side of the waist. The edge of the eye side of the waist is turned back on the wrong side about half the width of the pleat on the hook side, and stitched on the selvage.

Place the material on the front of the waist, always draping the right side first, with a generous seam on the shoulder. That is, raise it about 1 inch at the highest point above the neckline. Smooth it over the front of waist to the armhole, having the straight thread running across. Pin it securely across the chest, down the front, and around the armhole.

The draping of the remainder of the front depends on the fashion of the waist, and the prevailing mode in drapery. Sometimes fashion demands that all waists shall have a blouse or puff at the front of the waist. At other times the material is drawn down rather snugly to the waist belt. If a blouse or puff is desired, the material is raised at the center front into a puff or pouch and pinned securely at the waistline. Then the material is smoothed on a sort of bias which clings to the round of the form from the front armhole to the waistline and throws the necessary fullness to the puff or blouse. This fullness is gathered or pleated into the space from the center front to the front dart, and pinned securely. The material is pinned a little in front of the underarm seam, so that it may be placed in the seam or slip stitched over the back, which will have been sewn securely to the bone of the underarm seam.

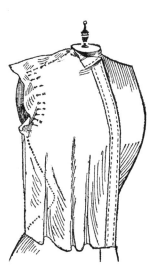

Figure 35. Draped waist front

Now remove the waist from the bust form. Baste the material securely where it has been pinned. (Be very careful not to remove the pins before basting.) Pin the waist together at the waistline and around the neck and armhole, so that each seam meets the corresponding one and the waist is even. Now pin the bottom of waist below the waistline, and trim it off to the desired length and shape. Do not cut it too short, as an allowance for turning the edge over the bones on the inside must be made. Cut the bones to the exact length of the waist.

Baste the edge, which will be about 1/2 inch wide, up on the inside of the waist; be sure that there is an even line for the bottom of waist. Cut a bias strip of the lining about 1 1/2 inches wide to face the waist. This facing may be sewn on the waist by placing the bias strip smoothly on the bottom and basting it through the middle of the strip. Then turn in both the edges and hem. The hemming stitch must not be caught through on the right side.

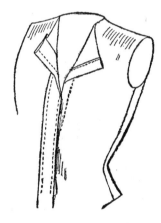

Figure 36. Draped waist taken from bust form

Another way of facing the waist is to sew the bias strip, with right side toward the turned-up edge of the waist, with running stitches. Then turn the facing up and turn in the edge to the lining and hem it onto the lining. Be very careful to begin the sewing of all facings with a couple of stitches to secure it, and to fasten with a firm stitch or two and a buttonhole stitch. The hemming stitches should be dressmaker's hemming stitches, and not the tiny stitches used in plain sewing. A dressmaker's hemming stitch is larger and more of a slide stitch, and when well fastened looks better and is just as reliable.

A belt tape is now placed in the waist to hold it down firmly on the body. This belt is measured to the waistline tightly, and fastened with a hook and eye, or belt buckle, such as is used on men's vests. The belt is secured to the three back seams of the waist, about 1/4 inch above the waistline. It is caught to the bones by cross stitches.

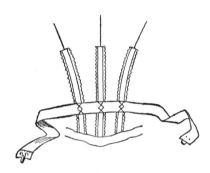

Figure 37. Belt tape

Draping the Sleeves

Sleeves are made in various ways. For a plain waist we will take a plain two-piece sleeve with fullness at the top of the upper sleeve, somewhat on the plan of a leg-of-mutton sleeve. The material for the undersleeve piece is cut exactly like the lining, but the upper sleeve has the number of inches desired added to the width and height from the elbow up to the top. This fullness on the width may be obtained by laying a tuck through the center from elbow up and adding a sufficient number of inches to the height to make a good shape.

The outside material is basted to the pieces of lining and put together in exactly the same way as was the lining. The sleeve is turned up to the required length and faced in the same way as was the bottom of the waist. It is then gathered at the top, the lining and outer material separately. The usual guide for the beginning of the gathers is about 4 inches from the front seam of the sleeve, and according to fullness from 4 to 5 inches from the back seam of sleeve. The lining gathers correspond to

the outside in extent, but are, of course, not so full. The lining and material are basted together. The gathering strings are fastened by drawing them up to desired space and then fastening them around a pin placed perpendicularly in the material.

The sleeve is now ready to baste into the waist. The front seam of the sleeve is placed exactly at the mark in the armhole, which is generally from 2 to 2 1/2 inches from the underarm seam toward the front. Pin the sleeve into the waist, holding the inside of sleeve toward you, so that the sleeve may be stretched into the waist bust from the front where the fullness begins, around to the back fullness, and adjust the gathers so that they will be at the top of the shoulder.

When the sleeve is basted in try it on the person. Make any alterations necessary, rectify, and stitch in by machine. Trim off the armhole seam and overcast the edges with a firm but loose stitch.

The Belt or Girdle

Waists usually have some sort of decoration for a finish a little below the waistline; this is called a belt or girdle. A girdle may be made of taffeta or satin, or, in fact, of any material which will lie in graceful folds around the figure. Another fashion for finishing the bottom of a waist is to shape a bias band to the shape of the waist, line it with crinoline, and stitch in rows about the width of the machine foot apart.

For a high girdle to be folded irregularly, one which reaches from 3 to 5 inches above the waistline, a true bias from 9 to 10 inches is necessary. The bias is drawn very snugly at the waistline and allowed to flare above and below, according to the curve of the figure. The material is then tacked onto the waist from the top to bottom on the bones of the waist. If the girdle is to close in front the ends should be folded in and sewn to the front waist bones, and the edge trimmed with little buttons. Or a small ruching may be placed over it to hide the opening. If the girdle is to be finished at the side, about 3 inches from the center is the proper distance where it should lap. When the girdle fastens in the last-named fashion, there should be no

extra material under it, as otherwise it does not allow the lap to lie flat on the waist.

Hooks should be placed on the lap side of the girdle sufficiently close together to hold the belt in place, and loops, either of metal or silk, placed in a corresponding position on the side over which it laps. The hooks should be sewn in from the edge of the lap about 1/4 inch and covered, save for the bill of the hook, with a piece of prussian binding or silk.

Trimming Waists

Many and varied are the fashions of trimming waists. Waists may be trimmed by making the designs on the pieces intended for the drapery, such as tucks put in in designs and insertions of lace set in between and across in any fashion the fancy dictates. Then there is the pleat which may run either vertically or around the waist. Shirring also forms a most attractive trimming. The fashion books will suggest many ideas, and are of great assistance in this way. Gimps, braids, medallions, are also very much used. Lace also, in its many designs, may be cut apart and readjusted in a thousand ways. Pretty little ruchings are made by shirring pieces of silk, chiffon, or net; these when applied to the waist make it very attractive. Hand embroidery is just now very fashionable for collars, cuffs, yokes, etc. Roses and flowers are made of silk chiffon and velvet and applied to the different parts of a gown.

All waists of net, chiffon, or any transparent material, should be interlined or veiled with mousseline de soie, as it softens the effect and hides all seams in the lining. When a transparent effect is desired for a yoke, a double layer of mousseline should be placed over the lining with seams on the shoulders. This must come below the line intended for the lace, or whatever material is used for the yoke proper, as seams and sewing are liable to pull the mousseline out of its place. Therefore it is well to be protected by 1 inch or so in reserve. Leave a good margin at the neckline as that also works away.

The material for the yoke must also be stretched over the mousseline without a seam on the shoulder, necessitating the finishing of the shoul-

Making a Waist

der seam first. This should be done by either turning the mousseline in with the lining shoulder seam, or making a plain fell of this seam. In any case, it must be a very small but secure seam.

The collar for such a yoke must also be transparent. It is made of double mousseline, boned, and is placed on the mousseline on the neckline and sewn there. The lace of the yoke is joined to the collar lace by applying one to the other. This does away with the harsh line of the collar joining the waist.

When the yoke and collar are secure, the waist lining may be cut out to the depth desired, and finished with a piece of seam binding sewn over it, or simply hemmed. The hooks and loops are placed on the yoke in the same manner as on the waist.

From Chapter IX
Lingerie Waists and Shirtwaists

Lingerie Waists

The lingerie waist is unquestionably the most popular waist of the day. The taffeta, crepe de chine, and various other silks so fashionable awhile ago are scarcely ever seen now. The lingerie waist speaks for itself. It can be made in so many attractive fashions, of such a variety of thin materials, and after laundering looks as fresh as ever, that it fills a need long felt. The lingerie waists are most attractive when buttoned in the back. Fine persian lawn, organdy, handkerchief linen, or other sheer materials, when trimmed with lace insertion, formed into designs or motifs, are very attractive. In fact, rows of insertions and tucks are very pretty, or allover tucking may also be made up in these materials.

A fine under waist should also be worn with a lingerie waist, and should be quite elaborate with lace and insertions or handwork. White ribbons are in better taste than colored ones, when run in the beading of the under waist.

When the figure is slight, ruffles of silk or muslin should be placed in the waist where they are needed: around the armhole, and across the front of the waist at the bust line. Usually three bias pieces are cut about 4 inches wide, and are sewed on the inside of waist at the bust line, one over the other, lapping about 1 inch. The edges of these ruffles may be pinked or hemmed. Pads are also made of cotton batting and hair, but both of these have proved to be so very uncomfortable that the idea of the ruffles in their stead has been hailed with delight. When the waist is taken off, these ruffles may be shaken out and aired, thus making the wearing of this kind of padding unharmful.

Sometimes when a low corset is worn, it is necessary to wear a little pad of tiny ruffles of muslin or silk in the front of corset at the hollow of the bust. This little pad consists of a number of little ruffles sewn to a heart-shaped piece of muslin or silk, and is slipped into the corset, point downward.

Shirtwaists

A good foundation pattern is absolutely necessary to the making of a well-fitting, good-looking shirtwaist. The plain, tailored shirtwaist is planned very much like a man's negligee shirt. Its seams are finished in the same way, and the collar and cuffs are of the same style.

To make a plain shirtwaist, cut two lengths for the front and one for the back. On the piece intended for the right side, make a box pleat from 1 1/2 to 2 1/2 inches wide, in the same manner as suggested for plain draped waists. Turn back the piece for the left side about 1 inch, and stitch like a hem. If one wishes to have pleats or tucks, they should be put in before the pattern is laid on and the waist cut out.

Place the straight edge of the pattern on the center of the box pleat in a straight line from the neckband to a point 4 inches below. Swing the edge of the material out from the edge of the pattern until the distance at the waistline is about 3 inches from the edge of the pattern to the edge of the material. For the back of the shirtwaist, lay the straight of the pattern to the center of the piece of material intended for the back, and cut out.

Join the shoulders and underarm seams, having the seams on the outside. Fit the waist with the seams in this position, as the alterations can be made and the seams stitched without reversing them. The edges are then cut so that one edge may be felled; that is, turned in over the other and stitched flat.

The fullness at the waistline of the back of the shirtwaist is gathered with two rows of sewing, 1/2

inch apart, into a space of about 4 inches. This will bring the width of the back at the waistline to about 9 inches from underarm seam to underarm seam. These proportions are intended for figures not over 27 inches waist measure. One's own judgment must be used in arranging the gathers for larger figures. A band of the material, cut on the straight, 1 inch wide, having the edges turned in all around 1/4 inch, should be stitched on the upper and lower edges to the waist, so as to cover the gathers. A tape is slipped into this casing at the ends. The tapes, when tied, serve to hold in the blouse or fullness of the front of the waist.

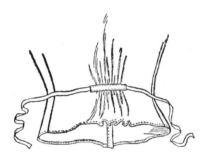

Figure 38. Gathers in back of shirtwaist

The collar-band pattern is placed on the material with the center of back on the straight fold of goods. It is cut with an allowance of 1/4 inch for turnings on both edges. Two of these bands must be cut, one for the foundation, and the other for the facing. The band intended for the foundation is placed on the inside of the neck of the waist, with the turned-in edge toward the waist. The band intended for the facing, or outside band, is placed with the edges turned in toward the foundation so that they meet exactly, then stitched close to the edge by machine.

The sleeves are cut with the center of the pattern to the center of the piece of material. They are then french seamed. An opening is made for a placket about 4 inches up from the bottom, into the sleeve, and about 4 inches from the front seam on the underside.

A shirt-sleeve placket is usually made in a tailored shirtwaist. A straight strip of material, 1 inch

longer than the placket opening, is sewn to the top or lap edge of the opening by placing the right side of the straight strip to the wrong side of the upper edge of the opening, both meeting evenly. The strip is then turned over on the outer side of the sleeve and basted to it; in this way the seam just made is hidden. The other edge of the strip or facing is turned in about 1/4 inch and basted flat to the sleeve. The extra inch is formed into a point at the top of the facing, for a finish. This point is basted close to the edge, flat to the sleeve.

The under or fly side of the placket is made by applying a straight piece of material and sewing it to the edge, with the seam to the wrong side of the sleeve. This strip is cut about 1 1/4 inches wide and 1/2 inch longer than the opening. After the seam is made, fold the strip of material to the inside of the sleeve. Turn in the edge, baste it back to the seam, and stitch. Turn in the edges of the top of this little fly, and catch the upper and undersides of the placket by making two rows of stitching across the facing at the top of the opening.

Figure 39. Shirtwaist sleeve placket

The sleeve is finished at the hand by a band or cuff. This band measures, for a normal wrist, 8 inches long and 2 1/2 inches wide. It is cut on the straight of the material, and must be of three thicknesses. That is, there must be an interlining of the same material or of "Indian Head," a kind of material like duck, which helps to stiffen the cuffs.

The waist is finished at the bottom by a hem. Usually the waist is fastened in front and at the cuffs by buttons and buttonholes.

From Chapter X
Coats and Wraps for Women and Children

To obtain the most satisfactory results, an all-wool material is the best selection of which to make a coat. It should be of sufficient body to lend itself to the shaping, or shrink to the form. All cloths do not respond to pressing in the same measure, so some need more than others.

Sponging the Cloth

The cloth for a coat or jacket must be sponged to prevent shrinking or spotting. To sponge cloth a sheet of muslin as wide as, and 1/2 yard longer than, the cloth should be thoroughly wet and wrung out. Place the wet muslin over a table. Place the cloth (leaving it in the fold) 1/2 yard from the end of the muslin. Fold the end of the muslin over on the end of the cloth and roll them smoothly together. Let them remain for about eight hours, so that the cloth may be thoroughly dampened. When the cloth has been removed from the muslin, place it over the pressing board or table. A table is to be preferred in this case as it allows the iron a greater sweep, and consequently a more even pressing. Press the cloth lengthwise with a hot iron. Be sure that you press with the nap of the cloth, which should smooth from the person. A cotton cloth should be placed over the goods while pressing, to prevent scorching. The cloth should be thoroughly dry before it is cut, as it is not well shrunken before it is dry.

A cambric pattern should be cut from the pattern to be used, and fitted to the person, and the alterations made on it, so that the cloth may be cut accurately. This cambric foundation is very often used as the interlining or foundation, particularly in coats of lightweight material.

Making the Foundation

To shrink canvas, put the piece into a vessel of water and thoroughly wet it. Wring the water out of it, place it on the ironing board, smooth the wrinkles out of it, but do not stretch it. Press it with a hot iron until it is smooth and thoroughly dry. Do not scorch the canvas.

The canvas is cut through the center, allowing half a width for each side of the coat. The cambric lining is placed on the bust form, wrong side out, and the canvas fitted to the right side of the front. The grain of the canvas is kept straight across the chest, and a dart is made from the bust line to the lower edge of the canvas at the waistline. The edges of this dart are lapped and basted flat. The canvas is basted to the cambric lining. A half yard of haircloth is cut through the center lengthwise, placed over the canvas, and fitted in the same way. The canvas is placed a little over the shoulder seam, but the haircloth is placed in such a manner that it will just reach the seam when it is stitched. The canvas is stitched in with the outside material when that is placed on the shoulder seam. The haircloth is basted firmly to the canvas around the point of the dart, and also around the shoulder, neck front, and armhole. This process of putting in the canvas and haircloth is repeated on the left side of the coat.

Then the coat is placed in the machine. Beginning at the front of the dart, a succession of circles is stitched 1/2 inch apart, through canvas, haircoth, and cambric, forming the shape for the bust. From the armhole line to the front of the waist and neckline straight lines of stitching are made in order to keep the coat in shape, as otherwise the canvas and haircloth might bulge. The edges of the haircloth, wherever they may occur, must be covered with a strip of cambric sewn flat over them to keep the little points of hair from pushing through the lining of the coat.

The coat foundation should now be placed over a firm, rounded pad; the point of the dart is well dampened and pressed into shape. The remainder of the shaped front is then dampened and pressed into shape. Should the shape of the bust be too high or too low, it may be dampened again and the form pressed to its proper position. It often happens that the canvas and haircloth do not sit in closely at the armhole. The remedy for this is a dart cut in from the armhole toward the point of the dart. The edges of this dart are also lapped, stitched, and pressed flat. The point of the little dart must also be so flattened by dampening and pressing as to be unnoticeable.

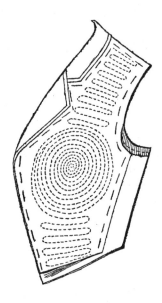

Figure 40. Canvas coat front

Trimming Off the Foundation

When the foundation of the coat has been tried on the person and the alterations made, if any are necessary, it is in condition to have the outside cloth applied or draped on it. If the design of the coat does not call for a revers and turned-over collar, the canvas extends to the front line, and the cloth is left 1 inch wider to allow for turning over the canvas. The canvas should be cut away at the proper line, and it should never be folded back with the cloth. The edge of the canvas is held in by sewing a narrow tape flat on the edge.

When a turned-over collar and revers, like those placed on men's coats, is desired, much care and very good workmanship is necessary. For this style of coat the canvas extends beyond the center front line as many inches as the revers will measure when finished, plus 1/2 inch allowance for work and shrinkage. The cloth for this style of front is cut the same width of the canvas, and is basted on the foundation around the neck, armhole, underarm seam, down the front line, and around the edge of the revers. The revers is then creased back on the front and shaped. The canvas is slightly eased on the cloth before padding, to allow the revers to roll back in position.

Padding

Padding or tailor's tacking is a succession of small stitches through the canvas and cloth to hold them together and to keep the revers in shape at all points, and to prevent the canvas from stretching. In padding, the stitch is a small, slanting basting. The larger stitch is made on the canvas, and the smaller one through the cloth. This last stitch is so small as to simply take up one thread, but nevertheless it serves to hold both materials together. The stitches are arranged in rows quite close together. The canvas is cut away to the exact size of the revers, and a piece of tape is run flat around the edge to preserve the shape and keep the edge from stretching. An allowance of 1/2 inch is left on the cloth outside of the canvas revers.

The facing of the revers is then cut. If the coat is to be double-breasted, the facing must extend the full length of the front of the coat. This facing must fit exactly with the straight grain of the goods or material. The front line of a double-breasted coat must be on the straight grain of the material. The right side of the material must be placed to the right side of the coat, placing the edges exactly together. The facing is then stitched by the machine just outside the edge of the canvas revers. The edges of the cloth are cut at the point of the revers, to avoid any bulk at the point. The facing is then turned over on the inside of the front and basted with little stitches. The seam must be on the very edge of the revers. The cloth is then basted over at the other edge of the canvas on the inside of the coat. The piece of cloth for the back of the coat is traced through the center; this tracing is placed exactly to the center back seam and basted to it.

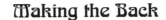
Making the Back

Plain backs are very rarely worn now. Pleats of some sort are usually made on both back and fronts. The pleats are made in the cloth before it is applied or draped on the lining. However, the principle is the same in both plain and pleated backs. The center must be placed to the center back seam, and the material drawn or smoothed on the straight grain across the back at the shoulders. The pleats or fullness must follow the lines of the figure tapering toward the waistline. The back is basted to the lining all around the neck, armhole, and underarm seam. The shoulders and underarm seams are traced and marked. They are then ripped apart and the cloth or outside material basted to the lining in the seam tracings, the marks placed together, and the seams basted exactly as they were fitted. The seams should then be stitched by machine and pressed flat. If necessary, these seams may be dampened.

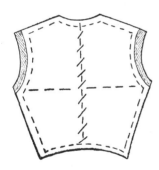

Figure 41. Back of plain coat or Eton jacket

Making the Collar

To make a turned-over collar, like a man's coat collar, take two pieces of canvas about 12 inches long and 5 inches wide, shrink them, and baste them together. Cut these pieces in half and stretch both the upper and lower edges by wetting thoroughly. Iron them with a hot iron curving the edges, the lower edge more than the upper; do not stretch the center of these pieces.

Place them on the neck of the person, or on the neck of the bust form. Join the pieces in the center back by pinning them together in a seam. Flatten the seam and shape the collar by molding it to the neck. This is done by turning the upper

edge over on the neck until the fold fits close to the neck. The under edge is cut in a curve at the corners so that it will not tighten the coat around the curve at the front of the neck. The top of the revers is placed on the collar and the place of joining marked on both collar and revers. A line is traced on the coat at the lower edge of the collar.

The collar is then removed from the coat. The center seam of collar is then stitched by machine and pressed very flat. Four pieces of cloth are cut the size of the collar, two pieces for the underside, and two for the top or outside. A seam of 1/2 inch is allowed on these pieces all around. The pieces for the underside are joined to fit the canvas. The seam is placed next to the canvas seam, which has been placed toward the outside of the coat, making a smooth surface for the facing proper to be placed on. The cloth is then basted to the canvas and padded, either by hand as the revers were padded, or by stitching rows and rows of machine stitching around the lower side of collar, which is placed on the coat. The turned-over part is stitched up and down. A tape is sewn all around the edge to hold it in place. The cloth, it must be remembered, extends 1/2 inch beyond the edge of the collar. The lower edge is cut just the required shape, and the cloth is basted back over the canvas, dampened, and pressed until it is perfectly flat. It is now basted around the lower edge to the coat on the traced line.

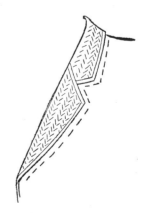

Figure 42. Padded collar

Fitting the Revers to the Collar

The fitting of the revers to the collar and making a neat joining is one of the most particular and exacting parts of the making of a coat. The collar is molded with the fingers around the neckline until it fits in its proper position; it must not be drawn out of this position in any way. The revers is fitted upon the collar and cut away. The collar is also cut away, leaving only a small margin to lap on the underside of the revers. The cloth on the edge of the collar is turned in and hemmed to the revers. The underside of the collar is now hemmed or machine stitched to the coat. The facing of the coat collar is next joined in a seam, to fit the collar and basted to the edge of cloth. The seam must be placed exactly on the seam of collar, the right sides of the cloth together. These edges must be machine stitched together, turned out after the thickness of the corners has been cut away, and basted close to the edge, the seam exactly on the edge of the canvas. The cloth is then stretched over the collar and basted around the neckline to hold it in place.

The joining of the outer collar and facing of the revers is the next consideration. Turn in both of these edges after they have been trimmed down to about 3/8 inch. Catch them together with an overhand basting stitch, which will hold them very closely together. This seam is slip stitched together with the finest of stitches.

Finishing Off the Edges

The bottom of the coat may be finished by turning the edge to the inside over a band of bias canvas. The edge of the material should be catch stitched to the canvas. The coat is now ready to be stitched all around the edges. This stitching should be continuous and of the same distance from the edge throughout. Beginning at the underarm, it should extend around the bottom, up the front, around the revers and collar, down the other side of the coat front, and around the bottom to the starting point. If one or more rows of stitching is made on the coat, they must be the same space apart throughout the entire coat, as this stitching serves as trimming or decoration.

The Lining

The coat lining should be of some substantial material, such as satin or silk. If a lining of either of these materials is used the coat will have not only a handsome appearance, but will hold its shape longer and give greater satisfaction all around. If the coat is an Eton coat, one width of the silk for the back and one for each of the fronts will be necessary. If the coat is an extra-large one, judgment must be used when calculating the number of yards necessary for the lining.

The silk for the back is laid in a pleat of about 1 inch. This pleat extends through the center of the silk from the neck to the bottom of the coat. When a coat is put on or taken off, there is more or less strain across the back at the shoulders. If the lining were of the same width as the outside material, it would split or tear. When the pleat is in the lining it opens or spreads and relieves the strain on the silk.

Coat linings are basted roughly into the coat, and then neatly arranged along the shoulder and underarm seams, the edges turned in, and hemmed all around the seams and edges with fine, firm stitches.

A Coat Sleeve

A coat sleeve is necessarily larger than the dress sleeve, and the elbow is less evident. The sleeve is always cut on the straight of the goods, the grain running perfectly straight on both upper and under portions around the upper part of the arm. Any swing from the straight is made from the elbow to the wrist.

The sleeve is placed together exactly like the waist lining sleeve. It is stitched with a 1/2-inch seam, and notched twice at the break of the arm on the front seam. When the sleeve is stitched it should be turned inside out and placed over the sleeve press board. Mark the sleeve the length desired. Place a piece of bias canvas at the bottom on the inside, and turn the cloth over it. Catch the edge of the cloth to the canvas. Machine stitch the edges once or twice to correspond with the stitching on the remainder of the coat. Press the bottom of the sleeve flat by placing the sleeve right side out on

the board and pointing the iron in the sleeve so that the bottom is pressed all around in a circular way. Never hold the sleeve together and press it flat in that way.

The lining is cut about 1 1/2 inches longer at the top and 1 inch longer at the bottom than the cloth sleeve. The lining is stitched together and slipped over the sleeve and basted in its proper position, the front seam of the lining to the front seam of the sleeve. The lining around the hand is folded into 1/4 inch from the bottom and hemmed. The lining at the top is basted to the sleeve about 3 inches from the edge.

The cloth sleeve is gathered around the top with two rows of fine running stitches, beginning about 4 inches from the front seam and extending to 4 inches from the back seam. The sleeve is sewn into the coat in the same manner as was the sleeve in the waist: the front seam to the notch at the front armhole. The gathers in the outside sleeve are pulled up to fit the required space on the coat, and basted in. The coat should be tried on the person and the fullness of the top of sleeve satisfactorily adjusted.

The sleeve should be stitched in by machine, the inside of the sleeve toward the person sewing. Almost a straight line should be preserved from the back armhole to the point where the fullness begins at the back of the sleeve. This straight line gives the coat a tailored effect, and shoulders a broader appearance. The fullness or gathers beyond the seam should be trimmed to a small margin. This margin should be turned back on the coat and sewn to the lining.

The sleeve lining must then be pinned in position. The gathers should be put in the lining at the top and drawn up to fit the sleeve. The edges should then be folded in and pinned so that the lining edge covers the machine-stitched seam. The sleeve lining is then ready to fell into the coat.

Pressing

To properly and successfully press a coat, it is absolutely necessary to have the proper press pads and boards. All the pressing should be done on the wrong side except the last, or finished, pressing.

The collar should be placed padded side up on the board, both edges stretched and dampened, and then pressed into shape by holding one end up and pressing in the form of a loop, so as to obtain a round effect. Dampen the revers on the padded side along the fold and press; stretch the edge a trifle and press until dry. This makes the edge of the revers fit closely to the coat, as it will follow the slope of the figure. To press the facing of a coat, take a piece of wet muslin–unbleached muslin serves this purpose very well–place over the facing and press. Remove the damp cloth, and finish pressing over a dry cloth. Press the collar and revers in the same way. Do not press the fold of the collar and revers flat at any stage of the pressing. The coat sleeve at the shoulder should be pressed over a pad.

The entire coat should be pressed on the right side, using a wet cloth and hot iron to give a finish. The cloth should be wet, wrung out, and placed over the coat. To remove shine caused by pressing, use a thoroughly wet cloth and a hot iron. Place the coat over a pad and lay the cloth over the shine. Hold the iron near the wet cloth with one hand and raise, with the other, the cloth against the hot iron. This will force the steam directly on the shine. Do not allow the weight of the iron on the cloth.

An Eton Coat

An Eton coat is a short coat which does not reach to the waistline, but fits the figure closely. To make this jacket or coat, a cambric pattern is fitted to the figure and used also as the foundation on which the jacket is built. One-half yard of tailor's canvas, which has been previously shrunken, and 1/2 yard of haircloth will be necessary to make the form for the front of the coat. All the canvas used on a coat should be shrunken before using.

A Box Coat

The cloth for a box or loose-fitting coat is usually of a weight sufficiently heavy to hold the shape. This style of coat may be made long or short, lined or unlined, according to the material. If covert, melton, kersey, or cloths of like weight are used, the seams are usually bound neatly and thoroughly

pressed, and no lining placed in the coat. If lighter weight cloth is selected, a silk or satin lining is used. Sometimes an interlining of flannel is placed in the lightweight coats. This interlining extends across the back and chest, and of sufficient length to protect the lungs. The collar of a box coat may be made like a man's coat collar, or may be stitched flat to the neck of the coat.

A piece of canvas should be cut to fit the armhole from the front armscye, joining the canvas and haircloth around the armhole to the shoulder seam. If the coat is interlined this piece of canvas is covered with a piece of silk, and is held in the coat by a close basting around the armhole. The reason for placing this canvas around the armhole is to make a firm foundation for the sleeve; if there was no stay at this part the cloth would wrinkle across the back. In lined coats this piece of canvas is attached by cross stitches to the interlining around the outer edge of the canvas.

A Tight-Fitting Coat

This style of coat must have all the portions cut separately and basted to the corresponding portions of common cambric. The lining should be eased on the cloth, particularly above and below the waistline, and the waistline marked and joined in the same manner as the tight lining is joined. The length from shoulder to waist is allowed 1/2 inch longer than this measure for a waist, and from 1/2 to 1 inch around the figure at waist and bust lines, allowing for the extra thickness of the dress waist worn under a coat. Particular attention must be paid to the lines of a tight-fitting coat. All the seams must be evenly stitched by machine and pressed flat. These seams may be stitched on either side close to the seam, or 1/2 inch from the seam, as a trimming.

The front of this coat must be cut with the center front line on the straight grain of the goods. Any shaping to the curve of the figure should, if possible, be made in the front dart. The fronts are lined with a piece of canvas the width of the buttonhole, plus 1 inch at least. This canvas must also be cut on the straight. Otherwise the edge of front

would stretch and ruin the appearance of the coat in a short time.

The collar for a tight-fitting coat is usually made like a man's coat collar. The bust should be made as usual, with canvas and haircloth, and the canvas placed around the armhole. (See Eton Coat.)

To line a tight-fitting coat the silk for the fronts must be cut large enough to allow a pleat 1 inch deep, which is placed at the center of the shoulder seam and extends toward the bust about 4 or 5 inches. This pleat is placed there for ease across the fronts.

The front dart of the lining, having been stitched and pressed, is placed exactly over the seam of the coat and basted to it with basting stitches. Ease the silk lining over the center front, turn it in about 1/8 inch from the edge, and baste. Ease the silk from the front dart back to the armhole. Turn in the silk at the shoulder line and baste the front silk over the back. Turn in the silk at the underarm seam and baste the front over the back.

The back is cut with a seam, allowing 3/4 inch for the back pleat. All the portions of the lining are cut 1/2 inch higher at the top and 1 inch longer at the bottom. The portions are all stitched together regularly and pressed, except the underarm seam and shoulder seams. Fold the pleat in the center back; pin it at the waistline and at the neck. Then pin the back portion along the rounding seam, turn back the free part, and sew the seam of the lining to the seam of the coat about 1/4 inch from the machine stitching. Turn the silk over and pin along the next seam and proceed as before. Ease the lining up to the shoulder seam around the armhole and over to the underarm seam, then baste. Turn in the lining all around the bottom and neck, being sure that the lining is full on the coat, and hem neatly.

Capes

Capes are rarely worn now except for evening wear. A very pretty model is the "Red Riding Hood" cape. This is cut like a circular skirt with a seam down the center back and fitted at the shoulder in one dart. To make this cape a warm one suitable for

winter wear, I would interline with flannel to the hip line. Be sure that the interlining is eased on the cloth, as it would tighten the cloth otherwise.

The hood is a circular affair lined with satin or silk. The lining and outside cloths are cut exactly alike. The right sides of both are placed together and machine stitched. These are then turned out and the edges basted. Two rows of machine stitching 1/2 inch apart are made about 1 1/2 inches from the edge, catching the silk and cloth together and forming a casing for the ribbon drawstring which, when drawn up, adjusts the hood to the shape of the head.

The lining is fitted to the cape and eased on the cloth. It is then hemmed all around to the cloth, which was previously turned up to the required length. The cape may be fastened with hooks and eyes, or by a cord and tassel placed around the neck and fastened at the center front to secure it in its place. This cord may be tied in one knot or in a bowknot, according to the thickness of the cord.

A pocket should be placed on one side of the cape lining just above the knee. This pocket may be made of a double piece of the lining cut 9 by 12 inches, and gathered at the bottom by two rows of hand stitching to the required width–about 4 inches. A casing is made at the top, into which is placed a piece of flat hat elastic about 4 inches long. This is placed in the top so that the pocket will admit the handkerchief, fan, etc. The pocket should be machine stitched down the sides and across the bottom to the lining.

This style of coat may be worn by a young girl or by her mother. It is usually made of broadcloth. For a young girl white, red, tan, lined with pale blue or pink, are very attractive. For an older woman black cloth, lined with white or some light-colored silk or satin, is most serviceable. Braid trimmings with a touch of gold thread or braid add much to the appearance of a black coat or cape. The hood attached to this style of cape is quite popular as a protection for the head, and incidentally very attractive.

From Chapter XI
Girdles, Collars, Sleeves, Etc.

Separate Girdle, Closed at Back

A girdle is a belt which may be made separately or attached to the waist. It is intended as a decoration or a finish to the waist. A very practical way to make a foundation for a separate girdle closed at the back is to secure a belt tape the size of the person's waist measure plus 1 inch for turnings. Mark the center and half the distance from the center front to the end of tape with pins. Cut five pieces of covered featherbone. The length of these pieces must be governed by the height intended for the girdle when finished. For a normal figure, that is, about 36 bust and 24 waist measure, a girdle with a bone 4 inches above the waistline and 1 inch below in the center front, another bone 1 1/4 inches above and 1/2 inch below the waistline at the underarm seam, and one 3 inches above and 3/4 inch below the waistline at each side of the center back, will prove a good foundation on which to build a girdle. The bones are pinned to the belt tape at the front, sides, and back, and sewn firmly to it with cross stitches of buttonhole twist or coarse cotton.

Figure 43. Girdle foundation

The covering for the foundation of the girdle may be of any material one desires. Taffeta, silk, satin, and sometimes chiffon and crepe de chine, as well as plain or fancy ribbons, are used with very charming effect. If silk or satin is used, it is well to cut the material on the bias. For a girdle of the pro-

portions given above 1/2 yard of silk on the straight will make one. Fold the silk so as to get a true bias, but not exactly across from corner to corner. Fold the corner over so that the center of the piece of silk will measure very nearly as many inches as the waist. About 8 or 9 inches along the selvage will be a sufficient width for the girdle. Then join the other piece to the selvage side of the bias and cut it to the same width.

Hem the bias edges of this piece either by hand or machine. Mark the center of the material and pin it in little folds to the center bone, turning the lower edge over the bone toward the inside. Arrange most of the fullness or folds from this point to about 2 inches above the waistline, making the folds of the silk scant at the top of girdle. Drape the material along the belt tape to the next bone, which of course will be shorter, and the folds will of necessity be crushed closer together. Pin securely to the bone. Drape the material to the back of the foundation, spreading the folds again.

The back of the girdle may be finished by a small heading, or ruffle, made of the end of the bias material. This little ruffle should be secured by two rows of fine gathers which reach to the outer edge of the bone. The ruffle will serve to hide the joining.

The girdle should be secured by four or five hooks sewn securely through the bone at the center back and far enough back on it to prevent the opening from spreading. The eyes on the other side of the belt should extend sufficiently to permit the hooks to slip into them. The belt should be adjusted to the figure so that it will pull around perfectly true, as the bias is apt to pull more to one side than the other, and thus render the girdle a most careless and untidy affair.

Girdle, Closed in Front

The foundation for a girdle which is closed in front or on the side should be made with three pieces of featherbone placed in positions on the belt tape corresponding to the back seams of a tight-fitting waist: one for the center back and one on either side of the center back. The distance between the center and these bones is about 1 1/2 inches for an ordinary waist measure. The center piece of featherbone should measure more in length than those at either side of it; these must measure exactly the same in length. Another bone is placed at the underarm seam, and one in the center front. The style of the girdle necessarily determines the length of the pieces of featherbone.

But there is one suggestion I would make emphatically, and it is that the top line of the girdle be of the height which would seem to balance. For instance, the front bone should not reach higher on the body than the bone at the center back. Otherwise the figure appears short waisted at the front and disproportionately long at the back. The underarm bone must also be carefully placed, so that it will not shove the material up into a point and thus spoil the even line desired.

The materials may be placed in a variety of ways on these foundations. I will give a few suggestions.

Figure 44. Girdle, opening in front and to side

Flowered Ribbon Girdle, Opening in Back

A ribbon girdle may be made in this manner after the foundation is satisfactorily fitted. A piece of ribbon 1 yard long and about 9 inches wide will be sufficient for a 24-inch waist measure. Find the center and mark with a tracing thread. Make a 1/4-inch tuck. Leave a sufficient length of the silk or twist to draw up when the shirred effect is made. Leave a space 1/4 inch on each side of the center. Run another tuck of the same depth as the center and leave the thread. Pull these threads so that the ribbon is a trifle wider than the bone, and fasten them well with two backstitches. Sew these tucks through the bone, as they must be very secure and firm. Drape the ribbon to the underarm bone and lay it in pleats, and fasten them to the bone. These fastening stitches must be so small as to be almost invisible. The reason for laying the pleats or folds at the underarm bone is to give the waist a trim appearance. Shirred tucks placed there would tend to increase the apparent size of the waist measure.

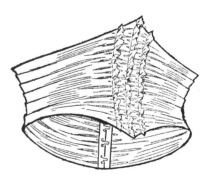

Figure 45. Flowered ribbon girdle, opening in back

Now drape the ribbon to the back bones. Mark with a tracing thread exactly the line where the belt meets, which will curve in slightly at the waistline. You will find a surplus amount of ribbon on each side. Measure on this piece the amount necessary for three 1/4-inch tucks, which will be 1 1/2 inches. Now measure that amount in on the ribbon toward the underarm bone and begin to make your tucks,

taking the last tracing line for your guide for the sewing of the tucks. The tucks must be made in the space between the tracings. The tucks will fit exactly into the position desired if these directions are closely followed. The back tucks must be sewn very firmly to the bones, as the strain will fall there when the girdle is pulled around the body.

The remaining edge of the ribbon may be turned back over the featherbone and the hooks and eyes sewn on. The hooks should be placed a sufficient distance, on the right-hand side, from the edge to slip into the eyes; on the left-hand side, in such a manner that the joining or opening may not be detected. The hooks and eyes should be faced with a piece of prussian binding or silk.

Trimmed Girdle

A very attractive girdle may be made by making the foundation to open a little to the left of the front. Three-quarters of a yard of soft silk or satin about 21 inches wide will make this girdle. Find the true bias by folding the selvage over until it lies across the piece on a straight line from selvage to selvage. The slanting or oblique fold thus made is the true bias. Cut through this fold. Then measure 10 inches on the selvage of the larger piece and cut across the material parallel to the first bias, preserving the same distance. Join the smaller piece to the larger along the selvage until sufficient length is obtained to reach around the body plus 2 inches.

Figure 46. Girdle lacing in front

Hem both the edges of this bias piece. Find the center and pin the material in flat folds to the bones in back and sew them through. Allow the hem to turn over the ends of the bones and sew it with a few firm stitches. The bones of this girdle should extend 5 inches above and 1/2 inch below the waistline in back, 2 inches above and 1/2 inch below at the underarm, and 3 1/2 inches above and 1 1/2 inches below the waistline in front.

The material is draped in folds at the underarm bone and sewn firmly through the bone. It is then draped to the front and pinned in evenly distributed folds on the bone. It may be found necessary to add another bone at each side of the front, of the same length, to hold the trimming in position. These bones will be placed about 2 inches either side of the front on the belt tape, and will extend 1/2 inch higher on the belt tape. The material is extended 3 inches beyond the center mark to lap over to the left side. Shaped pieces of thin silk are cut and interlined with thin crinoline, two pieces for the back the same width as the girdle, and two pieces for the front.

The edges of these pieces are turned over the crinoline and machine stitched in two or three rows as a trimming. Eyelet holes or buttonholes are made in these pieces opposite to each other. A silk or velvet ribbon is laced through these openings and tied in a bowknot at the bottom, or simply cut off and finished on the inside of the piece. This piece of trimming is slip stitched to the girdle along the firm line made by the bones. The front pieces are attached in the same way, except that the edge which is sewn to the lap of the girdle hooks over on the girdle proper.

This same style of girdle may be made very attractive by making, instead of buttonholes or eyelets, a latticework of small bands connecting the shaped pieces. The ends of bands may be finished with a small, fancy button.

A very beautiful girdle may be made of three shades of the same color, either of silk or ribbon. The darkest shade is placed at the bottom of the girdle, and the lightest at the top. The fastening at the back may be finished with small rosettes of the material of which the girdle is made.

Another pretty fashion is to make a bias girdle and fasten it with an attractive metal buckle, or some pretty design in appliqué or passementerie.

Tucked Net Collar

A very serviceable collar may be made of net tucked in little 1/4-inch tucks, made on the straight of the material. The tucked net is placed with the edge of the tuck forming the lower edge of the collar. The net is then stretched over the collar and turned over the top and bottom and caught with small stitches to the mousseline foundation. Bias strips of silk or satin, or small patterns of lace, may be applied to the net collar. There are many pretty devices in which small buttons may be introduced, and silk braids of narrow widths of various colors may also be used. Beads of silver or gilt give an attractive touch to these dainty neckpieces. A few colored beads or "cabochons" are often used, but discretion must be used in selecting them. They must not be large, as that would tend to make the collar appear heavy and the neck thick, two items to be considered in making collars.

When a collar is made of tucks only, they should run around the neck. When the tucks run up and down they give the neck a very thick appearance. If appliqués of lace are put on a tucked collar it does not matter in which direction the tucks run, as they will be held in place by the lace.

Fancy Sleeves

Fancy sleeves, so much in vogue, are draped. That is, the material is applied to a foundation sleeve of a lining of muslin, etc. To assist the home dressmaker in this matter, I would suggest a padded arm on which to drape the sleeve. The padded arm is made by fitting a strong muslin sleeve to each arm. Machine stitch it and pad it with tissue paper until it is perfectly firm and smooth from wrist to armhole. A piece of muslin is cut to fit the top of the sleeve or armhole. This piece is sewn over the armhole to keep the padding in place. Another piece of muslin is sewn over the opening at the bottom of the sleeve at the wrist.

Sleeves which reach to the elbow are very fashionable for coats and waists. When the lower arm does not look well in this style of sleeve, a high cuff of lace covers the arm and does not affect the style of the sleeve. The puff for a short sleeve of silk, muslin, or woolen should measure about 24 inches in width at the widest part, and should measure 1 inch more than the length of the arm from the armhole to the break of the arm on the front seam, and about 5 inches above the armhole to the top of the sleeve for the fullness. A leg-of-mutton shaped puff is also worn. This sort of sleeve fits close to the arm above the elbow, but grows fuller toward the top. The fullness of the top of the sleeve should be gathered in two rows of fine running stitches. An elbow sleeve is usually finished at the bottom by a cuff, or ruffles and pleatings of silk and lace.

A very attractive sleeve may be made entirely of tiny ruffles. They must overlap to give the proper effect. A foundation sleeve, of course, is used, onto which the ruffles or pleatings are sewn. This foundation should not be very full, about 4 or 5 inches more than the measure of the arm around the fullest part of the upper arm.

When the sleeve is to be draped on a foundation or lining, the lining should be placed on the padded arm and arranged in the proper position, the front seam on the front seam of the padded arm. If a draped effect is desired, the material should be pinned through to the foundation at irregular intervals until the desired effect is produced. The pins are left in the sleeve until it is removed from the arm. It is then tacked with two small running stitches and one backstitch; these stitches must be secure. Should the puff droop over the cuff or band at the bottom of the sleeve, the fullness may be laid in small tucks across the front seam.

Many of the sleeves made of thin materials have no linings, and are much trimmed with insertion and medallions of lace. When a transparent cuff is attached to an elbow sleeve, it should be made sufficiently long to reach over the elbow point, as it will otherwise be too short at the back seam when the elbow is bent. If a transparent cuff is made for a

silk or woolen sleeve it should be lined with mousseline de soie, as it will then hold its shape and add much to the appearance of the arm.

Batiste, which is so much used in trimming waists, may be made into very serviceable cuffs for woolen waists. It should be tucked in groups and have a narrow insertion of lace placed between the groups; the tucks and insertions to run around the sleeve. A ruffle of narrow lace at the hand would make a neat finish. The sleeves should correspond to a chemisette and collar made in the same design.

Coat sleeves when made elbow length, always covering the point of the elbow, are made either a puff or leg-of-mutton shape. They are usually finished by a cuff or band, and may be trimmed with braid, embroidery, or stitching. Pleated lace or silk adds to the finish when placed so that it falls from the inner side of the sleeve. The band or cuff may be made shaped to a pretty design. For example a leaf design which might be outlined with braid or fancy stitching, the same design to be made on other portions of the coat; the revers, vest, and collar for instance. When a band is used as a finish, it may be made of a bias strip of canvas cut the width desired and covered with the cloth or material designed for it.

From Chapter XII
Gowns: Their Choosing and Making

Materials

Each season naturally suggests the appropriate materials to be converted into gowns to be worn during that period. For winter we look for materials which will give warmth, and woolens hold first place. In the colder portions of our country heavy woolen materials are necessary. The milder climates call for the beautiful lightweight woolens and woolen mixtures so fashionable. Cashmere and henrietta cloth are manufactured in such attractive colors that they meet the demand for either street or evening gowns, and may be had in light or heavy weight. Henrietta cloth has a rich, glossy finish and is very serviceable. Voile, which is the French name for veiling, is a very popular material. It is a thin woolen or silk-and-wool fabric, usually transparent, and requires a silk lining throughout the gown.

While speaking of thin materials we must not forget the beautiful chiffons and chiffon effects. Silk mull has long held sway for inexpensive thin dresses, and some very beautiful gowns have been made from this material. A lawn lining is usually made in them which keeps the cost down to a very reasonable sum. Shirred tucks and insertions of lace or medallions add to the attractiveness of these gowns.

A gown made of either black or white net will prove a very valuable acquisition to a lady's wardrobe. Many styles might be suggested for a net gown, but here are a few suggestions which will hold good for any style. The first thought in making a net gown is for the lining. This should be of silk or satin, over which a veiling of mousseline de soie should be placed to give a softer appearance. A net gown should be made in such a manner as to allow for shortening, as the net will lose some of the dressing and sag somewhat after having been worn a few times. Net should not be weighted with a quantity of heavy jet or other trimming at the bottom of the skirt.

Silks are always fashionable; particularly is this true of black taffeta, which is worn for both dress and service. Every season brings forth a variety of handsome patterns and colors in silks. For street wear tweeds, serges, broadcloth, velvet, and velveteens are much worn.

Good Taste and Economy in Dressing

All the accessories must harmonize. Tan or reddish-brown gloves harmonize with most street gowns, whereas white or black kid gloves are worn almost entirely for evening. The silk glove in both black and white has had a tremendous vogue, particularly elbow lengths to meet the needs of the elbow sleeve. Black shoes are always and ever in good taste, except in the case of an elaborate white wedding gown. White shoes are at times very fashionable, particularly in the summer. White canvas ties and pumps are the most effective. Colored hose with white or black shoes are at all times in bad taste; only those seeking extremes in fashion would think of wearing them. The footwear should be in perfect harmony with the costume, but should not be conspicuous.

Choosing the Design

The whole design given in a fashion book need not be followed. Parts of one design may be used for the waist, and the skirt be taken from another. The trimming scheme, however, must be the same. If the trimming of the skirt should be ruffles, pleatings would hardly be in good taste for the waist. Taffeta trimming on the waist and velvet on the skirt, or a

Gowns: Choosing and Making

very fancy design for the waist and a walking skirt, is not good taste. The portions of a gown must balance well as regards the style.

The best plan for the home dressmaker is to secure a paper pattern which fits her and suits her style. The home dressmaker must not expect to get a paper pattern which will fit her form exactly without any alterations, unless her figure is of perfect proportions.

Measurements

The measurements for a pattern should be taken over the fullest part of the bust up under the arms, drawn snugly. For the skirt measure around the hips six inches below the waist measure. Measure around the waist tightly. Sleeves are measured around the upper part of the arms.

Patterns are sold by bust measures. The proportionate measures are:

Bust	Waist	Hips
32 in.	22 in.	39 1/2 in.
34 in.	24 in.	43 in.
36 in.	26 in.	45 in.
40 in.	30 in.	57 in.

Dressmakers' Terms

Terms and expressions which occur in fashion notes and books are very often unintelligible to many home dressmakers. Therefore, the introduction of them here may be helpful. We get our fashions from the French people, and many of them have never been translated into our own language, but always retain the French names.

Accordion pleating: One pleat laid on another by machinery, steamed and dried so as to retain this position.

Ajour: An open effect produced by joining two parts together by a cross or catch stitch.

Antique: A word used to designate an old-style material or fashion such as has been used in times long past—*moiré antique.*

Appliqué: Laces or embroidery joined to or applied to a material. It may be a piece, or a design of leaves, figures, etc.

Arabesque: A scroll effect or design which may be made with cords, stitchery, or applied pieces outlined.

Armure: A fancy weave of silk which has a small raised pebble design. It is much affected in mourning wear.

Bag seam: A seam stitched on the right side and then on the wrong, hiding the raw edges.

Basque: A tight-fitting waist which extends below the waistline; taken from the costume of the Basque peasants of France.

Batiste: A fine cotton muslin having a good deal of dressing, resembling lawn, batiste being slightly heavier.

Bayadere: A design in dress materials in which the stripes run from selvage to selvage giving a round appearance.

Beige: A soft, fine material made of yarns in the natural color. May be either twilled or plain.

Bengaline: A plain round-corded weave of silk and wool, in which the wool is used as a filling covered by the silk. It is smooth in surface and small in grain. When the cord takes a fancy appearance the fabric is called *crystal.*

Bertha: A ruffle or shaped cape following the line of a low-cut waist around the shoulders. It may be of lace, silk, or velvet.

Beurre: A name given to materials or lace having a yellow color resembling butter.

Bishop sleeve: Named for a sleeve in the robe of a bishop of the Episcopal Church. It is gathered at the top and again at the wrist with a straight cuff.

Blouse: A loose waist usually gathered on a drawstring at the bottom; to blouse a waist is to puff up from the waist, back and front.

Boa: A round neck scarf, either short or long, made of net, chiffon, lace and ribbon, and various soft materials. Fur and feathers are made into boas also.

Bodice: A tight-fitting waist; it is also applied to a high-fitted belt or girdle.

Bolero: A Spanish jacket; a small sleeveless jacket worn over a loose blouse. Many styles have this effect produced on lace or velvet.

Border: Any trimming put on an edge or above it and used as a finish to a garment.

Bouclé: A woolen material whose surface is raised in little tufts at regular intervals or in patterns; a rough material.

Bouffant: Used to express a very full or puffy effect—as *bouffant sleeves.*

Bouillouée: A narrow puffing used for fancy trimming, sometimes corded. It is often made in chiffon or soft satin.

Bourette: A kind of material on which rough threads or knots appear as straight or broken stripes.

Brandenburg: A military ornament of braid and loops with which a jacket is fastened.

Bretelle: A sort of cape which extends from the belt in front over the shoulders to the belt at the back of a waist. It is much wider at the shoulders and slopes at the waist.

Broché: An embroidered effect obtained by weaving; also called brocade.

Cabochons: A jet, glass, steel, or pearl flat bead or nail head, used for dress trimming or millinery.

Challis: An extremely lightweight dress fabric of cotton and wool, woven without twill; soft and free from dressing.

Chameleon: A changeable effect obtained by weaving two or three colors together.

Chiffon: The finest, sheerest silk material manufactured.

Chiffon cloth: A firmer fabric than chiffon.

Chiffon (Liberty): A chiffon cloth with a satin finish.

Chiné: Effects obtained by printing the warp before weaving, making the filling of a plain color.

Choux: A rosette of any soft material which will look like a cabbage.

Circular flounce: A flounce cut to fit the skirt at about the knee, but which flares in a circle at the foot of the skirt.

Collarette: A large collar or cape which fits the shoulders.

Collet: A small cape or large collar.

Covert cloth: Lightweight summer cloths, originally made of natural or undyed wool, resulting in gray, drab, or fawn colors.

Crash: A rough, loose linen material used for toweling and also for dresses. Often spoken of as *Russia crash.*

Crepe de chine: A soft silk fabric which lends itself to graceful folds.

Crepe tissue: A very fine transparent, crimpy material which is worn very much for mourning ruchings and trimmings.

Crepon: A woolen or silk-and-wool material with a crepe or crinkled effect.

Cuirasse: A perfectly plain tight-fitting waist.

Demassé: A fabric ornamented on the surface with a rich design, the running figure woven, but not printed, like damask.

Drap d'eté: An all-wool fabric with a twilled surface, woven as a twill and finished as a broadcloth.

Dresden effects: Warp-printed flowers and figures like those used on Dresden china.

Drop skirt: A lining skirt which is intended for one special dress, and is often hung or attached to the outer skirt.

Duchesse: The finest satin fabrics woven.

Dutch neck: A square or round neck cut only 2 inches below the throat.

Epaulette: A trimming which falls over the shoulders like a small cape.

Etamine: A canvas weave with a wide-open mesh rendering it more or less transparent. Sometimes woven with a silk stripe.

Eton: A short jacket or coat reaching to the waistline, dipping slightly to a point at the center back—after the style of uniform worn at the Eton School, England.

Faconni: Fancy, elaborate.

Fagoting: An embroidery stitch which fills the space between two edges, holding them together. It differs from the catch or herringbone stitch in being worked through the edges, and not flat on them.

Faille Française: A silken material having a soft cord with a cotton filling.

Featherstitching: Very much like bias or cord stitchery used in embroidery and with very good effect in dressmaking.

Fichu: A draped scarf or cape having long ends which fall from a knot at the breast.

Foulard: A soft, thin dress silk woven without twill. Twilled foulard is known as a silk serge.

French gathers: Made of one long stitch on the outside and one underneath, and alternating.

French knot: An embroidery stitch in which from four to eight or nine twists are made on the needle. The needle is pushed back through the same opening to the wrong side while the loops are held on the right side.

Frogs: Ornaments made of braid in a fancy pattern having a loop which fastens on the opposite button or olive. There are always a pair of these ornaments used for each fastening.

Full back: The straight-back widths of a skirt gathered in two rows at the top.

Galloon or passementerie: Trimming made of beads, spangles, or silk, into bands and fancy designs.

Gauffié: An effect seen in silk when the material is pressed into shapes or patterns.

Gauntlet: A cuff shaped like a gauntlet or riding glove, similar to the spreading cuffs seen on costumes of past centuries.

Gigot: A sleeve with a large puff at the top and fitting close to the lower arm like a leg-of-mutton sleeve.

Girdle: A belt of shaped cincture for the waistline.

Glacé: A shiny surface, applied to gloves and silk materials.

Granite: A raised pebbly effect in silk or woolen goods like armure.

Grenadine: An openwork diaphanous silk, wool, or cotton.

Grosgrain: A silk fabric with a cord or ribbed effect.

Guimpe: A yoke or waist usually made of white materials and worn with low-cut dresses—worn very much by children.

Habutai: A plain woven silk made in Japan on hand looms. It is smooth and even in texture.

Harlequin: Made of three or more separate colors.

Huckaback: A dicelike pattern, very heavy, used for toweling.

Iridescent: Changeable, having a rainbow effect.

Jabot: A trimming, usually of lace or chiffon, gathered full and allowed to fall in cascades or shells.

Jaconet: A fine muslin heavier than cambric, free from starch or dressing, but glazed by calendering.

Jacquard: Applied to materials made on jacquard looms, which automatically select the threads and make the designs, formerly produced by hand looms only.

Jardinière: Of many colors, resembling a garden of flowers.

Jupon: A short petticoat applied to double or triple skirts. The upper skirt is the jupon.

Khaki: A Japanese silk plain woven and less fine in weave than habutai.

Lancé: Shot effects, small dots—also called *petit pois*.

Liberty satin: A soft shiny satin.

Louis XVI; Regence; Directoire; Empire; Colonial: Certain styles peculiar to special periods in different countries.

Louisine: A soft, thin silk fabric.

Maline: A very fine gauzelike texture.

Matelassé: Woolen or silk cloth which has a raised pattern on the surface as if quilted or padded.

Medici: A collar for cloaks and dresses, very high and stiffened, rolling outward at the top.

Melangé: Mixtures of color applied in weaving; also mixtures of cotton warp and wool weft.

Melton: A stout smooth cloth used for men's clothing and women's coats. The nap is sheared close to the surface and is finished without pressing or glossing.

Mercerize: A chemical process of rendering cotton threads lustrous. The thread is shortened and hardened, producing a silky effect.

Merino: A soft woolen material.

Merveilleux: A satin fabric woven in a sort of twill pattern.

Mirror velvet: A smooth, shiny effect produced by ironing velvet with the nap.

Mitaine: A form of sleeve in which the lower part below the elbow resembles a mitten.

Moiré: A watered effect like spreading waves over a silk, cotton, or woolen material.

Motif: A portion of a design–as a leaf from a spray of flowers.

Mousseline de soie: A transparent, very thin material used for gowns or veiling satins or silks.

Nacié: A mother-of-pearl effect.

Natté: Like a basket weave.

Natural color: The grayish flax color–known as *undyed*.

Oriental; Persian; Cashmere: Names applied to a series of colors and patterns found in cashmere shawls.

Ottoman: A name applied to silk or woolen material with a large rep or cord.

Oxford: Originally a wool fabric in dark gray and white mixtures (90 percent of the former and 10 percent of the latter). Of late, heavy cotton and linen fabrics have been known by this name.

Pailette: Spangles of gelatin.

Panel: A piece of material placed either in the front or sides of a skirt, usually outlined by rows of trimming giving the appearance of an inlay.

Passementerie: Heavy embroideries or edgings and galloons, especially those made of rich gimps, braids, beads, silks, and tinsel.

Pastel shades: Very light tints, somewhat opaque in character.

Peau de cygne: One of the popular weaves of soft, highly finished silk; closely resembling peau de soie.

Peau de soie: A tough satin fabric.

Percale: A kind of cambric closely and firmly woven with more dressing than ordinary, and may be either printed or plain.

Picot: A small loop used as an ornamental edging on ribbons and laces.

Piping: A bias fold or cord put on the edge of a band or garment as a finish.

Placket: The opening left in a skirt to allow the garment to be put on and off the person; an opening in a shirtwaist sleeve.

Plastron: A full or draped vest for a waist.

Pleat: A trimming made by folding the material over on itself.

> Box pleat: A fold turned toward either side.
>
> Double box pleats: Box pleats having two folds.
>
> Kilt pleats: Large single folds turned one way.
>
> Knife pleats: Narrow folds turned to one side.
>
> Triple box pleats: Box pleats having three folds.

Plissé: Pleated.

Plumetis: A fine, sheer fabric in which a design is produced by means of loose tufts or spots.

Pointillé: Dotted with small spots or polka dots.

Polonaise: A waist and overskirt combined in one garment. It is taken from the Polish national costume.

Pompadour: Mixed colorings in light shades, such as were worn in the time of Louis XV and Mme. de Pompadour.

Pongee: A thin, soft silk fabric, woven from the natural uncolored raw silk.

Postilion: An extension of the back pieces of a basque or extra tabs set onto a basque at the back.

Pres de soie: A fine, cotton lining used for underskirts.

Princess: A style of dress in which the waist and skirt are made in continuous breadths from neck to feet.

Quilling: A narrow-pleated effect; a *rose quilling* is a very full triple box pleating stitched through the center, having the effect of a row of full-blown roses.

Redingote: An outside garment cut princess style, showing a skirt front beneath.

Rep: A style of weaving in which the surface has a crosswise appearance as a distinction from cords, which extend lengthwise in the fabrics.

Gowns: Choosing and Making

Revers: Pointed or square pieces usually turned back or reversed on the front of a waist or coat.

Ruche: A trimming of lace, silk, crepe, or chiffon, gathered or stitched in the middle.

Shantung: A heavy grade of pongee silk in which the natural color of the material is preserved.

Shirr: Two or more rows of gathers having a space between.

Sicilienne: A mohair of heavy weight, either plain or with a fancy pattern.

Smocking: Accordion pleating caught together alternately in rows, making an elastic fabric.

Soutache: Narrow worsted mohair or silk braid used in dress trimmings.

Stock collar: A full or plain collar in imitation of the stocks of 50 years ago.

Suede: Undressed kid; a skin from which the outer part has been rubbed off or skinned.

Surah: A soft silk woven in nearly invisible cords or twills.

Taffeta: A smooth weave of silk.

Tussah: A coarse silk produced by silkworms which are fed on oak leaves.

Tuxor: A soft, rich satin or silk cloth.

Vandyke: Pointed effects seen in laces, trimmings, etc.

Venetian: An all-wool material of a broadcloth construction, except that the face is twilled.

Vest: A flat center front trimming for a waist, also a separate garment.

Vigomeux: A worsted material which is printed in several colors, giving a melangé effect.

Voile or veiling: A wool or silk-and-wool fabric similar to the old-fashioned nun's veiling. Some voiles are extremely thin and transparent; these are called *chiffon voile*.

Watteau pleat: A box pleat down the center of the back of a princess gown which is laid from the neck to the waistline and then hangs freely to the bottom of the skirt.

Zibeline: A shiny, woolen material having long hairs.

From Chapter XV
Useful Hints

Miscellaneous Hints for Sewing

Armholes should be overcast or bound with a bias strip of soft lining silk or muslin. The front seam of a sleeve is placed about 2 or 2 1/2 inches from the underarm seam of the waist. Another very reliable guide is to fold the armhole from 1 inch back of the shoulder seam on a perfect bias. The point reached on the front of the waist is the guide to put the front seam of the sleeve at.

The shoulder seams should turn toward the front, to avoid any tightening which the reverse would make.

Dresses buttoned or hooked in the back should be fastened from right to left.

Pleating and Shirring

When full skirts are shirred in more than three rows of gathers, a staying piece must be placed under them. This piece should be fitted around the upper part of the hips, though not too closely, as every row of shirring must be invisibly sewn to this yoke or stay, and will tighten it if it is fitted too snugly. One can easily see how very necessary a stay is under cording or shirring; otherwise the fullness will not remain in its proper position. The skirt lining, if it is attached at the band to the upper skirt, will make a fine stay, both for the hip shirrs or cords and for those that are placed lower on the skirt, if there should be any.

If one intends to have a pleated back in a waist or shirtwaist, the tucks should extend the full length of the back. When the tucks or pleats end at the back yoke the fullness made by them gives a round-shouldered effect, unless when the tucks are so tiny that there is scarcely any fullness. When the pleats or tucks are large the piece of material should be tucked perfectly straight from top to bottom. When arranged at the waistline or belt they should be folded over until they taper with the figure from the armhole to the waist. Tucks made on the bias to give this slope are never successful, as they are bound to stretch on the edge, either in the laundering or wear.

Braid Trimming

A very nice way to sew on a skirt braid is to baste it to the bottom of the hem, allowing about 1/8 inch to extend beyond to protect the edge of it. Ease the braid on the skirt. Use a strong silk or cotton thread to sew it the first time near the edge. These stitches should be fine running stitches; they can be made almost invisible as the thread sinks into the braid. The top edge of the braid should be hemmed to the hem of the skirt with a fine, firm stitch, being careful to take no stitches through to the right side.

The braid should be joined where the ends meet in this way. A small end should be left on one side to lap over and turn in; this should cover the little joining. Hem all around this little lap and press it flat. While sewing on the braid, it should be held in as flat a position as possible.

From Chapter XVII
Gowns for Various Occasions

Outing Suits

Many women have become quite adept at contriving a good-looking as well as comfortable gown for sport. Here are a few fundamental guides to this sort of costuming. First, the material should be of good quality and of a color which will shed the dust and stand quite hard wear. The skirt should be short, at least 4 inches from the ground. As only a girdle is worn, the waist should be made on the blouse model. The neck should be finished by a turned-down collar, which gives freedom to the throat, and the sleeves elbow length. Bloomers should be worn in place of petticoats and undergarments. These suggestions are intended for outdoor sports.

The materials for these costumes are flannel, corduroy, tweeds, serges, and lightweight woolens; for the washable materials, piqué, linen, and denim are most serviceable. The skirt of an outing or athletic gown is best opened at the side of the front. It should be secured to the waist by hooks and eyes, or by a buttonhole tab sewn on the waist, and buttons on the skirt. The regulation gymnasium suit is usually made of blue serge, blouse and bloomers; these are made very full. Black stockings and gymnasium shoes complete the outfit. A bathing suit should accompany the gymnasium suit; this may be made of denim or brilliantine. The waist and bloomers are attached, the neck cut a little low, and the sleeves reaching above the elbow.

The Rainy-Day Costume

A short skirt of waterproof cloth or serge should be in every woman's wardrobe. The skirt should escape the ground by 4 inches, in order that the ankles may be kept dry. There should be two pairs of rubbers, a storm pair and a pair of sandals for damp weather. Cravenette cloaks are made full length from the neck to the feet, and are quite attractively gotten up in tans and oxford grays. There is, too, an arrangement of three capes which serves to keep the rain from the upper part of the body, but does not protect the skirt. A veil should also be provided for stormy weather, as it is almost impossible to keep one's hat in the proper position in a storm.

Maternity Gowns

As health, comfort, and a good appearance are the requisites, we will think of those gowns which will combine all three. To begin with, the weight, which should be as light as possible, must be suspended in some fashion from the shoulders, not from the waist or hips. The gown should be designed in such as way as to allow for expansion without altering the appearance. A gown which proved very successful had the darts in the waist lining laced, and as it became necessary the lacing was made looser.

A maternity gown should not be made of a conspicuous color for the street. Indistinctly striped cheviots, tweeds, or cashmeres are suitable materials. The skirt should be of a style which is fashionable, but one which may be adapted to this condition. The skirt should be made long; that is, to cover the feet. Particular attention must be given to the front gore. It must be cut broader at the top and longer; instead of being cut in a dip it must be longer in the center of the gore than at the sides. The waist belt should be much longer than usual, about 4 or 5 inches. This extra width may be held in by an elastic put in like a drawstring in a casing at the top of the skirt. The back of the skirt should be laid in pleats like an ordinary skirt. If the back below the waistline is very flat a little pad made of three or four silk ruffles may be worn in place of a bustle. It will add much to the appearance of the back. The

waist should be made with a puff or blouse in front. A coat effect, which should reach below the waistline over the hips, is most becoming and appropriate. The skirt should be attached to the waist by three hooks placed on the three back seams and three eyes sewn on the skirt at distances to correspond to the spaces between the hooks on the waist. In this manner the weight of the skirt is carried by the waist.

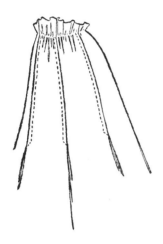

Figure 58. Maternity skirt

For the house tea gowns, loose flowing affairs of silk or challis or some other lightweight material, will help toward comfort and a good appearance. Short, fancy dressing sacks are also appropriate.

If a cloak or wrap is desired, the many styles of loose box coats seem to fill this need. Taffeta silks in dark colors, or lightweight cheviots, would make quite a comfortable wrap. A tight-fitting cloak or wrap should never be worn at this time. Every garment should be as loose and comfortable as taste will allow.

It is not necessary to dispense absolutely with a fitted waist. As a substitute for the corset which some women seem to need, I would suggest a Ferris waist or a corset cover made of heavy muslin into which a few strips of featherbone have been sewn. This waist will give the necessary support to the back. The darts could be laced and let out when necessary.

The petticoats and undergarments should be made of lightweight materials. If warmth is to be considered they may be made of woolen materials.

Correct Mourning

Good mourning, including crape, of course, is very handsome and refined in appearance.

When selecting mourning materials in the shops, insist upon having a good light on them, as there are different shades of black. Only the blackest shade is considered mourning. Blue blacks are not appropriate on account of the bluish shade, and the brownish blacks appear shabby and rusty.

The deepest mourning is that worn by a widow, who wears crape at least one year. Her gown should be of some soft, smooth, silky material such as henrietta. This gown may be trimmed with crape or mourning silk and should be made on the "simple elegance" plan.

Crape is made with the grooves or stripes running diagonally. When it is cut on the bias these crimps will be found running up and down; when cut on the straight the crimps run on the bias. Care must be taken before cutting the material, as a good quality is quite expensive, to have the pattern placed on the proper grain. Crape is so pliable that it can be shaped or molded to almost any shape. It should be basted smoothly on a foundation of soft crinoline which holds it in shape. The right side of crape is the raised side or the side on which the crimps run from left to right diagonally. Crape is not a very durable material, and should be placed on the gown in such a manner that it may easily be renewed or removed and some other trimming put on in its place. It takes the dust and becomes rusty looking after very little wear.

When crape is laid aside plain black gowns and hats are worn, and these in time give place to black and white, grays, and lavenders. Many widows wear only black as long as they remain in that state, which in many cases means the remainder of their lives, particularly when they have passed middle life.

The crape veil is not worn very much in America; it is replaced by a nun's veiling and net veils which may be had ready to wear. The nun's veiling has a border woven in it so that it is ready to put on the hat when bought. The net veils are more elaborate. Many of them are made of a heavy net with a very coarse mesh. A double hem of crape is slip stitched around the four sides, making the veil quite handsome.

For a parent, mourning is worn two years; black for one year and black and white, grays, etc. during the second year. For a sister or brother about the same rule is followed. Crape is very little used for any except the husband or parent.

Black is so very somber and unbecoming at the neck that even widows wear a band of white at the throat. White shirtwaists with black skirts, belts, etc. are far more sanitary and sensible in hot weather than black ones, and many wear them after a few months have elapsed. A string of black beads will help carry out the mourning idea.

When mourning is put aside it is very poor taste to put on any very bright or conspicuous colored dresses. Dark blue, brown, or mixed cheviots or serges are very appropriate materials for this time.

Pure white is considered deep mourning. It must be dead white, not cream white, and is usually worn in the house. Ostrich feathers, velvet, jet, and gold jewelry are not worn during the term of mourning. For first mourning folds and tucks are considered the most appropriate arrangement of trimming. Crochet buttons and chiffon trimming are also in good form. Black taffeta silk is considered mourning, provided it has not a great luster.

A Bridal Trousseau or Outfit

The station in society which the bride-to-be occupies before marriage and the one she will occupy when she marries must determine the extent of her wardrobe. Every girl should at the least have six full suits of underwear, one half dozen pairs stockings, one dozen handkerchiefs, two or three white skirts, two pairs of shoes and one pair of slippers, two or three kimonos or dressing sacks, one silk or nice dark petticoat, a good comb and hairbrush, a

nailbrush, toothbrush, and other toilet articles which her own habits will suggest. She should also have a bath robe or long gown of some sort.

For the outer clothes she must have a good woolen dress of a dark color, well made and not too much trimmed. A tailor-made suit would be a fine foundation around which to plan her other gowns. Besides this there should be a black or dark blue skirt which would serve to wear with shirtwaists; and of these she should have at least one half dozen. A pretty fancy dress of some light material of a dainty color would be one which she could wear on many occasions, as many invitations are extended to brides. She would not care to appear every time in her wedding gown, and a little gown of silk or fancy material would just do. If the bride intends to do her own work she should have a couple of nice gingham house dresses or shirtwaists and skirts.

A wedding gown is supposed to be made of white material, as white is symbolic of purity. Whether the gown be elaborate or simple I would recommend white. If the wedding is to be solemnized in the summer what prettier material could be suggested than swiss or chiffon organdy? It may be made very elaborately with lace, tucks, and insertions, and lined with taffeta silk. If a softer lining is more to her taste a pretty soft lawn trimmed with lace and insertion will do just as well. With a dress of this style a dainty summer hat of white leghorn trimmed in some pretty fashion with white would be appropriate. A bridal veil should never be worn with a short dress; a veil calls for a dress with a train.

White voile, eolienne, net, crepe de chine, chiffon crepe, chiffon cloth, and the different weights of satin are all appropriate for wedding gowns; any one of these requires a silk lining throughout. Lace robes are very fashionable and can be bought ready to put together. The skirts have the flounces sewn on, and all that is necessary to complete the robe skirt is to join the back seam and hang it. A lace robe should be lined with silk or satin and interlined with mousseline de soie. The waist of a robe usually requires quite a little plan-

ning. This may be made easier if the mesh of the robe is matched when the dress is bought, and a couple of yards of net secured to help out in the making of the waist.

Allover valenciennes lace may be made into a very handsome wedding gown. Flouncing to match the allover lace may be had. If the lace has a creamy color it makes it more elegant. Old family heirlooms of lace have a creamy or yellowed appearance and are much prized, especially for wedding gowns or trimming for them.

Crepe de chine will always be a popular material for wedding dresses. It has a clinging tendency and falls in very graceful folds. The trimming may be made of the material in tucks, shirring, cordings, bands, joined by a catchstitch or fagoting. In fact any and all manner of handwork is appropriate for crepe de chine. With a transparent yoke the gown will be handsome enough for either a church or a home wedding. With this style gown a veil may be worn if the skirt is trimmed.

Satin, of course, is one of the most pretentious of materials. It should be made in the princess style, a lace yoke or bertha of some fine lace being a most beautiful trimming for the waist. The lower part of the sleeve might also be of lace. The lines of a princess gown should be beautifully fitted and stitched, as any deviation from an even stitching will be very apparent.

The train of a white satin princess gown should rest on the floor at least 1 yard, a 72-inch train. That, measuring from the waist to the end of the train, is the usual length. Some extreme trains have been of sufficient length to rest 2 yards on the floor. A reliable pattern of a train should be secured, as it is a very difficult matter to make a successful one. The lining of the skirt should extend to the end of the train. It should be padded on the inside to the depth of 1/2 yard with sheet wadding; this padding should be hidden with a facing of taffeta or the lining of the dress. Padding gives weight to the bottom of a skirt; little lead weights should be covered with pieces of silk and sewn at intervals around the bottom of the train. A dust ruffle must be placed on the inside and one on the outside of the lining

to give a soft finish to it. The satin should be tacked to the lining with tie tacks–long stitches taken through both skirts and pulled out so as to make a 1/2-inch space between them. These threads are buttonholed and in this way secure the skirts together.

Orange blossoms are considered the proper flowers for a bride. Some of them may be arranged at the front of the corsage.

The tulle which is worn for bridal veils is manufactured especially for this purpose, and is about 3 yards in width. The veil should be a little longer than the length from the top of the head to the end of the train; this extra length is to allow for the graceful fall which it must have. It should be long enough to fall over the face to the knees, and may be arranged on the head by a milliner who has taste in such things. Orange blossoms are also worn in the hair.

Long gloves of white suede or glacé kid should be worn. One of the seams of the ring finger should be ripped; it may be slipped back from the finger during the ceremony, in this way avoiding much confusion. The stockings worn with an elegant costume of this kind should be of white silk, and the shoes of fine white satin or kid.

For a quiet wedding after which there is no reception many brides prefer to wear their going-away gowns; gray is the prime favorite. A tailored suit is quite the proper kind of a gown, and may be very handsomely trimmed with stitching, buttons, braid, or embroidery. With this suit (skirt and coat), as very few tailored cloth waists are worn now, a handsome white lingerie waist may be worn. This waist may be quite elegant with handwork and lace, etc. Black ties or shoes should be worn and white or gray gloves. The hat should be a smart affair to set off the gown. A veil of chiffon or lace, either gray or white, should complete the costume. Blue, brown, or tan are worn at weddings, but gray seems to be the most appropriate, next to white.

A long coat of pongee, rajah, or mohair is a very useful addition to a bridal outfit. It saves the dress from dust, and as every bride wishes to look her best on arrival at her destination, this wearing

403

of a traveling coat will help her to this end. It may be made of the box coat model, reaching to the very bottom of the skirt. It may be made with a cape or set of capes. The sleeves should be made quite full, gathered into a cuff at the wrist. The fronts should be double breasted, or arranged in such a manner that the coat will cover the entire gown when it is necessary.

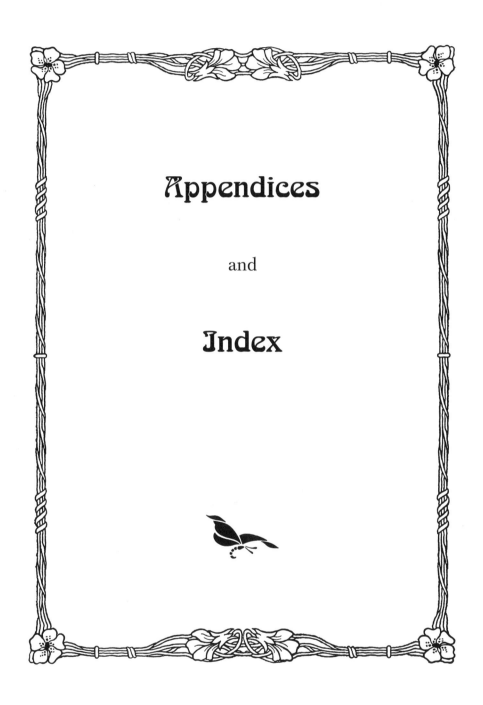

Appendices

and

Index

Appendix A
American System of Cutting Rulers

To aid you in enlarging the *Edwardian Modiste* patterns, I had the American System of Cutting rulers reconstructed from the patent application (see appendix B). They may be used either for drafting or to determine the size a pattern piece should be projected to.

Instead of inches, the patterns are labeled with numbered (whole) units and lettered (fractional) ones. Unit size varies with the ruler, so the same number of units is used for any size pattern. To draft a bodice with a 34-inch bust, you would choose the size 34 ruler to draw all horizontal lines. To draft a bodice with a 36-inch bust you would use the size 36 ruler, and so on. Two rulers are required for each pattern piece, one to draw horizontal measurements and the other to draw the vertical baseline. A tab has been added to each ruler to indicate the inch measurement it is used for, plus the (rounded) metric equivalent.

The rulers are uniformly scaled, enabling you to draw patterns for any size even if no ruler is specifically supplied for it. Where a smaller measurement is needed, you use the ruler that is double in size. To draft a bodice with a 15-inch back waist length, you would use the size 30 ruler to draw the vertical baseline and count the stipulated number of units. To draft a bodice with a 50-inch bust, you would use the size 25 ruler to draw horizontal lines and count twice as many units.

Only ten units have been provided for each ruler, as described in the patent application (plus a little extra length to facilitate pasting). These rulers are too short to draw some pattern lines. The book page size prevented me from lengthening them. In fact most rulers had to be broken into halves. However, a ruler long enough to draw any line can be created by photocopying.

First figure out which rulers you need to enlarge the desired pattern (see the introduction and "Using the American Garment Cutter System"). Then find the longest line to be drawn with each ruler. The number of units the line requires is indicated on the end farthest from the baseline. Lengthen the ruler to at least that many units.

The rulers read top to bottom for vertical lines and right to left for horizontal ones, due to the placement of the pattern baselines. If a ruler was not broken into halves, copy it as many times as required. Cut out the copies. Lay the first segment of the ruler vertically on a table with the identifying tab at the top. On the second segment, fold under the tab at the heavy line under the label. Align this line with the line indicating the "10" unit on the first segment, covering the "1" of the "10." Tape or glue in place. Use a pen to rewrite the covered "1," or change it to "2" to indicate 20 units. Paste any additional segments the same way.

If the ruler was broken, make one copy of each half. Paste the 6–10 segment to the 1–5 segment. Copy and paste this ten-unit ruler as described above.

The rulers may then be glued to cardboard or inexpensive yardsticks and used for drafting. Or they may be used for measurement only, and lines drawn with a yardstick.

19 in.
48 cm

20 in.
51 cm

21 in.
53 cm

22 in.
56 cm

22 in.
56 cm

23 in.
58 cm

23 in.
58 cm

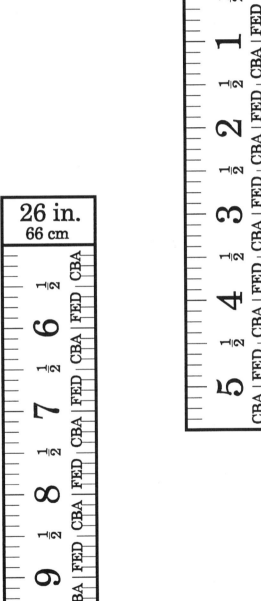

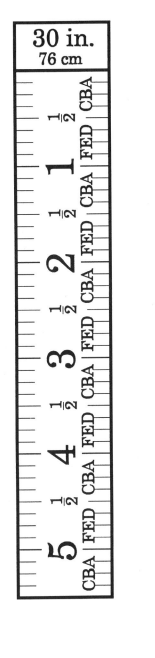

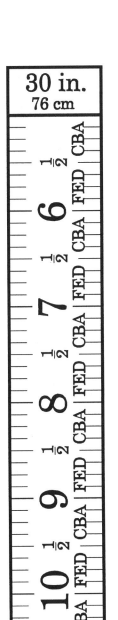

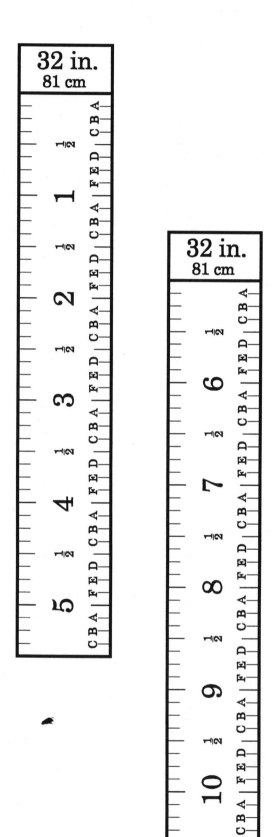

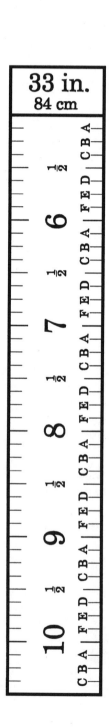

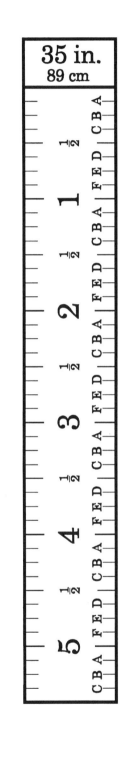

415

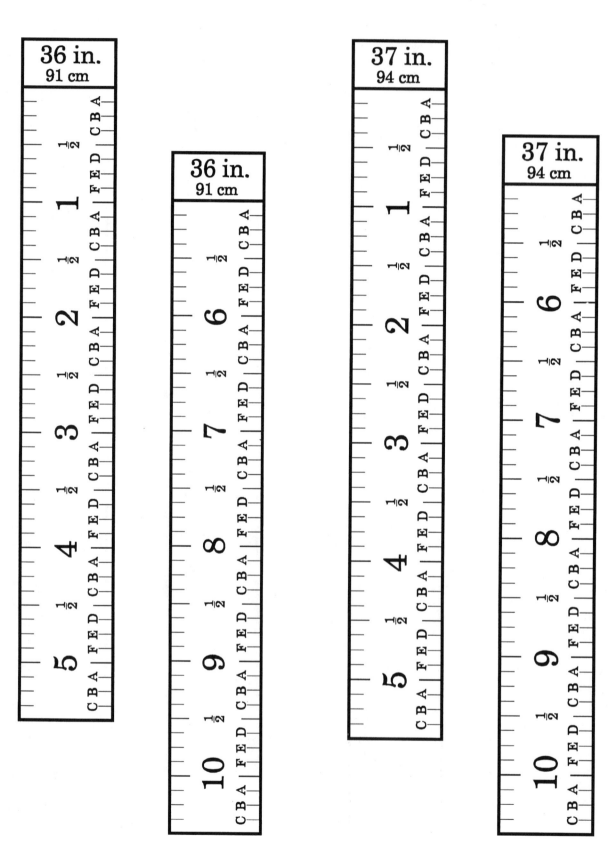

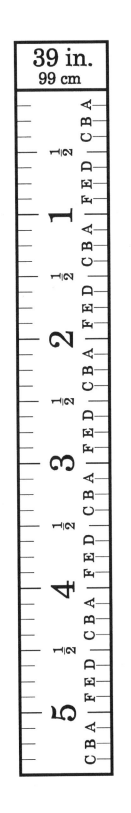
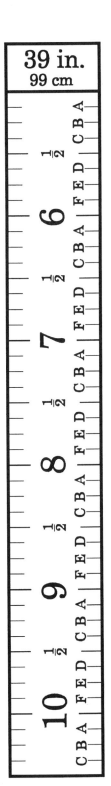

417

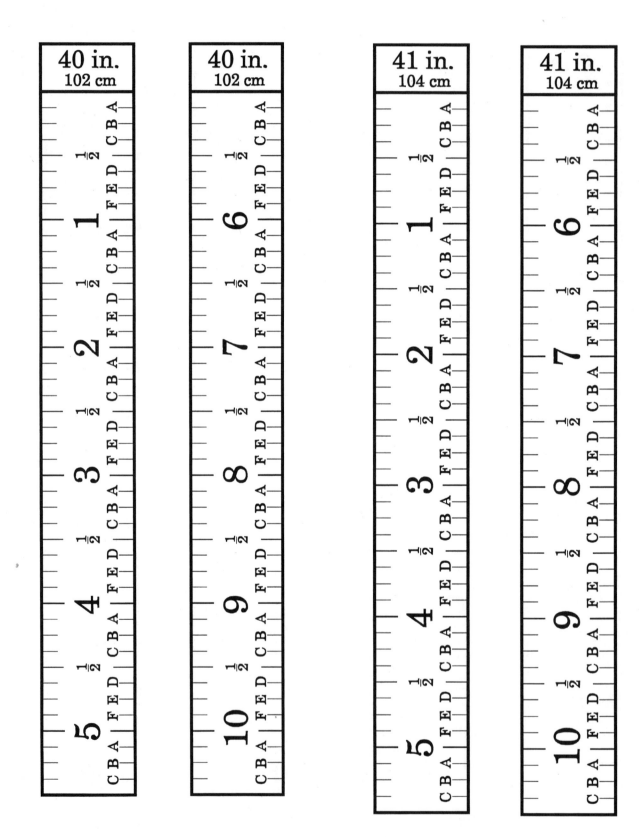

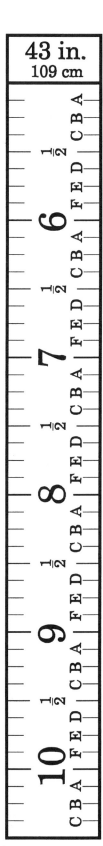

42 in.
107 cm

A B C D E F
1 ½ 1
D E F C B A
2 ½
F E D C B A
3 ½
F E D C B A
4 ½
F E D C B A
5 ½
F E D C B A

42 in.
107 cm

A B C D E F
6 ½
D E F C B A
7 ½
F E D C B A
8 ½
F E D C B A
9 ½
F E D C B A
10 ½
F E D C B A

43 in.
109 cm

A B C D E F
1 ½ 1
D E F C B A
2 ½
F E D C B A
3 ½
F E D C B A
4 ½
F E D C B A
5 ½
F E D C B A

43 in.
109 cm

A B C D E F
6 ½
D E F C B A
7 ½
F E D C B A
8 ½
F E D C B A
9 ½
F E D C B A
10 ½
F E D C B A

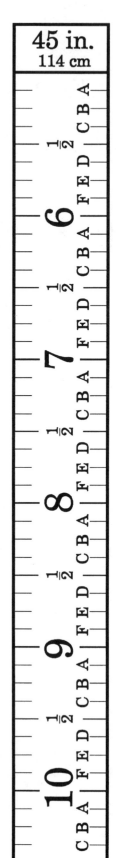

46 in.
117 cm

A
CBA
1½
1
FED
CBA
2
FED
CBA
3
½
FED
CBA
4
½
FED
CBA
5
FED
CBA

46 in.
117 cm

A
CBA
6
½
FED
CBA
7
½
FED
CBA
8
½
FED
CBA
9
½
FED
CBA
10
FED
CBA

Appendix B
Patent Application for the American System

United States Patent Office
Jonathan Nelson
of Warsaw, Indiana
Garment-Scale

Specification forming part of Letters Patent No. 717,253, dated December 30, 1902.

Application filed September 12, 1902. Serial No. 123,057. (No model.)

To all whom it may concern: Be it known that I, Jonathan Nelson, a citizen of the United States of America, residing at Warsaw, in the county of Kosciusko and State of Indiana, have invented certain new and useful Improvements in Garment-Scales, of which the following is a specification.

My invention relates to certain new and useful improvements in garment-scales; and its object is to provide suitable means by which, a standard pattern being provided, garments of any desired size may be cut therefrom, preserving at all times the proper proportions.

To this end my invention consists in certain novel features shown in the drawings and described in this specification.

In the drawings, Figures 1, 2, and 3 are views of three of the scales in use, and Figure 4 is a view of one of the patterns intended to be used in connection therewith.

The scales, preferably twenty-eight in number, numbered from 19 to 46, inclusive, are laid off as shown in the drawings. Each scale is divided into ten main divisions, the main divisions being numbered from "1" to "10," and each of these ten divisions is in turn laid off into eight divisions, which

are lettered "A," "B," "C," "1/2," "D," "E," and "F," as shown. The actual length of each one of the rules is one-third of the number of inches corresponding to the number of the rule—that is to say, the rule No. 30 is ten inches long, rule No. 19 is six and one-third inches long, and so on. The large numbers at the ends of the rules correspond to the number of inches in the bust measure of the person for whom the garment is to be made—that is to say, if a garment is to be made for a person having a thirty-inch bust measure rule No. 30 is used for making all measurements. If the person has a nineteen-inch bust measure, rule 19 is used, and so on. In each case, then, the rule to be used bears a certain definite proportion to the length of the bust measure of the person for whom the garment is to be made.

The pattern is marked as shown in Figure 4, one standard pattern being provided for all sizes in a given style of garment. It will be noted that the markings commence at the lower right-hand corner and are marked in terms of the figures appearing on the rules. The second figure to the left of the starting-point, marked "0," will be seen to be "6F." This means that from the point zero is measured off with the rule to be used six main divisions and seven minor ones—that is, to the point "F" between "6" and "7." This system will of course be quite obvious in reference to the rules.

The operation of the entire system will now be quite evident. The person for whom the garment is to be made is measured, and the rule corresponding to his or her bust measure is selected. The standard pattern of the garment of the desired style is selected, and an outline similar thereto is laid off with the previously selected rule. This of course makes the garment when cut out of exactly the same shape as that of the standard pattern and of exactly the right size in bust measure for the per-

422

son for whom it is intended. It will be seen that this is a very great simplification of the ordinary methods of laying out patterns and an exceedingly desirable improvement.

I claim as new and desire to secure by Letters Patent—

A rule laid off into a plurality of equal divisions, each of said divisions being laid off into a plurality of subdivisions, said subdivisions being designated by letters of the alphabet, the rule being adapted to be used in connection with a pattern, the various points on which are provided with indicating figures and letters, corresponding to the figures and letters on the rule, substantially as described.

In witness whereof I have signed the above application for Letters Patent, at Chicago, in the county of Cook and State of Illinois, this 8th day of September, A.D. 1902.

——Jonathan Nelson

Witnesses:
    Russell Wiles
    S. Bliss

Appendix C
Metric Conversion Table

This table contains the English and metric equivalents of measurements often used in sewing. Numbers running to several decimal places and (most) fractions under 1/16 inch have been rounded for easy use.

English Measurement	Metric Equivalent	Metric Measurement	English Equivalent
1/8 in.	3.2 mm	1 mm	1/32 in.
1/4 in.	6.4 mm	2 mm	1/16 in.
3/8 in.	9.5 mm	3 mm	1/8 in.
1/2 in.	1.3 cm	4 mm	5/32 in.
5/8 in.	1.6 cm	5 mm	7/32 in.
3/4 in.	1.9 cm	6 mm	1/4 in.
7/8 in.	2.2 cm	7 mm	9/32 in.
1 in.	2.5 cm	8 mm	5/16 in.
1 1/4 in.	3.2 cm	9 mm	11/32 in.
1 1/2 in.	3.8 cm	10 mm (1 cm)	13/32 in.
1 3/4 in.	4.4 cm	2 cm	3/4 in.
2 in.	5.1 cm	3 cm	1 3/16 in.
2 1/4 in.	5.7 cm	4 cm	1 9/16 in.
2 1/2 in.	6.4 cm	5 cm	2 in.
2 3/4 in.	7.0 cm	6 cm	2 3/8 in.
3 in.	7.6 cm	7 cm	2 3/4 in.
3 1/4 in.	8.3 cm	8 cm	3 1/8 in.
3 1/2 in.	8.9 cm	9 cm	3 1/2 in.
3 3/4 in.	9.5 cm	10 cm	3 15/16 in.
4 in.	10.2 cm	15 cm	5 7/8 in.
4 1/2 in.	11.4 cm	20 cm	7 7/8 in.
5 in.	12.7 cm	25 cm	9 13/16 in.
5 1/2 in.	14.0 cm	30 cm	11 13/16 in.

Metric Conversion Table

English Measurement	Metric Equivalent	Metric Measurement	English Equivalent
6 in.	15.2 cm	35 cm	13 3/4 in.
6 1/2 in.	16.5 cm	40 cm	15 3/4 in.
7 in.	17.8 cm	45 cm	17 11/16 in.
7 1/2 in.	19.1 cm	50 cm	19 11/16 in.
8 in.	20.3 cm	55 cm	21 5/8 in.
8 1/2 in.	21.6 cm	60 cm	23 5/8 in.
9 in. (1/4 yd.)	22.9 cm	65 cm	25 9/16 in.
9 1/2 in.	24.1 cm	70 cm	27 9/16 in.
10 in.	25.4 cm	75 cm	29 1/2 in.
10 1/2 in.	26.7 cm	80 cm	31 1/2 in.
11 in.	27.9 cm	85 cm	33 7/16 in.
11 1/2 in.	29.2 cm	90 cm	35 7/16 in.
12 in. (1 ft.)	30.5 cm	95 cm	37 3/8 in.
1/2 yd. (18 in.)	45.7 cm	100 cm (1 m)	39 3/8 in.
3/4 yd. (27 in.)	68.6 cm	1.25 m	1 yd. 13 3/16 in.
1 yd. (36 in.)	91.4 cm	1.50 m	1 yd. 23 1/16 in.
1 1/4 yd.	1.14 m	1.75 m	1 yd. 32 7/8 in.
1 1/2 yd.	1.37 m	2.00 m	2 yd. 6 3/4 in.
1 3/4 yd.	1.60 m	2.50 m	2 yd. 26 7/16 in.
2 yd.	1.83 m	3.00 m	3 yd. 10 1/8 in.
2 1/2 yd.	2.29 m	3.50 m	3 yd. 29 13/16 in.
3 yd.	2.74 m	4.00 m	4 yd. 13 1/2 in.
3 1/2 yd.	3.20 m	4.50 m	4 yd. 33 3/16 in.
4 yd.	3.66 m	5.00 m	5 yd. 16 7/8 in.
4 1/2 yd.	4.11 m	5.50 m	6 yd. 9/16 in.
5 yd.	4.57 m	6.00 m	6 yd. 20 1/4 in.
5 1/2 yd.	5.03 m	6.50 m	7 yd. 3 7/8 in.
6 yd.	5.49 m	7.00 m	7 yd. 23 9/16 in.
6 1/2 yd.	5.94 m	7.50 m	8 yd. 7 1/4 in.
7 yd.	6.40 m	8.00 m	8 yd. 26 15/16 in.
7 1/2 yd.	6.86 m	8.50 m	9 yd. 10 5/8 in.
8 yd.	7.32 m	9.00 m	9 yd. 30 5/16 in.

Appendix D
Further Reading

Ben-Yusuf, Anna. *Edwardian Hats: The Art of Millinery*. Mendocino: R. L. Shep, 1992.

Reprint of a 1909 millinery guide.

Bryk, Nancy Villa, ed. *American Dress Pattern Catalogs, 1873–1909*. New York: Dover Publications, 1988.

Includes a complete 1909 McCall's catalog.

Cabrera, Roberto and Patricia Flaherty Myers. *Classic Tailoring Techniques: A Construction Guide for Women's Wear*. New York: Fairchild Publications, 1984.

Information on molding and shaping garments, which can be adapted to period styles.

Elite Styles Co. *Elite Fashions Catalog, 1904*. Mineola: Dover Publications, 1996.

Reproduces the majority of fashion drawings from the May 1904 Elite Styles pattern catalog.

Gordon, S. S. *Ladies' Tailor-Made Garments*. Berkeley: Lacis Publications, 1993.

Reprint of a 1908 drafting manual, with patterns for women's tailored clothes. Supplemented by three period dressmaking articles and some fashion plates.

Grimble, Frances. *After a Fashion: How to Reproduce, Restore, and Wear Vintage Styles*. San Francisco: Lavolta Press, 1993.

Covers medieval through Art Deco styles for women and men. Guides readers through each stage of a reproduction project and advises them on all aspects of collecting vintage clothes.

Hopkins, J. C. *Edwardian Ladies' Tailoring: The Twentieth Century System of Ladies' Garment Cutting*. Mendocino: R. L. Shep, 1990.

Reprint of a 1910 drafting manual, with patterns for women's tailored clothes. Supplemented by fashion plates.

Kidwell, Claudia. *Cutting a Fashionable Fit: Dressmaker's Drafting Systems in the United States*. Washington: Smithsonian Institution Press, 1979.

A history and analysis of 19th-century patent drafting systems.

La Barre, Kathleen M. and Kay D. La Barre. *Reference Book of Women's Vintage Clothing 1900–1919*. Portland: La Barre Books, 1990.

Illustrations from fashion magazines pasted up alphabetically by category—bags, belts, bathing suits, etc. and details such as skirt lengths and trims—and by year within each category. Alongside runs text that probably summarizes the original descriptions.

National Cloak & Suit Co. *Women's Fashions of the Early 1900s: An Unabridged Republication of "New York Fashions, 1909."* New York: Dover Publications, 1992.

Reprint of a mail-order catalog showing suits, day and lingerie dresses, wrappers, blouses, skirts, coats, lingerie, and accessories.

Shaeffer, Claire B. *Couture Sewing Techniques*. Newtown: Taunton Press, 1993.

Construction as practiced in couture workrooms, where Edwardian techniques are still used.

Index

A

accessories, 393, 400–403. *See also* belts; neckwear
American System of Cutting
 drafting with, 2, 8–9, 407
 patent application, 422–423
 rulers, 1–2, 8, 407–421

B

basting, 9, 368, 371, 373, 377, 386
bathing suits. *See under* sports outfits
belts
 belt tape, 376
 corset cover, 367
 girdles, 377
  closed at back, 388
  closed in front, 389
  flowered ribbon, 389–390
  trimmed, 390–391
blouses. *See* dresses; waists
boning, 372–374, 388–390
box coat, 385–386, 401, 403
bridal wear, 402–404

C

camisoles. *See* corset covers
capes, 386–387
chemises. *See* slips
cloaks
 colors, 168
 materials, 168, 221
 maternity, 401
 rainy day, 400
 trims, 168
coats. *See also* suits
 backs, 383
 box, 385–386, 401, 403
 bridal, 403–404
 collars, 383

colors, 138, 221, 320
 Eton, 385
 fitted, 386
 foundation, 381–382
 hemming, 384
 lining, 384–386
 materials, 96, 189, 221, 381, 384–386
 padding, 382
 patterns
  Artistic Directoire Coat, 260–263
  Evening or Opera Coat, 290–293
  Ladies' Auto Coat, 156–160
  Ladies' Auto Fur Coat, 81–85
  Ladies' Dressy Paletot, 31–34
  Ladies' Empire Coat, 17–20
  Ladies' Empire Raincoat, 341–343
  Storm and Motor Coat, 217–220
 pressing, 385
 revers, 382, 384
 shrinking, 381
 sleeves, 384–385, 392
collars. *See* neckwear
colors. *See also* specific garment patterns
 bridal, 402–403
 capes, 387
 cloaks, 168
 coats, 138, 221, 320
 dresses, 96, 247, 269, 298
 mourning, 401–402
 suits, 96, 112, 138
 vests, 168
 waists, 97, 138, 247, 347
combinations. *See also* corset covers; drawers
 Ladies' Combination Suit, 245–246
corset covers
 making, 367, 379
 maternity, 401
 patterns
  Fitted Corset Cover, 297
  French Corset Cover, 358–359

Index

Ladies' Corset Cover, 68
One-Piece Corset Cover, 167
Seamless Corset Cover, 67
crape, 401
cuffs. *See* sleeves
cutting out
    skirts, 368–370
    waists, 371–372

D

drawers, 365–366
dresses. *See also* suits; waists
    bridal, 402–403
    colors, 96, 247, 269, 298
    designing, 393–394
    lining, 393
    materials, 69, 96–97, 138, 189, 247, 269,
        320, 393
    maternity, 400–401
    patterns
        Afternoon Toilette, 206–209
        Attractive Model for Summer, 227–231
        Dressy Reception Gown, 40–44
        For Autumn and Winter, 264–268
        For Day or Evening Wear, 280–284
        Gown for Dressy Occasions, 275–279
        Ladies' Afternoon Gown, 123–127
        Ladies' Dinner Gown, 86–90
        Ladies' Empire Gown, 55–57
        Ladies' Evening Dress, 181–185
        Ladies' Evening Gown, 70–73
        Ladies' Jumper Suit, 113–117
        Ladies' Princess Gown, 35–39
        Ladies' Reception Gown (1), 76–80
        Ladies' Reception Gown (2), 107–111
        Ladies' Reception Gown (3), 144–150
        Ladies' Reception Gown (4), 253–259
        Ladies' Reception Gown (5), 337–340
        Ladies' Reception Gown (6), 348–351
        Ladies' Visiting Gown, 222–226
        Pretty Creation for Summer, 236–239
        Reception Toilette, 26–30
        Shirtwaist and Skirt, 210–213
        Smart Design for Easter, 313–317
        Stylish Evening Gown, 309–312

        Stylish Street Gown, 304–308
        Unique Style for Summer, 321–324
        White Linen Suit,190–194
    trims, 59, 96, 168, 269, 298, 393–394, 401,
        403
dressing sacks. *See under* robes

E

edgings, 366
Eton coat, 385

F

fabric. *See* materials
facings, 370, 382
fastenings, 373–374
fitting
    skirts, 369
    waists, 371–372
french seam, 365

G

girdles. *See* belts; specific dress patterns
gowns. *See* dresses
guimpes, 65, 107, 320

H

hemming
    coats, 384
    skirts, 369, 403

I

insertion, 366

J

jackets. *See* coats; suits

L

lingerie. *See* specific garments
lingerie waists, 379
lining. *See also* specific garment patterns
    capes, 387
    coats, 384–386
    dresses, 393
    guimpes, 320
    skirts, 368–369

waists, 168, 371–372

M

materials. *See also* specific garment patterns
    belt, 388, 390
    bridal, 402–403
    cloak, 168, 221
    coat, 96, 189, 221, 381, 384–386
    dress, 69, 96–97, 138, 189, 247, 269,
       320, 393
    maternity wear, 400
    mourning, 401
    skirt, 247, 368
    sports outfits, 400
    suit, 96, 112, 138, 189, 221, 269, 320, 347
    vest, 168, 189
    waist, 69, 97, 138, 189, 221, 269, 298, 320,
       347, 379
maternity wear, 400–401
measurements, 7, 365, 394
mourning, 401–402

N

neckwear, 69, 189, 221, 320, 378
    coat collar, 383
    fitting, 374
    shirtwaist collar, 380
    tucked net collar, 391
nightgowns, 366–367

P

padded arm, 391
padding stitch, 382
patterns. *See also* specific garments
    altering, 368
    drafting, 2, 8–9
    finishing, 2–3
    projecting, 2
petticoats
    Ladies' Petticoat, 360–361
    making, 366
    maternity, 401
    styles, 247
plackets, 366, 369, 380
pleats, 369–370, 379, 383–384

preshrinking, 381
pressing, 385

R

robes
    Japanese Robe, 161–163
    Kimono Wrapper, 214–216
    Ladies' Dressing Sack, 65–66
rulers. *See under* American System of Cutting

S

shirtwaists, 379–380
skirts. *See also* sports outfits; suits
    circular, 370
    cutting out, 368–370
    fitting, 369–370
    hemming, 369, 403
    length, 69, 112, 247, 269, 298, 320, 400
    lining, 368–369
    making, 112, 269, 368–370
    pleated, 369–370
    slot seam, 370
    styles, 247
    trains, 403
    trims, 96, 112, 138, 247, 269, 298, 370
sleeves
    coat, 384–385, 392
    fancy, 391–392
    form for draping, 391
    making, 373, 377, 380
    styles, 247, 269
slips. *See also* petticoats
    Ladies' Chemise, 136–137
    Princess Slip, 344–346
slot seam, 370
sports outfits
    materials, 400
    patterns
        Golf and Outing Suit, 240–244
        Ladies' Bathing Suit, 332–336
        Outing Suit, 327–331
suits. *See also* coats; skirts; sports outfits
    colors, 96, 112, 138
    materials, 96, 112, 138, 189, 221, 269,
       320, 347

Index

patterns
    Chic Toilette, 232–235
    Dressy Redingote, 169–174
    Dressy Street Costume, 98–101
    Dressy Street Suit, 299–303
    Dressy Tailor-Made Suit, 151–155
    Easter Model, 195–200
    Effective Street Design, 248–252
    Ladies' Shirtwaist Suit, 21–25
    Ladies' Street Costume, 49–54
    Ladies' Street Suit, 131–135
    Ladies' Traveling Suit, 139–143
    Ladies' Visiting Gown, 118–122
    Practical Street Suit, 270–274
    Season's Newest Mode, 201–205
    Smart Creation for Street
      Wear, 285–289
    Spring Costume, 102–106
    Stylish Street Suit (1), 175–180
    Stylish Street Suit (2), 352–357
    Visiting Costume, 45–48
trims, 96, 112, 138

T

tight-fitting coat, 386
trims. *See also* specific garment patterns
    bridal, 402–403
    cape, 387
    corset cover, 367
    cutting out, 370, 401
    drawers, 365–366
    dress, 59, 96, 168, 269, 298, 393–394, 401,
      403
    mourning, 401–402
    for patterns, 3
    skirt, 96, 112, 138, 247, 269, 298, 370
    sleeve, 391–392
    suit, 96, 112, 138
    waist, 97, 112, 138, 221, 247, 298, 377–378
trousseau, 402–403
tucks, 365–366, 391

U

under waists. *See* corset covers
underwear. *See* specific garments

V

vests, 168, 189. *See also* specific suit patterns
veils. *See* accessories

W

waistcoats. *See* vests
waists. *See also* dresses; sleeves
    belt tape, 376
    boning, 372–374
    colors, 97, 138, 247, 347
    cutting out, 371–-372
    draping, 374–377
    fastenings, 373–374
    fitting, 371–372
    lingerie, 379
    lining, 168, 371–372
    materials, 69, 97, 138, 189, 221, 269, 298,
      320, 347, 379
    patterns
      Dainty Waist, 186–188
      Draft for Medium and Slender
        Forms (1), 13
      Draft for Medium and Slender
        Forms (2), 15
      Draft for Medium and Slender
        Forms (3), 16
      Dressy Afternoon Waist, 318–319
      Dressy Separate Waist, 58–60
      Dressy Shirtwaist, 63–64
      Good Draft for Medium Stout
        Forms, 14
      Ladies' Evening Waist, 61–62
      Ladies' Jumper Blouse, 128–130
      Ladies' Separate Waist (1), 74–75
      Ladies' Separate Waist (2), 164–166
      Practice Waist, 10–12
      Pretty Net Waist, 294–296
      Silk and Net Waist, 325–326
    shirtwaists, 379–380
    styles, 91–95, 112
    trims, 97, 112, 138, 221, 247, 298, 377–378
wedding dresses. *See* bridal wear
wrappers. *See* robes

After a Fashion
How to Reproduce, Restore, and Wear Vintage Styles

By Frances Grimble
Illustrated by Deborah Kuhn

Medieval through Art Deco styles for women and men
8 1/2" x 11" quality paperback, 352 pages, 147 line drawings

A complete guide to the reproduction, restoration, and wearing of vintage styles. ... There's a large and unique section on making your own patterns from a variety of sources, such as from gridded scale drawings or pattern drafts from books, scaling pattern drawings with a projector, copying original garments, writing your own sewing instructions once you have the pattern, and even using vintage patterns. [The book includes] detailed sections on taking body measurements and altering patterns, and on repairing and altering vintage garments.

———*Threads*

The techniques are shown on each of the periods, but in ways that apply to all, so you get the maximum benefit throughout the book. With practical instructions and clear illustrations, the author and illustrator lead you through research, pattern drafting, choosing the best patterns and materials, reproduction techniques, mending and altering period or vintage garments, and much, much more. A large appendix of resources, books, supplies, periodicals, and organizations is a treasure trove. The author ... openly shares all the tips and hints she's learned along the way.

———*Reenactor's Journal*

Most of the book's sewing instructions are numbered and illustrated, and they're among the clearest I've seen in any sewing resource. The entire book is organized for easy reference.

———*Sew News*

The introduction to this book states that it "is for everyone who wears historic styles, reproduction or real" including reenactors, vintage clothing collectors, dealers, and others who need to produce their own costumes. If you are any of the above and if you could buy only one book, this book should be it. ... Should become the standard source on this subject.

———*Rags*

After a Fashion can be purchased for $35 in bookstores or ordered from Lavolta Press at 20 Meadowbrook Drive, San Francisco, CA 94132. If mail ordered, shipping is $4; California purchasers must add sales tax. Prices subject to change without notice.